I0124797

A Leftist Critique
of the Principles of
Identity, Diversity, and
Multiculturalism

A Leftist Critique
of the Principles of
Identity, Diversity, and
Multiculturalism

Richard Anderson-Connolly

LEXINGTON BOOKS
Lanham • Boulder • New York • London

Published by Lexington Books
An imprint of The Rowman & Littlefield Publishing Group, Inc.
4501 Forbes Boulevard, Suite 200, Lanham, Maryland 20706
www.rowman.com

6 Tinworth Street, London SE11 5AL, United Kingdom

Copyright © 2019 by The Rowman & Littlefield Publishing Group, Inc.

All rights reserved. No part of this book may be reproduced in any form or by any electronic or mechanical means, including information storage and retrieval systems, without written permission from the publisher, except by a reviewer who may quote passages in a review.

British Library Cataloguing in Publication Information Available

Library of Congress Cataloging-in-Publication Data

Names: Anderson-Connolly, Richard, author.
Title: A leftist critique of the principles of identity, diversity, and multiculturalism / Richard Anderson-Connolly.
Description: Lanham : Lexington Books, [2019] | Includes bibliographical references and index.
Identifiers: LCCN 2019012157| ISBN 9781498590679 (cloth) |
ISBN 9781498590686 (electronic) ISBN 9781498590686 (pbk) Subjects:
LCSH: Multiculturalism--Political aspects. | Equality. | Civil rights. | Socialism.
Classification: LCC HM1271 .A558 2019 | DDC 305.8—dc23
LC record available at https://lccn.loc.gov/2019012157

Contents

List of Tables and Figures

Introduction

Massive and unavoidable are the signs of strain in American society today. Economic inequality matches a level last seen just prior to the Great Depression. Yet instead of genuine solutions the federal government delivers economic austerity, on the one hand, and surveillance and repression on the other. Local governments too are cutting social services while expanding the powers of the police. Our political structure seems incapable of responding to—or sometimes even recognizing—the problems faced by most citizens. Neither party represents the interests of the majority of Americans, who reside in the middle and working classes. The Supreme Court promotes a corporate agenda, justifiably earning one of its lowest public opinion ratings in history.

The details of the assault on the middle class and the nearly complete corporate takeover of our democracy do indeed make a morbidly fascinating story of power and propaganda. But this book does not intend to be another telling of this history. It has been told by those who have seen it from the inside, like former Secretary of Labor Robert Reich (2012) or former U.S. Representative Bob Ney (2013). John Perkins (2004, 2007), a former "economic hit-man," has provided his personal and riveting account of the schemes behind the largely successful imposition of the so-called Washington Consensus around the globe. Outside the beltway, the most celebrated recent treatment of inequality is Thomas Piketty's *Capital in the Twenty-First Century* (2014), which raised both academic and popular awareness of the issue.[1] In short, the wealthiest Americans have used the powers of our semi-democratic state to further their short-term interests against the interests of the large majority of citizens. Concentrated political power and extreme inequality have mutually reinforced each, while weakening both our civic institutions and the economy. For the most part we know—or should know—where the problems lie.

And we even know how to reverse direction. The notion that there is no alternative to our political-economic state of affairs—what I refer to as neo-liberalism—is itself part of the ideology that props up the current top-heavy arrangement. The Economic Policy Institute's initiative, *Raising America's Pay* ("The Agenda to Raise America's Pay" n.d.), lists 11 policies to address wage stagnation, the "country's key economic challenge":

1. Raise the minimum wage
2. Update overtime rules
3. Strengthen collective bargaining rights
4. Regularize undocumented workers
5. Provide earned sick leave and paid family leave
6. End discriminatory practices that contribute to race and gender inequalities
7. Support strong enforcement of labor standards
8. Prioritize very low rates of unemployment when making monetary policy
9. Enact targeted employment programs and undertake public investments in infrastructure to create jobs
10. Reduce our trade deficit by stopping destructive currency manipulation
11. Use the tax code to restrain top 1 percent incomes

Other progressive economic policies include universal healthcare and low-cost or even free college. But political-economic problems are not, of course, only economic. We need to strengthen civil liberties by downsizing our criminal justice system and by restricting the powers of surveillance agencies. Economic inequality and political repression are never independent phenomena. Aggressive policing and mass incarceration are one type of political response to the social problems and unrest generated by inequality and poverty. Yet we could choose the other way, what we might call a new New Deal.

So how do we get there? Because the status quo benefits the economic and political elite, implementing any solutions will require a broad and sustained social movement that can force change. Social movements, for their part, require a sufficiently motivated segment of the population. Finally, this motivation depends upon people having a certain explanatory framework for the way the world works as well as holding a particular set of core values that are threatened by the current arrangement. A citizenry that misreads its situation or has a muddled morality is unlikely to participate in collective action to improve its welfare.

This work intends to explore that last step. I want to approach our political-economic crisis by examining the misunderstanding of our current situation. I want to avoid blaming the victim. The misapprehensions of the citizenry result from the failures of those responsible for their education and information.

Americans have not been given an adequate model to explain their plight and have been offered unsophisticated moral arguments. This work is intended to complement the other explanations of our political-economic crisis that focus on the maneuvers of the political and economic elite. We know, more-or-less, how they pulled it off in D.C. and on Wall Street. I start with different questions: Where were progressives over the last 40 years as economic inequality skyrocketed and civil liberties were eroded? And what are progressives doing now, as we continue to move in the wrong direction?

I believe that liberals and progressives—without gainsaying all the systemic biases arrayed against them—have been ineffective in fighting the rightward shift because they have misdiagnosed the problem. They are intellectually rooted in—and blinded by—some version of what is commonly referred to as identity politics. I will refer to this paradigm as the Identity, Diversity, and Multiculturalism Program and argue that it is compatible with the inequality and injustices in our political economy.[2] It should be already clear but—because the potential for misunderstanding is considerable—I will repeat: this is not another right-wing diatribe; I will waste no time with the paranoid conservative take on issues of identity politics or with their strawman of political correctness. My goal is to reach out to supporters and sympathizers of the Program as potential political allies. I situate myself in the leftist tradition as it has come down to us from the Enlightenment and the rise of the industrial working class. I am motivated by the urgent need to address the damage done to our society, that is, to the welfare of actual human beings. The United States has the most unequal distribution of resources among the industrialized democracies (and more unequal than many developing economies).[3] Our (official) child poverty rate is consistently around 20 percent.[4] Over most of the last half century, the middle class has seen stagnating or even falling wages. Concurrently, and not coincidentally, the repressive apparatus of the state has expanded and we now face the crisis of mass incarceration. Throughout most of that time the Identity, Diversity, and Multiculturalism Program has been in ascendance, at least among progressives, and—where I have the most familiarity—certainly among progressives inside the academy—faculty, students, and administrators. I am not claiming that the Identity, Diversity, and Multiculturalism Program directly caused our inequality but rather that the adherents have done almost nothing to prevent it because they were fighting the wrong fight. Furthermore, and just as importantly, I will argue that the program is ill-equipped to reverse the true crisis. The IDMP has confused progressives, diverting their attention and activism away from the real problems of inequality and repression.

It is therefore no coincidence that many politicians in both major parties have embraced the rhetoric and have skillfully used Identity, Diversity, and

Multiculturalism as tools to manipulate the electorate. Indeed, the Democratic Party has largely replaced any real leftist policies with faux progressive Identity, Diversity, and Multiculturalism. We might expect such maneuvers from politicians but the real tragedy is that many self-identified progressives have jumped fully on board. Even the corporate sector, which we might presume is less willing to focus on unprofitable activities, now appropriates much of the language and even organizational structure of the IDMP. The very corporations that dominate our political process—Walmart, Exxon-Mobil, Bank of America, and many others—embrace Identity, Diversity, and Multiculturalism. It all makes perfect sense: the IDMP poses no threat to the interests or agendas of the economic and political elite. On the contrary, Identity, Diversity, and Multiculturalism has been put into service of the neoliberal project.

But we cannot overlook the growing signs of discontent among progressives. The neoliberal consensus in the Democratic Party is breaking down. Not among the elites who remain committed to a pro-business agenda, but among the rank-and-file. Yet the base is confused. Even while recognizing the historic economic inequality, the inflated criminal justice system, the unrestrained militarism promoted by both parties, they are still intellectually hamstrung by the dominant paradigm of Identity, Diversity, and Multiculturalism. Some even recognize that neoliberals are using "identity politics" to avoid talking about the difficult issues of justice. But even those who are uncomfortable with IDMP often soften their critique. Like the early Protestants who saw themselves as returning Christianity to its true, original path before it was corrupted by the mundane world, so too the present reformers allege that neoliberalism has distorted the otherwise valid message of Identity, Diversity, and Multiculturalism. This is precisely what I challenge. There is nothing of intellectual or moral substance for leftists to take from the Identity, Diversity, and Multiculturalism Program.

This work serves three purposes for three audiences. For leftists and progressives who are already suspicious and uncomfortable with "identity politics" it provides a set of conceptual, theoretical, and empirical arguments they could use to critique the IDM Program. The arguments cannot in any (reasonable) way be characterized as racist; indeed, they are solidly left, maybe even a bit radical for some. For those who embrace Identity, Diversity, and Multiculturalism it poses a challenge: What is the defense of IDMP from leftist—not from right-wing—criticism? If, upon reflection, the Program cannot be reconciled with your fundamental values, please engage in leftist action, either social movements or electoral politics. Finally, I offer the centrists, those who have not yet formed an opinion either way on "identity politics," a critique from the Left instead of the Right. I fear that the excesses and nonsense coming out of the IDMP, some of it an unfair caricature, to be sure, are nonetheless being fruitfully exploited by conservatives who are attempting to portray the political agenda of the Left as entirely circumscribed by "identity politics." Thus, we are losing allies, people we might otherwise get to join social movements against repression, inequality, and militarism.

DOING IDENTITY, DIVERSITY, AND MULTICULTURALISM

Identity, Diversity, and Multiculturalism has rooted itself in mainstream U.S. politics. As the leading example, consider the boost given to Obama and his neoliberal agenda during his presidency. He remains popular now, despite his failure to deliver on any of his promises to help the middle class. Conservatives, of course, hated him and still do. I'm speaking of progressives, who gave him a pass and continue to do so out of all proportion to his actual record. The fact that we elected our first black president was a laudable achievement of the Civil Rights Movement. Americans demonstrated that we are now, indeed, willing to elect a black person to the highest office. At the same time, leftists must admit that the Obama administration, despite the rhetoric of his presidential campaign, was not leftist or progressive and indeed betrayed our values of economic equality, civil liberties, and peace. Entering office with the opportunity to dramatically curtail the power of Wall Street due to the financial crisis, the Obama administration instead protected, even strengthened, the position of big banks and investment firms.

Progressives in the IDMP often use a convenient rationalization of blaming Republicans for Obama's failures. Most Republicans were, of course, almost irrationally obstructionist. But it was not the GOP who picked former Wall Street counsel Eric Holder for Attorney General (celebrated by the IDMP as the first black person to hold the position) or who put in power any of the other New Democrats like Rahm Emmanuel, Timothy Geithner, Jeh Johnson, Ron Kirk, Michael Froman, and Gary Gensler. The executive branch has substantial power beyond the control of Congress and Obama often used it in ways contrary to leftist principles. It was not the GOP who deported and detained more Latino immigrants than President Bush. Nor was it Congress that continued the executive branch's warrantless surveillance of Americans. It was the Obama administration that prosecuted more journalists than all previous administrations combined. And it was Obama who expanded the drone assassination program without a congressional declaration of war. Republicans in Congress may have been supportive of these actions, and a Republican president would probably have done much the same, but that simply proves the point. In far too many ways the Obama administration was simply a continuation of the neoliberal and neoconservative project he inherited.

Of course, none of these Obama appointments or policies is directly the fault of those in the Identity, Diversity, and Multiculturalism Program. Their mistake lies in giving Obama a free pass and thereby abetting another eight years of increasing inequality, waning civil liberties, and militarism. With Trump in power it has become acceptable again to criticize policies that were ignored or defended under Obama. The root of the problem is the presumption in the IDMP that having "Diverse" people in power is progressive of itself. Then, after seeing them in power, the advocates of Diversity either become blind to the faults of the powerful or else willing to excuse them. The result is a stifling of criticism and popular resistance from leftists. Progressives were properly outraged by things like the PATRIOT Act, drone strikes, and Wall Street bailouts when they were the policies of President Bush but most of the criticism faded as soon as Obama continued—or even expanded—all of them. Shortly after leaving office, Obama was paid $400,000 by the Wall Street firm Cantor Fitzgerald for a single speech. Justifiably, one might think, criticisms were raised. But Trevor Noah of the Daily Show, as tapped into the zeitgeist of the liberal class as any program, tweeted (April 28, 2017): "People are saying Obama shouldn't accept the money for his speech. So the first black president must also be the first one to not take money afterwards? Fuck that, and fuck you."

Gender generates a similar reaction. For example, there were feminists, even self-proclaimed socialist feminists, who backed Hillary Clinton over Bernie Sanders for president even though the policies of Sanders would have done more to improve the lives of women (and men). Why would a socialist ever support Clinton? "I want a woman president," proclaimed Suzanna Danuta Walters, Director of the Women's, Gender, and Sexuality Studies Program at Northeastern University, writing in The Nation (2016, 14). "I support her less for her specific political positions . . . than for the iconic value of electing the first woman president of the United States." The willingness to sacrifice actual improvements in the material well-being of real humans for symbolic victories is one of the worst consequences of the IDMP. Conspicuous displays of Identity are especially common among progressives and Democrats but it's such a simplistic ploy that it has been adopted by the right wing. Republican administrations have given us "Diversity" in the form of Gina Haspell, Elaine Chao, Ben Carson, Clarence Thomas, Condoleezza Rice, and Colin Powell. All these symbolic victories have worked diligently against leftist principles of justice. These uncomfortable truths are often simply ignored in the progressive discourse that is dominated by considerations of Identity, Diversity, and Multiculturalism.

The Nation magazine, a longtime leading voice of the left in the U.S., struggles with the ideas of Identity, Diversity, and Multiculturalism. At times,

The Nation continues to vigorously defend leftist principles of economic inequality and civil liberties. For example, in the same issue referred to previously, it published "Why this Socialist Feminist in not Voting for Hillary" by Liza Featherstone, who made the genuinely leftist point that "Socialist feminism assumes that redistribution is the best way to begin improving life for the vast majority of women, both materially and socially" (2016, 13). And they deserve credit for endorsing Bernie Sanders, one of the few social democrats in federal office, over Hillary Clinton.

Yet at other times they promote the identity politics of the IDMP. Nation columnist Katha Pollitt penned a piece called, "Why Bernie Didn't Get My Vote," after supporting Hillary Clinton in the 2016 New York Democratic primary. I suppose it's a good sign that both Pollitt and Walters felt the need to defend their position and seemed to recognize the tension between the calls for economic and social justice, on the one hand, and identity politics, on the other.[5] Like Walters, Pollitt admitted that, "his [Sanders's] politics are closer to mine than Hillary Clinton's" (2016, 6) So why vote against Sanders? "The problem is less that Bernie focuses on class and economic inequality than that he doesn't seem to understand that the economy, like society generally, is structured by gender and race." *Structured by* is common enough phrasing in IDMP circles. It comes across as an incisive diagnosis of the problem. In reality, it has no clear, operational meaning in economics or in politics, or even among leftists. If Pollitt means that women face discrimination and segregation and earn less money than men, then, well, every "traditional leftist" like Sanders knows that, and his policies speak to solving those problems. Sanders real failing (in addition to his gender) was not, I suspect, a supposed misunderstanding of pseudo-analytical concepts like "structured by," but rather his tone. Pollitt explains that even though Sanders's policies might "benefit more women than men . . . they do not speak directly to the rage and fed-upness that so many women, in every class, justly feel." Can we infer that Pollitt believes Clinton has the proper righteous rage? And that this rage makes her a better choice despite her worse policies? Or that she understands what is meant by "structured by gender" because she's a woman? It's an argument whose fundamental weaknesses are concealed to those who already accept the ideology of Identity, Diversity, and Multiculturalism.

At the same time, individuals who might seem to have the right Diversity qualities will be dismissed if they don't conform to the "right" narrative. While Hillary Clinton was running to the be first female president, and often that was the strongest argument in her favor, Bernie Sanders was running to be the first Jewish president. Yet Bernie got no Diversity credit. On the contrary, the representation of Sanders on a T-shirt for sale at the 2016 Democratic National Convention, in which he seemed to be morphing into a rat, would not have been especially out of place in Kristallnacht Germany. In 2018 Alexandria Ocasio-Cortez, a young Latina, ran against incumbent Democrat Joe Crowley, most distinctly white and male, for a New York City congressional seat. Absent was any notion of "I'm with Her" from the crowd that was quick to jump on any opposition to Hillary as sexist. While Crowley lacked any Diversity attributes, he was one of the leading recipients of Wall Street money (OpenSecrets.org), an alliance that trumped that Diversity brought by Ocasio-Cortez. Ben Jealous, a progressive in the Democratic Party who ran for governor of Maryland in 2018, saw members of his own party offer tepid support. Despite the fact that he was black and running against a white Republican, some Democrats didn't endorse him and some had high praise for his Republican opponent (McCartney 2018).Celebrations of Identity, it seems, are reserved for those whose politics do not threaten the established interests.

For further displays of Identity, Diversity, and Multiculturalism we can turn from politicians to their symbionts in the corporate sector. It is probably clear how Identity, Diversity, and Multiculturalism could be used as an easy way for politicians to gain some popular support, especially among those who already buy into the framework, but it might not be as easy to find the corporate angle on IDMP. After all, profiting-making seems to be far removed from the activities of statecraft, which must make at least a pretense of concern for social justice. Yet many large corporations tout their Identity, Diversity, and Multiculturalism, justified perhaps not as plans to promote social justice, but rather as simply smart business. Yet the language of social justice is implicit, and they want credit for being good corporate citizens.

As exhibits I offer three leading firms—ExxonMobil, Walmart, and Bank of America—from different sectors—energy, retail, and banking—of the economy. None could be considered a friend of the Left. These firms (along with most other large companies) provide ample information about their principles and plans regarding Identity, Diversity, and Multiculturalism (or alternatively Inclusion or Inclusiveness). The following, for example, was taken from various pages on the ExxonMobil Global Diversity report (2017):

Our Global Diversity Framework is the foundation for our long-term, career-oriented approach to employment, with three interrelated objectives:
- Attract, develop and retain a premier, diverse workforce from the broadest possible pool to meet our business needs worldwide;
- Actively foster a productive work environment where individual and cultural differences are respected and valued, and where all employees are encouraged to contribute fully to the achievement of superior business results;
- Identify and develop leadership capabilities to excel in a variety of international and cultural environments.

ExxonMobil's global policies promote diversity and inclusion and prohibit any form of discrimination or harassment in any company workplace, anywhere around the world. These broad policies encompass all forms of discrimination, including discrimination based on sexual orientation or gender identity.

Walmart, the world's leading employer, goes even further in their *Culture, Diversity, & Inclusion* report (2018). Their mission is to "is to create an inclusive culture where all associates are engaged to deliver on our purpose." And they have put some resources behind their words, holding an African American Forum, an Inclusion Forum, and an Interfaith Summit, and creating a Global Women's Development Series. The report lists a number of *Diversity and Inclusion Commitments* including,

- Accelerating progress in the representation of women and women of color in executive/senior level positions over five years.
- We will continue to make our workplaces trusting places, where complex —and sometimes difficult—conversations about Diversity & Inclusion are possible.
- We will implement and expand unconscious bias education. By helping our employees recognize and minimize their blind spots, we aim to facilitate more open and honest conversations.

Walmart, we should remember, is where Hillary Clinton once served as a member of the board of directors. It is notoriously anti-union and "pays its employees so little that many of them rely on food stamps, health care and other taxpayer-funded programs." The organization, Americans for Tax Fairness, estimates that Walmart receives approximately 7.8 billion dollars annually in subsidies and tax breaks (2014). By no standard is it a progressive company, yet it seems more than willing to do Identity, Diversity, and Multiculturalism.

Finally, consider Bank of America, one of the largest financial firms on the planet, making the list of *too big to fail* under George Bush and *too big to jail* under Obama and Eric Holder. Bank of America's Global Diversity and Inclusion Council (GDIC), chaired by the CEO and staffed by senior executives, provides the diversity leadership. From their *Supporting Inclusion* webpage as of July 2018:[6]

As part of our ongoing commitment to being a great place to work, we encourage our employees to have courageous conversations as a way to promote inclusion, understanding and positive action by creating awareness of different experiences and perspectives . . . We also invest in our employees and inclusive workplace through a variety of development and learning programs that help drive a culture of mutual respect, and promote teamwork and positive engagement at every level of our company.

- Unconscious Bias—This training has been rolled out globally to more than 41,000 employees since 2013.
- Diverse Leader Sponsorship Program—Targets top-performing diverse talent and assigns each participant a senior leader sponsor who helps accelerate her or his visibility, advocacy and development over the course of the 10 month program. Protégés and sponsors continue to meet after the program is over. We've found participants to be twice as likely to be promoted as a result of their participation in this program. Sponsors are just as diverse as their protégés, many being women, people of diverse races and ethnicities and LGBT leaders.
- Disability learning—In 2017, we added over 20 courses covering topics related to proper use of disability terminology, hiring, accommodations and inclusive communication. Over 1,200 employees participated in this self-directed learning in 2017.
- D&I Learning—Focused on celebrating diversity and practicing inclusion, the program had more than 200,000 completions in 2017 alone.
- LGBT learning—Offers training modules and events for employees to become better informed about the issues facing the LGBT community, and how together we can help promote an inclusive working environment. To date, LGBT training sessions have been delivered to more than 19,000 participants worldwide . . .

The enthusiastic embrace of the rhetoric of the Identity, Diversity, and Multiculturalism Program by neoliberal politicians and their corporate allies might suggest to its progressive supporters that it cannot possibly be a radical, leftist project. The rejoinder might be that in the process of widespread adoption the real meaning has been distorted and debased. The celebration of Martin Luther King Jr. Day, while ignoring much of his message, could be given as another example. Or the popularity of Che Guevara T-shirts among bourgeois youth. I argue, however, that unlike King's Poor People Movement or Guevara's Marxism, the IDMP is simply not a leftist project and there is no need to twist its message to make it palatable. I claim it never offered a radical critique that corporations needed to twist. My argument depends, of course, on definitions—on what the IDMP actually means, and on how we define the Left. We turn to these conceptual tasks soon.

As perhaps most tragic example of the influence of Identity, Diversity, and Multiculturalism we should discuss the movement known as *Black Lives Matter*. The movement was sparked by a number of well publicized (and video recorded) incidents of police brutality against, for the most part, black men. BLM is responding to decades of mistreatment at the hands of the police as well as excessive punishment in the criminal justice system more generally.

Yet despite the justness of the cause, the broader cultural effectiveness of the Black Lives Matter movement has been hampered by a moral philosophy and political strategy informed by the Identity, Diversity, and Multiculturalism paradigm. Let me make clear that I, along with virtually everybody else on the Left, believe that excessive force by the police is a significant problem in this country. As leftists, we oppose three-strikes laws, long and mandatory prison sentences, and the resulting mass incarceration. I am concerned that the strategy of BLM will undermine the likelihood of achieving these objectives. The movement is built upon a foundation of racial divisiveness, a clear contrast to the unifying message of the Civils Rights Movement and the Poor People's Campaign. It therefore also stands in opposition to core values of the Left that come to us via the Enlightenment, which emphasized universalism and equality. The Civil Rights Movement embraced these core values and demanded that America make good on the promise. The problem, in other words, was not Enlightenment values but the failure to follow them, a stance that even opponents had trouble rejecting. The *Black Lives Matter* movement, on the other hand, has put progressives into a difficult position. We do indeed need a social and political strategy to radically remake our criminal justice system, yet the racial divisiveness stimulated by the movement is contrary to our core values and, as a practical matter, will likely impede the realization of our goals. We properly object when the leaders on the Right arouse racial consciousness and animosity in their base. Let's not use the same dangerous tool on the grounds that our objectives are morally superior.

Thus, I find fault with the framing of the movement, not to the idea that black lives matter, nor to the objectives of equal treatment, nor to a more humane criminal justice system. Taken as a statement, *black lives matter* is the conclusion to a syllogism parallel to the classic exercise in deductive logic proving that *Socrates is mortal*. It goes something like this:

All lives matter (major premise)
Black lives are lives (minor premise)
Black lives matter (conclusion)

As with all syllogisms the truth of the conclusion is contained in the truth of the premises. Supporters of the movement believe that *black lives matter* is a truth that America needs to acknowledge. Those who prefer to say that *all lives matter* are to be dismissed as racists. There was a minor moral panic on my campus (and others, I hear) when somebody put up a poster claiming "It's OK to be white." The headline on the front page of the campus newspaper: "White Supremacist Posters on Campus" (Schiff 2018). The placarder may indeed be a white supremacist, or maybe was simply a prankster looking to trigger the exact overreaction he got, but the meaning itself is true (every skin color is OK). Treating the trivial message as an "incident of bias and hate," instead of simply taking them down without fanfare, probably scores points with those who are already on-board with the Program but it cannot possibly gain support among those, especially whites who might infer that the university takes the position that it's not OK to be white, who are not. I fear it may send potential political allies toward the Right, where they never fail to characterize displays of "identity politics" as representative of the entire Left. So before we label incidents as hate or people as racists we might want to consider some reasonable alternatives.

I suspect that very few critics—or even outright opponents—of the Black Lives Matter movement would reject the full syllogism if it were presented to them in this form (which it never is). This is important because it means that the major and minor premises—all lives matter and black lives are lives—are not the source of the problem. Neither is the conclusion when it follows the premises. The problem arises only when there is insistence on the mutual exclusivity of the major premise and the conclusion: *Do all lives matter or do black lives matter?*, goes the question at a Democratic primary debate.[7] Yet it would be absurd to engage a debate regarding whether all men are mortal or whether Socrates is mortal (except among philosophy students). We should not take the bait when the question involves race. And we should not discount all the skeptics. Black lives matter precisely because all lives matter and black lives are lives. Yet many progressives are willing to overlook the divisiveness by saying things like, *Yes, white lives matter too but right now we focusing on black lives*, or, *People already know that white lives matter and now they need to acknowledge that black lives matter*. Or they might dismiss the questioners outright for showing their white privilege. Criticism of the Black Lives Matter movement is considered bad form by many progressives because it could be misinterpreted as a denial of the problems faced by many black people during encounters with the criminal justice system. Yet no leftist denies racism and the none of the defenses of the movement gets around the problem with the "or." Do all lives matter *or* do black lives matter?

Liberals should not suppose that the divisiveness created is solely the fault of those who take offense or that only racists believe that all lives matter. Poor whites, for example, might justifiably be put off by suggestion they "just don't get it" because of their white privilege. They could respond that we need a new movement: Poor white lives matter. Judging by how well they are treated in our society, it's simply not true that everybody knows that poor white lives matter. But why stop there? Let's go further: Latino lives matter. Latina lives matter. Native American lives matter. Muslim lives matter. Gay lives matter. Then we can start with the intersections. Poor Latin/x lives matter. Lesbian immigrant lives matter. And on and on and every group would be correct, just as the conclusion to the syllogism is correct, but where would that leave the Left? Divided by an ideology created by progressives, and totally ineffective as a social force.

Black lives matter vs. *all lives matter* is both bad moral philosophy and bad politics. It downplays the fundamental Enlightenment values of equality and universal human rights and it contradicts a key organizational principle of the Left: building class solidarity across other social differences. We can recognize that blacks disproportionately suffer from problems of poverty and police violence without insisting that other groups do not suffer. The Civil Rights Movement took equality as a core value and solidarity as an organizing principle. Howard Zinn's classic, *A People's History of the United States* (2003), relates that in colonial American history race was used, virtually manufactured, by the wealthy elite to divide and rule poor workers and farmers. Later, many whites in the working class, including in unions like the AFL, bought into the racist system. And while unions today fortunately hold a more encompassing notion of solidarity, the IDMP has ironically now become the problem, using a new ideology to make it more difficult for the working and middle classes to realize their best interests in an increasingly plutocratic system. Leftist values demand that we criticize not only social problems like policing and economic inequality but also the tribal divisiveness stimulated by the Identity, Diversity, and Multiculturalism Program, and manifested, for instance, in Black Lives Matter. Leftists today, like those in the Civil Rights Movement of the last century, should nurture an ethos of universal humanism and a practical commitment to social-movement solidarity.

This is not a matter of morality or the politics of compromise. There is a real danger to maintaining the current posture of smugness taken by many progressives when they talk about the angry white man, the working class, white southerners, evangelical Christians, and others regarded as hostile to Identity, Diversity, and Multiculturalism. It may be true that a certain percentage, probably even a disproportionate number, of the individuals in these groups are racists, homophobes, Islamophobes, or various other forms of nativists and xenophobes. At the individual level we can indeed renounce and condemn these right-wing populist beliefs. In private we might want to ridicule them (although it still strikes me as bad form). But at the sociological level we should think about the conditions that nurture such individual traits and direct our energy at correcting these problems. To make an argument by analogy: we condemn individuals who commit crimes like domestic violence and robbery while working at the same time to change the social, cultural, and economic conditions that contribute to them. I'm suggesting that instead of doling out self-righteous mockery, progressives should work on fixing the political-economic problems that form the substrate for the cultural problems of the populist Right and alienated center.[8]

The peril of failing to act is that we continue to foster a set of beliefs that would permit or even encourage an increasingly authoritarian and perhaps even fascist political regime. Is this hyperbole? I fear not. In his study of Nazi Germany, the sociologist Hans Gerth found the group most supportive of nascent fascism in the 1920s was the anxious and declining middle class.

> The common element in the situations of all these different strata was their despair and lack of social and economic security, the wide differential between self-esteem and actual status, between ambition and accomplishment, between subjective claims for social status and the objective possibility of attaining these goals through competitive orientation toward "market chances," or opportunities for social ascent through bureaucratic careers (1940, 528).

Despite the different causes of the political-economic crises—the one in Germany resulting from the loss in WWI, the reparations required by the Treaty of Versailles, and the Great Depression, while the one in the U.S. coming more as a self-inflected, internal decline—the social consequences of decline are uncomfortably alike. An air of moral superiority toward those who "just don't get it" will be no protection from a repressive state or violent thugs if the situation takes a similarly dark turn here. It is thus enlightened self-interest to pursue a social and political strategy that creates as large a coalition as possible. Fortunately, there is plenty of common ground for just about everybody in the working and middle classes, regardless of race, sex, gender, sexual orientation, religion, or any other identity or any of their intersections.

A LEFTIST CRITIQUE

What do I mean when I say that the Identity, Diversity, and Multiculturalism Program is not leftist? The claim is so contrary to the world taken for granted among progressives that it will certainly be met with some incredulity for those who identity as supporters. In some cases, I will make the strong claim that the IDMP is in fact conservative or neoliberal (both of these terms will be clarified in chapter 1). Some of their policies, I maintain, are worse for the groups they claim to want to help than policies they reject as racist. Other elements of the program are simply *not leftist*; some ideas might be characterized as politically centrist. And while the Center may not be as bad as the Right, it isn't the Left either. Finally, some elements of the Program might not easily be placed on a political or philosophical spectrum that goes from left to right; they are simply apolitical or amoral. What this means—whether it is right-wing, centrist, or politically irrelevant—is that the Identity, Diversity, and Multiculturalism Program does not promote a leftist or radical agenda for social justice. At best we might hope it does no harm, but on balance it is detrimental to the leftist cause because it pulls people away from more constructive activities and abets the neoliberal forces in society. Progressives should spend their time and energy on issues and campaigns that will promote leftist values.

The leftist standpoint adopted here separates it from other works on Diversity and identity politics by its liberal critics, notably those of Walter Benn Michaels (2006), Jim Sleeper (1997), and Mark Lilla (2017). Michaels in his insightful and influential work, *The Trouble with Diversity*, speaks of altering "the political terrain of contemporary American intellectual life" (7). In addition to pushing for more radical remedies, my argument is more socio-economic (I'm a social scientist and Michaels comes from the humanities[9]) yet I share his objective of creating space in which criticism can be voiced without being labeled as conservative, racist, sexist, homophobic, privileged, and so on. In *Liberal Racism,* Jim Sleeper also tends to downplay a leftist political-economic analysis in favor of a cultural critique of our obsession with race. Of course, the cultural side is important (I engage it in chapters 4 and 5) and I fully accept his claim that "precisely because the United States is becoming more racially, ethnically, and religiously complex, liberals should be working overtime to identify and nurture at least a few shared national principles and bonds that deepen a sense of common belonging and nourish democratic dispositions" (177). Mark Lilla in *The Once and Future Liberal* properly emphasizes the need for liberals to return to actual politics, ending the anti-politics and pseudo-politics of the last 40 or so years. This requires "the priority of institutional over movement politics; the priority of democratic persuasion over aimless self-expression; and the priority of citizenship over group or personal identity" (104). We disagree, however, on the details of that political engagement: The Democratic Party, led by someone like a Barack Obama, would seems to satisfy his demands for justice. It should be clear already, but I maintain that Obama and the Democrats are behind the twin problems of neoliberalism, on the one hand, and the IDMP, on the other.

I personally know a number of progressives who have doubts about Identity, Diversity, and Multiculturalism. Many, however, are hesitant to voice a critique, particularly when there is some risk for stepping out of line and saying the "wrong" thing. I would hope that this book could provide some additional cover for dissenting viewpoints. There is a tipping-point aspect to all of this. The more doubts that get raised the easier it becomes to voice even more. Some people might be waiting for criticism of Identity, Diversity, and Multiculturalism to become a bit safer before jumping in. I see this as a perfectly rational strategy. At the same time, I hope that some will take a risk, step forward, and be among the first in their personal and professional circles to publicly criticize the Program from a leftist perspective.

My objective is to offer a choice to progressives in the Program: To be consistent one can either be a leftist or one can support the Program. Because the Left should be seen as the more fundamental set of principles, the reasonable response to any state of cognitive dissonance would be to affirm one's leftist commitments and to discard or modify one's attachment to the IDMP. Realistically, I have little hope that those officially attached to the program will react in this way because material rewards make such an honest reassessment nearly impossible. Furthermore, those followers who embrace the Program as something akin to a religious faith will not easily be dissuaded. But I am much more optimistic about young people. College students in particular have been in the vanguard of many recent social movements and their engagement is probably necessary if we want to fix the current problems in our country.

More modestly, I would be satisfied if this work weakened the *presumption* that Identity, Diversity, and Multiculturalism is somehow progressive, leftist, or radical. I hope to shift the burden of proof onto the supporters of the program. Progressives who support the IDMP should demonstrate—and not merely assume—that the program promotes justice according to leftist values and principles. Whichever side we take, we must provide arguments—that is, logic and evidence—for our positions. And we must be wary of the many fallacies, including *ad hominem*, along the way. I look forward to joining a dialogue on Identity, Diversity, and Multiculturalism that is not premised on the conservatism, racism, sexism, or homophobia of the critics. I hope for something of a dialectic process in which my critique produces a response by the defenders in which they modify their positions and I, too, must go back and revise my own thinking. We may not move toward each other but rather into some new, perhaps unexpected, synthesis.

In order for the Left to be of value to society, to shift its attention from symbolic games to the substantial problems of inequality and repression, to engage in the popular struggle for greater equality and liberty, it is necessary to displace Identity, Diversity, and Multiculturalism with a more humane and reasonable paradigm. It is not leftist to have supported Barack Obama—who oversaw a massive decline in black wealth by choosing to help banks instead of homeowners—because he is black, or Hillary Clinton—who supported cuts to welfare at home and military intervention abroad—because she is a woman. Elizabeth Warren, instead of trying to establish her Identity *bona fides* by taking a DNA test to prove she was Native American, should have joined the fray when the Standing Rock Sioux Tribe and their allies nonviolently resisted a violent onslaught by private and public policing forces at the behest of Energy Transfer Partners, whose aim was to build the Dakota Access Pipeline (Sainato 2016). The Black Lives Matter movement, despite a valid criticism of police repression and mass incarceration, undermines its own cause by falling back onto tribalism instead of universalism as a motivating framework. Given the magnitude of our social problems and the role that social movements must play in any solutions, the pressing task before us is therefore to build a leftist case against the Identity, Diversity, and Multiculturalism Program so that the Left can better organize itself.

My critique does not ignore the fact there are many people already doing good work and most of them sympathize with Identity, Diversity, and Multiculturalism. Indeed, I am counting on their good will and intellectual honesty in order for my arguments to get a fair hearing. Because the thesis of this work violates conventional wisdom—most supporters view themselves as part of a leftist, even radical, program—we must spend some time conceptualizing the key terms in a clear and consistent manner. Foremost among them are terms like the *Left* and the *Identity, Diversity, and Multiculturalism Program,* but our analysis will also involve other important concepts like *racism* and *colorblindness*. I have already mentioned that liberty and equality are values central to the Left, but that still leaves a lot to resolve, including the content of those terms and the ways to handle any trade-offs between them. But let's postpone a fuller interpretation of the Left as a political and philosophical orientation, as well as the conceptualization of race and racism, for later chapters. Here in the introduction I want to start by examining the object of my leftist critique, that is, the Identity, Diversity, and Multiculturalism Program, especially its core principles.

THE FOUR TENETS OF THE IDENTITY, DIVERSITY, AND MULTICULTURALISM PROGRAM

What, exactly, are the main principles of Identity, Diversity, and Multiculturalism? Potentially this is a very long list of things. The Program is intrinsically a big, complex, social, political, and academic phenomenon. It includes all manner of intellectual and organizational activity—the statements, proposals, plans, initiatives, conferences, committees, panels, forums, and so on. It would be impossible to get even the supporters of the program to agree on everything. Reasonable people can interpret it in many ways or highlight different components.

Yet it would hardly be fair to critique the Program without offering a clear statement of its key principles, unless I wanted to critique it on the grounds of vagueness, a charge that might have some merit but avoids the bigger issues. Instead of attacking a long list of points that are potentially contentious among the adherents, or pulling out some of the more outlandish statements and actions by its enthusiasts (now a thriving industry by conservatives on social media), I have opted to evaluate a smaller set of core themes that recur frequently among the academic practitioners of Identity, Diversity, and Multiculturalism, as well as among scholars in associated fields like African-American Studies, Gender Studies, Queer Studies, etc. As discussed previously, many of these ideas have been consumed and adopted in the broader culture and in the political economy, but here I will focus on colleges and universities as the primary producers of the principles. The academic manufacturing and marketing of the Identity, Diversity, and Multiculturalism Program is an important part of the overall production of new cultural knowledge. Ideological and explanatory frameworks that start on campuses get transmitted to the rest of society with each graduating class.

Drawing from the academic literature and from other activity of campus, I identity four central tenets of the Identity, Diversity, and Multiculturalism Program. I state them here in brief, with a discussion to follow.

1. *Diversity as Justice*: The most important struggle for justice today is increasing the representation throughout society of individuals from historically marginalized groups by ending discrimination on the grounds of race, gender, sexual orientation, and similar characteristics;
2. *Colorblindness as Racism*: Race-neutral solutions to the problems caused by racism are harmful to blacks;
3. *Race as Culture*: Members of different races belong to different cultures;
4. *Culture as Virtue*: Cultures should be respected and celebrated.

My thesis can now be more precisely stated: none of the four tenets of the Identity, Diversity, and Multiculturalism Program is a leftist value or principle. The tenets are either right-wing, centrist, or irrelevant to leftist notions of social justice. Thus, they distract and divert many potential progressive activists away from genuine leftist projects. Detailed and specific critiques of the four tenets will be developed in subsequent chapters but in the remainder of this introduction I will expand and clarify the meaning and context of each tenet. The reader who is already familiar with these themes may wish to skip to the actual critiques in the subsequent chapters while readers not as acquainted with the Program, especially as manifested in the academy today, may benefit from the following primer.

Tenet 1: Diversity as Justice

Diversity as Justice refers to the belief that discrimination on the grounds of race, gender, and sexual orientation is the main cause of inequality and injustice in the U.S. today. Seen from the other side, *Diversity as Justice* asserts that whiteness, along with maleness, heterosexuality, and perhaps a few other identities, are the main sources of unjustifiable privilege. The tenet maintains that those who believe in justice should, above all, fight against racism and other forms of discrimination, on the one hand, and the corresponding privilege on the other. *Diversity as Justice* maintains that discrimination on the grounds of racism, sexism, homophobia, and cisnormativity prevents blacks, women, and LGBTQ individuals from occupying highly paid jobs and other positions of power and influence. If we could end such discrimination by whites and others with power and privilege, we would see the fair representation of those who have been historically excluded.

Many groups presumably face such discrimination, and in principle the tenet would include them all. In practice, however, Diversity focuses above all on race and racism. That is, *Diversity as Justice* is concerned above all with the relative treatment and representation of blacks and the privilege of whites. In most hiring situations, at least in the academy, race is the most important "diversity" factor. Women and LGBTQ certainly count as Diversity, but not as much as race, and furthermore some non-whites are better than others. For this reason and to minimize repeating the names of all the groups and categories that potentially face mistreatment, my critique of the first tenet will presume a narrower focus of *Diversity as Justice* on race, and even black and white more specifically. Many elements of the critique, however, are easily generalized to other racial (or ethnic) groups and other forms of discrimination and privilege like gender, gender identity, sexual orientation, and the like.

My critique of *Diversity as Justice* is leftist. It does not deny or even minimize the extent of racism and other forms of discrimination, as do most right-wing assaults. In fact, I call for a fuller realization of equal opportunity, one that would undo racial inequality to a much greater extent than that called for by appeals to Diversity. But that argument will have to wait until later. Now, the task is simply to clarify the objective. That is, where, specifically, can we find manifestations of *Diversity as Justice*? Most colleges and universities—from the University of Oregon to the University of Virginia, from Minnesota to Arizona—now have Offices of Equity (alternatively called the Office for Equity and Diversity, or the Office of Equity and Inclusion, or the Office for Institutional Equity, or something similar). While *equity* seems to be a safer term than either *justice* or *equality*, the organizational missions are not and cannot be value-neutral. A concern with justice is clear. I do not suggest, of course, that everybody on these campuses is committed to *Diversity as Justice*; my interest is with the progressive supporters of the Program. Most practitioners certainly see themselves as working on a just and progressive cause for their campuses and for the larger society.

Many colleges and university have endorsed *Diversity Statements* (or similarly titled documents), and most are available on the internet. The statements often speak to efforts in recruitment, admissions, and hiring in order to increase minority representation among students and faculty. At the University of Puget Sound, the liberal arts college where I teach, the Diversity Strategic Plan states that "We continuously work to increase the structural diversity of the Puget Sound campus community."[10] While at Stanford the president writes that, "Diversity is a wonderful and empowering characteristic of our 21st century existence, here at Stanford and in the broader world. Inclusion is an essential set of practices that must continually focus each of us on the meaningful participation and support of all members of our community. Equity is a fundamental goal as we seek together to create a society of fairness, character, and integrity."[11] The Strategic Objective at the University of Kentucky is to "Enhance the diversity and inclusivity of our University community through recruitment and retention of an increasingly diverse population of faculty, administrators, staff, and students, and by implementing initiatives that provide rich diversity-related experiences for all to help ensure their success in an interconnected world."[12]

These initiatives are part of the broader academic environment, but what's going on inside the classrooms? Teaching and scholarship in many fields strongly promotes the notion of *Diversity as Justice*. I would not be surprised if the most commonly assigned article in introductory courses on race or African-American studies turned out to be Peggy McIntosh's, *White Privilege: Unpacking the Invisible Knapsack* (2008). It seems to be de rigueur to include it in anthologies on *Race, Class, and Gender*.[13] In McIntosh's famous piece she argues that we must look at the other side of the coin: the disadvantage of blacks implies an advantage for whites. White privilege includes not merely the clear manifestations of advantage that accrue from acts of intentional discrimination against people of color but also "an invisible package of unearned assets." The heart of the piece is a list of 26 *white privileges*. Wherever blacks face oppression—from interactions with the criminal justice system to contact with mortgage lenders—whites must logically receive a corresponding unfair advantage.

The academic writing on white privilege provides *the* central framing for the notion of *Diversity as Justice*. A search in Google for the term *White Priv-*

ilege produces 158 million hits (as of late 2018); a search limited to Google *Scholar* finds nearly a million documents. For those in the field, white privilege is an important concept because it argues that whites receive an unjust advantage and thus have a moral responsibility not simply to avoid overtly racist acts against blacks but also to change the current system. The discourse around white privilege inseparably involves the issue of justice. Note that privilege is not merely an advantage—tall people have a legitimate advantage in basketball—but rather an advantaged that is morally unjustifiable. In McIntosh's formulation the language is clearly value-laden, and she is far from alone. In *Confronting One's own Racism* Joe Feagin and Hernan Vera (2008) write that "all whites can confront their racist views and propensities and seek to become egalitarian and antiracist" (153). Tim Wise (2010), often referred to as a leading anti-racist, writes, " . . . there is the issue of fairness itself. For whites to have such a relative advantage over people of color, and in such large measure because of the inertia carried over from past unequal opportunity, as well as ongoing discrimination, is unjust. These advantages are not earned, and thus to benefit from them is ethically dubious" (135–35). The likelihood of misinterpretation is so high that I need to be especially clear about my position here or, rather, what my position will be when I critique the tenet in the next chapter. While the term is often used imprecisely, I do not dismiss the notion of white privilege. In fact, in chapter 2, I explicitly incorporate one manifestation of white privilege into a model of economic inequality. And I certainly do not object to academics involving themselves in a struggle for justice. I would like to see more of it, especially outside the classroom and into the realm of politics, where it is the most appropriate and most beneficial. The modest claim here is that the academic work on white privilege is an important instance of the tenet of *Diversity as Justice*. In the next chapter I will critique that tenet from the Left—a critique that has almost nothing to do with the existence or degree of white privilege. It follows that an assertion of the existence of white privilege, however impassioned, cannot be used to rebut the leftist critique of Diversity. In other words, believing in white privilege does not suffice to make one a leftist. The political and personal demands are far more stringent.

Tenet 2: Colorblindness as Racism

It is widely supposed that solutions to the problems of racism will require policies that specifically benefit historically disadvantaged racial groups. The tenet of *Colorblindness as Racism* is stronger still: laws and programs intended to reduce racial inequality but that make no reference to race are, *ipso facto*, racist. Even policies targeting income differences—something ostensibly quite progressive—are suspect. The motives of those who advocate colorblind policies are often explicitly regarded as racist.

Among the general public, the tenet of *Colorblindness as Racism* would be contentious. After all, it was Martin Luther King, Jr. who, in perhaps his most cherished speech, dreamt of a world in which children "will not be judged by the color of their skin but by the content of their character."[14] Although King may be passé among academic supporters of Diversity, he is widely respected in the larger society, and the notion that people be judged not by their color still receives broad support off-campus. In the academic world, however, the disdain for a colorblind approach can be observed by considering the titles of some recent books by scholars friendly to Identity, Diversity, and Multi-culturalism:

- *"Color-Blind" Racism*, by Leslie Carr (1997)
- *Racism without Racists: Color-Blind Racism & the Persistence of Racial Inequality in Contemporary America*, by Eduardo Bonilla-Silva (2010)
- *Color-Blind: The Rise of Post-Racial Politics and the Retreat from Racial Equity*, by Tim Wise (2010)
- *The Price of Progressive Politics: The Welfare Rights Movement in an Era of Colorblind Racism*, by Rose Ernst (2010)
- *Colorblind Injustice: Minority Voting Rights and the Undoing of the Second Reconstruction*, by J. Morgan Kousser (1999)
- *The New Jim Crow: Mass Incarceration in an Age of Colorblindness*, by Michelle Alexander (2012)

And consider a few book chapters and academic articles:

- *The Sweet Enchantment of Color-Blind Racism in Obamerica*, by Eduardo Bonilla-Silva and David Dietrich (2011)
- *We Aren't Just Color-blind, We Are Oppression-Blind!* by Abby L. Ferber (2014)
- *Toward a Critical Understanding of Gendered Color-Blind Racism within the U.S. Welfare Institution*, by Shannon Monnat (2010)
- *The Linguistics of Color Blind Racism: How to Talk Nasty about Blacks without Sounding "Racist,"* by Eduardo Bonilla-Silva (2002)
- *The Color-Blind Bind*, by Lee D. Baker (2001)
- *Color-Blind Racism and Racial Indifference: The Role of Racial Apathy in Facilitating Enduring Inequalities*, by Tyrone Forman (2006)
- *The Legitimation of Black Subordination: The Impact of Color-Blind Ideology on African American Education*, by Dawn Williams and Roderic Land (2006)

- *Whiteness and White Privilege: Problematizing Race and Racism in a "Color-blind" World and in Education,* by Paul Carr (2016)
- *Color-Blind Racial Ideology and Psychological False Consciousness Among African Americans,* by Helen Neville et al. (2005)

As seen from the titles, it is acceptable in the academy to associate *color-blind* (or *colorblind*) with racism and other negative terms and concepts. A leading proponent of this perspective and the author of several of the above mentioned pieces is Eduardo Bonilla-Silva, professor of sociology at Duke University. He elaborates (2010): "I have attempted to conceptualize racism as a sociopolitical concept that refers exclusively to racial ideology that glues a particular racial order. Thus, I have suggested that *color-blind racism* is the ideology of the 'new racism' era" (173; emphasis added).

Another leading voice, Tim Wise, author of *Colorblind,* offers a similar depiction of colorblindness, which he refers to also as "post-racial liberalism." Wise (2010) declares that, "colorblindness, by discouraging discussions of racial matters and presuming that the best practice is to ignore the realities of racism, makes it more difficult to challenge those biases, and thus increases the likelihood of discrimination. . . . In the final analysis, the problem with colorblindness and post-racial liberalism is that they ignore the different ways in which we experience the society around us" (18–19). This position will be rebutted in chapter 3 but simply note here the facility of the linkage between colorblindness and racism.

Among scholars in African-American studies or among those who label themselves as *anti-racist* there are very few who espouse or defend color-blindness. There is some debate, but it tends to go from colorblindness as wrong-headed liberalism, on the one hand, to colorblindness as insidious conservatism, on the other. Critical race theory, an important paradigm among progressives in law schools, provides an example of the subtler "critique of liberalism" by maintaining that "color blindness . . . will allow us to redress only extremely egregious racial harms . . . Only aggressive, color-conscious efforts to change the way things are will do much to ameliorate misery" (Delgado and Stefancic 2012, 27). Bonilla-Silva (2002), on the other extreme, asserts that, "Color blind racism's racetalk avoids racist terminology and preserves its myth through semantic moves" (61). He offers additional advice to help his colleagues break through the "rhetorical maze" of unwanted data in order to get to the right answer:

If there is a new racial ideology that has an arsenal of rhetorical tools to avoid the appearance of racism, analysts must be fully aware of its existence and develop the analytical and interpretive know-how to dissect *color blind nonsense* . . . It is the task of progressive social scientists to expose color blindness, show the continuing significance of race, and *wake-up color blind researchers* to the color of the facts in contemporary United States. (63, emphasis added)

From personal and professional interactions, admittedly a non-random sample, it is my sense that most of those who teach at the university level and align themselves with Identity, Diversity, and Multiculturalism readily accept the equivalence of colorblindness and racism. They support and assign the writings of scholars like Wise and Bonilla-Silva. They instruct their students to make the same association. A student once shared with me a quiz on race he was given by a professor at the beginning of the semester. An item from the quiz:

"Color blindness" is a strategy used by some to ignore race and often involves stating that one does not see or notice the race of another human. A colorblind stance argues that our society is "post-racial." For contemporary America, a colorblind strategy:

   A. is not a useful approach to racism and would not be effective in ending racism.
   B. can not work to end racism in a society where wealth and economic opportunity are not equal.
   C. may be born of good intentions, come from home training or reflect a desire not to have to deal with race and racism.
   D. is not supportive of people of color and generally not seen by them as a compliment to them.
   E. perpetuates racism.
   F. All of the above.
   G. I don't like any of these so I am writing my own answer.

In political science this might be called a push poll. It seems as much designed to shape one's opinion on the topic as to measure it. A student unfamiliar with the issue would easily understand that the professor believes the correct answer is "All of the above." There are no favorable descriptions of colorblindness included in the "quiz." Presumably colorblindness would be racist if were true that it "would not be effective in ending racism" and would even "perpetuate racism."

A final anecdote. I arranged to give a talk at my college on the same topic as this work, that is, a leftist critique of Identity, Diversity, and Multiculturalism. The flyer on campus had a line that read, "Colorblind is not Racist." When I arrived at work one morning I discovered that several of the flyers in my building had been altered overnight by markers to block out the word "not." Certainly these students (I assume they were students) believed very strongly that colorblindness was racist even without hearing the counter-arguments. Their attitude toward free and open debate on campus is a bit troubling but, leaving that aside for now, we can plausibly infer they had learned to associate colorblindness and racism in some of their classes. It seems equally likely they had never come across any argument in favor of colorblindness. Nor, it seems, did they care to.

Of course, I should not overgeneralize from these experiences. Most professors do not administer push polls and most students are willing to consider the other side of a debate. Still, among academics who work in the area of Identity, Diversity, and Multiculturalism the notion of *Colorblindness as Racism* holds the dominant position. It may not be as well-advertised outside of the academy but only because it would not be well-received by a citizenry that is regarded as naïve enough to still largely agree with Martin Luther King, Jr.

Tenets 3 and 4: Race as Culture and Culture as Virtue

The final two tenets, *Race as Culture* (members of different races belong to different cultures) and *Culture as Virtue* (cultures should be respected and celebrated), are distinct ideas but they are easily and often lumped together. In fact, the notion of *Race as Culture* tends to be implicitly accepted in discussions of *Culture as Virtue*. Different cultures must exist, after all, if we should bother to regard them as virtuous. It is convenient, therefore, to discuss here the two tenets together under the broader heading of Multiculturalism.

Manning Marable (1997) writes that "multiculturalism . . . is a recognition that this nation's accomplishments are not reflected in the activities of only one race (white), one language group (English-speaking), one ethnicity (Anglo-Saxon), or one religion (Christianity)" (251). While many progressives, like Marable, endorse these ideas it's interesting to note how successful they have been even in the wider society. Although conservatives might reject Multiculturalism in order to defend a white, male, and European canon, both the Multiculturalist and the conservative accept the validity of *Race as Culture* and *Culture as Virtue*, the former fully and the latter with a caveat. Marable claims that four characteristics—race, language, ethnicity, and religion—can be used to form distinct cultural groups. The conservative would presumably agree: Blacks and whites (and Christians and Muslims, and so on) represent different cultures. By speaking of *accomplishments,* Marable endorses the notion of *Culture as Virtue*. And while conservatives might doubt the accomplishments of black culture for white people, they certainly see the value in white culture for white people and many might even grant that black culture is just fine for black people.

Although the critiques of *Race as Culture* and *Culture and Virtue* must wait until chapters 4 and 5, respectively, I should note that it will not directly engage the debate between Multiculturalists and conservatives. Instead I will undermine the foundation that unites them. My critique challenges the liberal as much as it challenges the conservative view of multiculturalism because both sides accept both tenets. I would grant that if the assumptions behind the debate were correct—if races were distinct cultures and if culture were virtuous—then we indeed should all be Multiculturalists now. I will make no leftist argument for allegiance to a European canon; education in the social sciences and humanities should be more comparative. While the European Enlightenment is the historical basis for the contemporary Left in the United States, a philosophical commitment to reason, liberty, and equality is not a uniquely European phenomenon and can be arrived at independently via other historical, philosophical, or personal routes. It's obvious that many Westerners do not have such commitments and many non-Westerners do. The leftist values should be judged on their own merit and not according to any particular geographical genealogy.

Nathan Glazer, who takes something of a middle-ground in the debate, offers a description of Multiculturalism similar to Marable's: "Multicultural-ism, for its advocates, becomes a new image of a better America, without prejudice and discrimination, in which no cultural theme linked to any racial or ethnic group has priority, and in which American culture is seen as the product of a complex intermingling of themes from every minority ethnic and racial group, and from indeed the whole world" (1998, 11). Many Diversity Statements (or similar documents) speak to the benefits to the organization when multiple races and cultures interact. Indeed the Supreme Court's deci-sion in *Regents of the University of California v. Bakke* (1978), which permit-ted race to be used in admission decisions, hangs on exactly this empirical presumption. On the surface, these are not entirely unreasonable points but they do presume the veracity of both *Race as Culture* and *Culture as Virtue*.

Statements of something like the two tenets can be found in the works of many other social theorists. According to Gary Peller (2011), for example, Multiculturalism is

> the notion that American society should be understood as a collection of diverse cultural groups, rather than a single, unified national body on the one hand or as simply an aggregate of atomized individuals on the other . . . it takes the status of group membership as a positive, meaning-generative value . . . a multiculturalist sensibility implies the government must recognize and respect, if not nurture, the diversity and integrity of racial and ethnic communities. (100)

The two tenets are foundational for Multiculturalism as it comes to us out of the field of education. Beverly Daniel Tatum, a psychologist and author of the best-selling *Why Are All the Blacks Kids Sitting Together in the Cafeteria,* explores the role of racial identity in individual development. Both of the tenets receive ample support in her work. "We all must be able to embrace who we are in terms of our racial and cultural heritage, not in terms of assumed superiority or inferiority, but as an integral part of our daily experience in which we can take pride" (2003, 107). These feelings of pride convey the notion of *Culture as Virtue*. Making the connection between race and culture even more explicit, she describes a strategy in which "a Black student can play down Black identity in order to succeed in school and mainstream institutions without rejecting his Black identity and culture. Instead of becoming raceless, an achieving Black student can become an emissary, someone who sees his or her own achievements as advancing the cause of the racial group" (64). This formulation suggests that one has a race and that it carries a distinct culture. Similarly, when one has more than one race, one has more than one culture. In discussing "biracial children" she endorses the work of Robin Lin Miller and Mary Jane Rotheram-Borus by suggesting that "if parents are going to encourage a biracial identity, they need to provide substantial positive exposure to both racial groups to help the child understand what it means to be a participant in both cultures" (177).

In describing a similar process of racial identity formation Mary Dilg (2003) writes,

> As students of color come to embrace their racial identity more fully, they may move into a period of wanting to surround themselves with overt signs of their own culture and to remove themselves from those in the dominant culture. In the classroom, for many of our students this is reflected in taking pleasure in studying the history and literature of their own culture . . . By their later years in high school, many of our students of color describe looking at themselves and others from a position of maturity, comfort, and pride in relation to their own identity. One young black woman wrote that . . . she had come to realize she could appreciate both her own culture and the culture of others. (64–65)

The adherents of Multiculturalism believe that "each racial grouping in the United States has, over past centuries, developed separate and distinct cultures. There is an African American culture, a Native American culture, an Asian American culture, a Latino/Hispanic culture, an Arab American culture, and a white culture" (Barndt 2007, 185). They speak about "the value of cultural membership" (Kymlicka 1989).[15] The tenets of *Race as Culture* and *Culture as Virtue*—and not the call for opening the western canon—will be critiqued. Thus my critique should not be casually dismissed as Eurocentric. On the other hand, the reader who rejects leftist values on their own merit can reject the critique offered. But establishing the inconsistency of the IDMP and the Left is, of course, the entire point.

SUMMARY AND CONCLUSION

In this work I will argue that the Identity, Diversity, and Multiculturalism Program is not a leftist project. I operationalize this task by critiquing from a leftist standpoint the following four tenets:

1. *Diversity as Justice*: The most important struggle for justice today is increasing the representation throughout society of individuals from historically marginalized groups by ending discrimination on the grounds of race, gender, sexual orientation, and similar characteristics;
2. *Colorblindness as Racism*: Race-neutral solutions to the problems caused by racism are harmful to blacks;
3. *Race as Culture*: Members of different races belong to different cultures;
4. *Culture as Virtue*: Cultures should be respected and celebrated.

My attempt to capture the main principles of Identity, Diversity, and Multiculturalism in plain language in these four tenets does afford the defenders an obvious way out. They could claim that I missed the point and deny that the four tenets are actually part of the program. Or they could allege that these four are minor aspects and that I missed the core of the program. But if I did somehow fail to nail down key principles of the Program, I could reasonably request that the supporters state the *true* tenets in language that is as clear and succinct as possible. And, just as importantly, to defend them as leftist. If that cannot be done, then allegations that the four tenets miss the mark might be seen as an attempt to avoid instead of to face head-on the cognitive dissonance.

The book will proceed as follows. In chapter 1, I start with the critique of *Diversity as Justice*. In chapter 2, I offer a model of inequality that complements that argument and provides a causal framework that will be useful for the subsequent critique of *Colorblindness as Racism* in chapter 3. The notion of *Race as Culture* is critiqued in chapter 4. *Culture as Virtue* is treated in chapter 5. In the concluding chapter I pose to the reader, particularly to the progressive and idealistic young person, the choice between the IDMP and Left. This conclusion includes a consideration of the rhetoric of the Program and an attempt to preemptively address the likely objections to my critique. The idea that one must choose between the Left and the IDMP will certainly strike many as unacceptable. I imagine great efforts will be made to confuse the issue or otherwise avoid it. Nonetheless I believe that, in the end, Camus (1955) was right: "A man is always a prey to his truths. Once he has admitted them, he cannot free himself from them. One has to pay something" (31).

NOTES

1. Robert Reich, one of our leading public intellectuals, is currently a professor of economics at U.C. Berkeley and previously served in the Clinton administration. Bob Ney was a U.S. Representative from Ohio who was forced from office after pleading guilty to charges of fraud. He gives an account of the corruption of the American political system from the perspective of a person who was, admittedly, corrupted. Other good accounts of our political-economic situation include Chris Hedges, *Death of the Liberal Class* (2011), Bill Press, *Buyer's Remorse: How Obama Let Progressives Down* (2016), and Robert Scheer, *The Great American Stickup: How Reagan Republicans and Clinton Democrats Enriched Wall Street While Mugging Main Street* (2010).

2. I will mostly avoid and only occasionally use the term *identity politics*. The connotations and emotional baggage it carries make it less than ideal. Instead I will use *Identity, Diversity*, and *Multiculturalism*, either singly or collectively. I will capitalize the terms to indicate that they have taken on some new and additional meanings. I take (lowercase) identity to mean the answer to the question, "who are you?" The ordinary dictionary meaning of *diversity* is variety and that of *multiculturalism* is a state where individuals from different cultures are present. These standard meanings capture neither the denotation nor especially the connotation of the terms as currently employed by their supporters. Further I will refer to the *Identity, Diversity, and Multiculturalism Program* (IDMP) or just the *Program* by which I mean the intellectual and social movement, in all its various manifestations, that support the agenda or embrace the rhetoric of Identity, Diversity, and Multiculturalism. The key principles, or tenets, of the IDMP will be introduced shortly.

3. The most common measure of inequality is the Gini index, a number that ranges from 0, meaning a completely egalitarian distribution, to 1, indicating that one person (or household) has all the income in the country. According to the CIA Factbook (n.d.) the U.S. Gini index is 0.45, putting us in the company of China and Russia. Sweden, among the world's most equal countries, has a Gini index of 0.23 and Germany, the largest economy in Europe, has a Gini index of 0.27.

4. The leading source of official data on poverty is *Income and Poverty in the United States*, revised annually and released in September as part of the Current Population Survey of the Census Bureau (Semega, Fontenot, and Kollar 2017). The September 2017 release has data for the year 2016. At that time the official poverty rate for those under age 18 was 18 percent. There are, however, methodological problems with the official poverty threshold and a more complete survey of household budgets by the Economic Policy Institute indicates that the true threshold should be much higher (Gould, Wething, and Sabadish 2013). This would mean, of course, a much higher rate of actual poverty.

5. Pollitt was easily outdone by *Nation* writer Joan Walsh, who spoke of "Bernie Bros," a supposed legion of young, white, male progressives who hated Clinton because she was a woman. See, for example, her absurd *Bernie Sanders is Hurting Himself by Playing the Victim* in which she avers that Sanders risks becoming "the messiah of an angry, heavily white, and male cult" (2016).

6. Available at https://about.bankofamerica.com/en-us/what-guides-us/support ing-inclusion.html#fbid=1Hr-BXYjXtj.

7. The debate in Des Moines, Iowa, on November 14, 2015. The video is available at http://www.cnn.com/videos/politics/2015/10/13/bernie-sanders-democratic -debate-black-lives-matter-27.cnn.

8. At the same time, I don't deny that mockery or political satire, like that of The Onion, may indeed play a useful role in social change. It can help to erode the legitimacy upon which all social systems ultimately rely. But satire, I believe, is best directed at those with political-economic power, not at those at the other end of the hierarchy, however misinformed and misguided the latter might be.

9. Of course there is plenty of good social science and moral philosophy in Michaels's work, but our approaches to the problem differ. As an economic sociolo-gist I hope to push the analysis a bit further in these directions.

10. Strategic Goal number one for the 2017 Diversity Strategic Plan, available at http://www.pugetsound.edu/about/diversity-at-puget-sound/diversity-strategic-plan/.

11. The Message from the President, available at https://facultydevelopment.stan ford.edu/about-us/presidents-statement-diversity.

12. Available at http://www.uky.edu/sotu/diversity-and-inclusivity.

13. Paula Rothenberg edits a popular anthology titled *White Privilege* (2008) and dedicates it to McIntosh, "Who led the way."

14. *I Have a Dream*, August 28, 1963, The King Center, available at http://www. thekingcenter.org/archive/document/i-have-dream-1.

15. This is the title of chapter 8 in *Liberalism, Community, and Culture* by Will Kymlicka.

Chapter One

A Leftist Critique of Diversity as Justice

In this work I critique, from an unmistakably leftist perspective, the Identity, Diversity, and Multiculturalism Program (IDMP). In the introduction, we explored some of the displays of Identity, Diversity, and Multiculturalism in political and corporate contexts. We examined its intellectual foundation in the academy and found many illustrations of its four central tenets:

1. *Diversity as Justice*: The most important struggle for justice today is increasing the representation throughout society of individuals from historically marginalized groups by ending discrimination on the grounds of race, gender, sexual orientation, and similar characteristics;
2. *Colorblindness as Racism*: Race-neutral solutions to the problems caused by racism are harmful to blacks;
3. *Race as Culture*: Members of different races belong to different cultures;
4. *Culture as Virtue*: Cultures should be respected and celebrated.

In this chapter we consider the first of these tenets: *Diversity as Justice*. I claim that *Diversity as Justice* does not promote a leftist vision of justice but instead falls safely within the center of current political thinking. Many people, almost by definition, will fall in the center of any distribution, so this is not necessarily a criticism by itself. The critique has bite, however, because most supporters believe they bravely fight in the vanguard of a radical struggle against inequality, oppression, and all manner of right-wing injustice. What accounts for this perception? Much of the confusion among supporters, I allege, can be traced to improper conceptualization of some key terms. Some concepts are poorly defined and some perhaps not at all. This is a common occurrence, of course, in all matters discursive. Terms often have multiple meanings—a ubiquitous issue with language—but the real problem is that many participants in the debate are not aware of the ambiguity and are often oblivious to the fact they are using the same word with different meanings. For example, I suspect that many supporters could not give an adequate definition of equal opportunity, one that did not loosely refer to racist discrimination, sexist discrimination, and the like. More surprisingly, given its importance for the IDMP, even *racism* is a vague and ambiguous term. People can be racist, and also laws, ideas, words, images, a hiring or admission decision, or even the entire economy or educational system. These might all be perfectly valid uses but we should recognize that they are qualitatively different and that an awareness of these differences might be necessary for a proper understanding of the problem at hand. Discrimination is obviously related to racism but it is not always clearly specified how. I believe that, in large part, the fuzziness in these terms encourages the false belief that ending racism, sexism, and the like would be tantamount to achieving equality of opportunity and even satisfying the demands of justice for the Left.

Leftists, too, can be guilty of imprecision. What is meant by the *Left* as a political and philosophical standpoint? Many people could readily place themselves on the political spectrum but I suspect most would be unable to define what is meant in the abstract by left or right (progressive or conservative in the contemporary vernacular). They could probably state their views on social issues like abortion or gay marriage and on some economic issues like minimum wage and healthcare. But when pressed to find some logic that might unify their positions on the various issues they will run into trouble. To some degree it seems likely that political identification is a matter of conforming to group norms—family, friends, school, church, and so on.

But peer influence could not possibly account for all of it. It seems more plausible that there exists some intuitive understanding of our political moral philosophy. Our position on various issues will "hang together" for some reason, even if we cannot quite put it into words. For many purposes that moral intuition will suffice. Actions or outcomes that strike us as intuitively wrong would probably still do so even if we became aware of a deeper logic. For some problems, however, this imprecise expression of our values is not enough. Our intuition might fail us. It might be inconclusive or it might actually point in the wrong direction.

I suggest that this is true of Identity, Diversity, and Multiculturalism. By far the greatest portion of its supporters would identify as politically left or progressive. On college campuses, they might even say radical. The presumption that the Program expresses leftist values is, I claim, a failure of moral intuition. The social environment and media framing encourage this error. Progressives talk as if it were a force for social justice. The contrapositive is even more strongly stated: those who oppose Identity, Diversity, and Multiculturalism *must* be conservative.[1]

In large part, therefore, the leftist critique of Diversity as Justice is a matter of proper conceptualization. Once we understand the meaning of the relevant terms—racism, discrimination, and the leftist principles of justice—the incompatibility between the Left and the IDMP becomes quite clear. I turn first to a conceptualization of the Left. Definitions are merely agreements that words will stand for other words and thus can be neither objective nor permanent but communication would be impossible if words were free to flop around without any anchor. The contemporary meaning of *leftist*, while always in a process of evolution, is most certainly anchored in the thinking and politics of the Enlightenment. It is thus to a brief historical sidebar that we must first turn.

THE ENLIGHTENMENT ORIGINS OF THE MODERN LEFT

"There is a hardly a single ideal of the left that does not derive from the Enlightenment," writes Stephen Eric Bronner (2004, 60), a leading scholar of that historical period. Although the genealogy of the Left is perhaps not strictly necessary for a leftist critique of Identity, Diversity, and Multiculturalism today, as with many social ideas and institutions, the parallels with the past enrich our understanding of the present. Originally designating a physical, spatial relationship, the current usage of the word *left* in a philosophical and political sense comes to us from the French Revolution, certainly the most dramatic event of the Enlightenment. Those who favored a republic quite literally sat on the left side of the president in the National Assembly and later in the Legislative Assembly.

Like all such historical designations—Hellenistic Greece, the Roman Empire, the Middle Ages, the Renaissance—the boundaries of the Enlightenment are fuzzy. We never find a complete social revolution where previous ideas and institutions are fully obliterated. Furthermore, however strong the break with the past might have been, every era has its own diversity of thought and practice such that any attempt to summarize must necessarily oversimplify. As in biology, we cannot point to a single mutation as the moment of speciation yet, looking back over time, we can say that, at some point, the dog is no longer a wolf. Historians can continue to debate when and even what the Enlightenment was but I take the beginning of the era to be the philosophy of Rene Descartes in the middle of the seventeenth century and the ending to be the works of Kant, who popularized the German term *Zeitalter der Aufklärung* (Age of Enlightenment) to describe the movement around the end of the eighteenth century.² Enlightenment thinking as philosophical and political discourse continued throughout the nineteenth century and up to the present day, but the historical epoch, proper, can be conveniently bookended by the century and a half spanned by these two thinkers.

During the Enlightenment changes occurred throughout society—in economics, politics, philosophy, culture, religion, art, and so on. Out of the many changes, I emphasize two philosophical assumptions as of central importance to the present-day Left. The first was a change in the very meaning of *reason*. It would be an overreach to say that science was invented in the Enlightenment but we could say that a scientific outlook expanded and science as a practice became institutionalized. Mathematics similarly flourished. The key aspect for the Left, in any case, is not science itself, although it was a related phenomenon, but rather a change in the more fundamental concept of reason. Prior to the Enlightenment, reason was a theological construct representing the intellect of god. Henceforth, reason would refer to the intellectual endeavor of humans to understand reality, not the plan of God. "The Enlightenment in large part was created by this shift from reason as the perfect intelligence to reason as the law of nature" (Hankins 1985, 6). Humans came to believe that the universe could be understood at least in part by the application of science, that is, by observation and cogitation.³ *Sapere aude!*—Dare to reason!—was Kant's motto for the Enlightenment.

If the first fundamental change—the move from divine to human reason—involved the relationship between humans and a deity, the second involved our relationship with each other. *Liberté, Égalité, Fraternité!,* the famous slogan of the French Revolution, captures this spirit. Despite various counter-revolutions and other reactionary fits, the French Revolution symbolized the end of the age of monarchy, replaced with an audacious model of governance in which the people ruled themselves, that is, democracy.⁴ Those revolutionaries challenged, or at least began to challenge, the notion that any person was innately superior to any other, able to command others out of some birthright. Philosophically, it is the assumption of the equal moral worth of all individuals. Politically, it is the belief that sovereignty rests with the people. Some individuals can lead—hierarchy was not eliminated—but only by the consent of the led. Thus was established the cultural belief in democratic legitimacy.

I do not make the sweeping historical claim that these two cultural shifts—belief in human reason and moral equality—were the main societal changes to occur during the age of the Enlightenment. Already by the fourteenth century the social institution of feudalism was being replaced in certain parts of Europe by what can be called capitalism, not industrial capitalism as we now see it, but nevertheless a system increasingly built around the privatization of land and market exchange. Merchant republics in present-day Italy and the

Low Countries were established even earlier, but the scope and pace clearly accelerated during the 150 years of the Enlightenment. In reality, the spread of merchant capitalism and the scientific discoveries leading to industrial capitalism may have been the most important historical factors of this age. The cultural changes almost certainly required this materialistic foundation. Nevertheless, once established, the philosophical system had a logic that was somewhat freed from these economic moorings. Furthermore, capitalism itself represented progress in many ways compared to the previous feudal class structure.[5] While further societal changes were still needed before we finally arrive at the modern Left, the fixing of new beliefs in human reason and moral equality were necessary ingredients in subsequent political and philosophical progress. It turns out that the complex interplay between the progressive cultural beliefs of the Enlightenment, on the one hand, and the less noble imperatives of capitalism, on the other, form the basis for the leading political philosophies and conflicts that exist up to this day.

Enlightenment thought thus divided into two main branches: The Left and the Right. The left branch evolved into nineteenth-century socialism and twentieth-century social democracy. The right branch, just as much the intellectual legacy of the Enlightenment, brought us libertarianism and neo-liberalism. But these two new ideologies did not exhaust the political and philosophical landscape. Many people, including a lot of priests, politicians, and philosophers, embraced neither of these currents in Enlightenment. The time of the Enlightenment was full of superstition, ignorance, and cruelty. This reactionary political and philosophical faction formed the *Counter*-Enlightenment, the third major group and progenitor of fascism, conservatism, and neoconservatism. This, too, we call the Right, despite the obvious differences with classical liberalism and modern libertarianism. Let us first take the left branch before exploring the two paths on the Right.

THE MODERN LEFT

Although two key values were inherited from the Enlightenment—a belief in human reason as the only valid (albeit imperfect) arbiter of truth and a commitment to the equal moral worth of all individuals—they are not yet a full statement of principles for the modern Left. We look to the Enlightenment to find the wellspring of our core values, not for a blueprint for political action in the twenty-first century. The modern Left must work out the implications of those fundamental assumptions given current social conditions. Leftist principles help us align our contemporary societal arrangements with these key Enlightenment values.

What are the key principles today for those who embrace those values? In the introduction I suggested that they involve two commitments: first, to a strong set of political and civil liberties, and second, to a high level of economic equality. Any movement that we might recognize as leftist is motivated to expand either liberty (or civil rights or human rights) and/or equality (or otherwise improve the material well-being of the working and middle class). There are differences among these movements, of course. Furthermore, there are difficulties in specifying the exact degrees of liberty and equality, and the ways in which possible trade-offs will be addressed. Yet *Liberté, Égalité, Fraternité* still captures—more than two centuries later—the essence of leftist politics even if it leaves the practical details unresolved (something completely appropriate for a slogan!).

Yet in order to build a leftist critique of Identity, Diversity, and Multiculturalism one must commit to certain details. In this work, I take as the exemplary statement of leftist principles the theory of justice as fairness proposed by John Rawls, whom the Internet Encyclopedia of Philosophy refers to as "arguably the most important political philosopher of the twentieth century."[6] Many may claim to support Enlightenment values but Rawls (2001) exhorts us to "take seriously the idea that citizens are free and equal" (39). Cheap talk and political rhetoric are so common that we may fail to give proper consideration to the implications of a genuine commitment to the Enlightenment value of equal moral worth. If we are serious, however, then we are obliged to accept certain consequences.

As stated in Rawls' 2001 work, *Justice as Fairness: A Restatement*, the two principles of justice are

a. Each person has the same indefeasible claim to a fully adequate scheme of equal basic liberties, which scheme is compatible with the same scheme of liberties for all;
b. Social and economic inequalities are to satisfy two conditions: first, they are to be attached to offices and positions open to all under conditions of fair equality of opportunity; and second, they are to be to the greatest benefit of the least-advantaged members of society (the Difference Principle). (39)

The prose is dense but I can offer a simplified and pragmatic interpretation at the cost of some philosophical rigor. The first principle requires a generous system of civil liberties, something the U.S. Bill of Rights and similar documents in many other democracies will approximate. They protect freedom of speech, assembly, and religion. Also the right to vote (although this is found unfortunately only in case law and not in the U.S Constitution) and to hold political office. They include rights to privacy and various protections for the accused.

The second principle gets at the notion of economic *equality* by establishing the amount of *inequality* that is morally permissible. To comprehend its meaning, we must distinguish between inequality of outcome and inequality of opportunity. They are conceptually distinct but empirically related because excessive inequality of outcome prevents the realization of equality of opportunity. It is not today possible, for example, for children born into poverty to have the same opportunities as children born into wealth. The first part of the second principle asserts that inequality of outcome is permissible but must be kept within limits that allow for full equality of opportunity (more on this below). The second part, named the *Difference Principle*, further limits inequality of outcome by requiring that it (inequality of outcome) be to the benefit of the poor. Thus Rawls accepts the possibility that some inequality of outcome might benefit even the poorest, perhaps by increasing the size of the economic pie via incentives for effort, education, and so forth.

The Rawlsian position is therefore not strictly egalitarian. Inequality of outcome can exist in a just society but it is clearly subject to some strong restrictions. The satisfaction of these requirements would certainly produce a very high level of equality of outcome, albeit not complete equality. Furthermore, according to Rawls the principles are to be realized in the order stated. The first principle is prior to the second, and equality of opportunity comes before the Difference Principle. In other words, trade-offs are not permitted among the various desiderata. In a just society we do not sacrifice our system of liberties in order to achieve more economic equality. Instead we promote economic equality within a framework that protects liberty.

I offer the Rawlsian principles of justice as my preferred statement of modern leftist principles, but rigid adherence is not my litmus test for the Left.[7] Leftists who take seriously the key Enlightenment values—the notions of human reason and moral equality—ought to adopt principles of political liberty and economic equality in the *neighborhood* (to borrow a term of philosophers when trying to add precision to something a bit fuzzy) of the Rawlsian principles of justice. Philosophers may reasonably want to explore the importance of the technical details. For example, Amartya Sen asks a fundamental question, "equality of what?" and considers both "(1) the actual achievement, and (2) the freedom to achieve" (1995, 31). And within those he notes that we must further select a "focal variable" like income, wealth, primary goods, resources, or utility. Well, philosophers must decide such things. Leftists need not fully embrace or understand the philosophical arguments because their political values will be relatively similar in any case. For the purpose of the critique of the Identity, Diversity, and Multiculturalism Program we can identify leftists by their support for (1) extensive civil liberties and (2) a high level of economic equality, nearing complete equality of opportunity but permitting some modest degree of inequality of outcome.

In short, I define the Left as those who share a commitment to the two fundamental Enlightenment values—confidence in human reason and belief in the moral equality of all—and a commitment to something like the two (Rawlsian) principles of political liberty and economic equality. Leftist social movements are attempts to realize this vision of a just society. Getting more specific still, leftists will build their political platform and policy positions upon these foundations. Leftists will disagree among themselves about the best set of practices—this is normal and even useful—but they will share a commitment to a more or less common destination. Leftists can disagree, say, on the balance between income and wealth taxation when the time comes to write legislation. Or whether we spend our limited and precious time fighting for voting rights or raising the minimum wage. Reasonable people might take different routes to the realization of leftist principles, or might, for matters of personal preference, pursue certain issues over others.

The upshot of the critique of *Diversity as Justice* is the claim that the IDMP does not share a commitment to this leftist destination. Furthermore, the disagreements are not minor policy details or personal preferences. Participating in movements inspired by the Program does not help move us toward a leftist notion of a just society. In fact, many of its elements pull us toward the political Right, or keep us stuck in the center-Right. This is a strong claim, and requires that we better understand what is meant by the Right. While we might be able to define the Right as simply the opposite of the Left, the Right has its own internal logic which, like the Left, comes to us out of the time of the Enlightenment.

THE RIGHT-WING PATHS OUT OF
THE AGE OF THE ENLIGHTENMENT

The two other significant political and philosophical movements are the conservative and the (neo)liberal. I will refer to both as right-wing even though they differ from each other in important ways. We can trace conservativism back to the earliest political and philosophical reaction against the social and economic changes during the Enlightenment. After the French Revolution conservatives were those who defended the *Ancien Régime*, the political-economic system that dominated the feudal epoch. Conservatives formed the Counter-Enlightenment, aligned with the Church and the aristocracy, both attempting to defend their historical privileges from secular reasoning and the rising capitalist class. "Where the Enlightenment valued liberty, discursive persuasion, and the critical exercise of reason, the Counter-Enlightenment stood for obedience, coercive authority, and tradition" (Bronner 2004, 67). Today conservatism still retains this notion of looking and longing backward, perhaps not quite so far as feudalism (but maybe to the mythically idyllic 1950s).

Conservative beliefs are often explicitly located in and justified by tradition, which for many in the United States means an interpretation of the Judeo-Christian Bible that purports to be literal, that is, fundamentalist. The sexist and homophobic attitudes that are still too common among conservatives are defended on religious or traditional grounds. For example, it is supposed that heterosexual marriage is superior simply because it is rooted in tradition. Women were traditionally the primary care-givers for children, thus they should continue in this role. Homosexuality is presumably denounced somewhere in the Old Testament and for that reason should still be condemned today. What many *conservatives* claim to *conserve* are biblical values and the supposed mores of a previous, and presumably better, era. It is not relevant whether such an interpretation of either the Bible or history is correct. The facts don't really matter—history is not around to stand up to the historical imaginations of those in the here and now. Conservatives are able to create a tradition and use it as the underlying justification for their beliefs and actions. Given the supposed theological foundation for their values, conservatives commonly tend to believe in one divinely revealed truth—valid for all peoples for all times. Some believe that non-Christians will quite literally burn in hell.

From this moral certitude it seems a short step to lend one's support to "coercive authority," the state-sponsored repression of social reformers and "deviants," an enduring position among conservatives. Consider, for example, the idolatry of guns and the Second Amendment. Although this bellicosity does not seem entirely consistent with Christianity, a religion whose founder returned violence by turning the other cheek, well, so much the worse for moral consistency. For some social conservatives Christianity is actually a tough, manly business. But for others, especially *neoconservatives,* the explicit rhetoric of Christian values is often minimized in favor of a tradition built around nationalism, nativism, and xenophobia. A supposed clash of cultures thus becomes justification for an aggressive foreign policy. Both social (Christian) conservatives and neoconservatives quite often support violence to "defend" their core values, which are often perceived as threatened by groups trying to change America from within or threaten America from without. Interestingly, we can trace these traits of the Right all the way back to their origins in the Counter-Enlightenment, even though the details of the culture war have changed a bit.

But there is another face to the modern Right—neoliberalism—and it comes from a very different source. In fact, liberalism (or classical liberalism) was part of the Enlightenment itself—not the Counter-Enlightenment as was conservativism. Both *liberal* and *neoliberal* share an obvious etymological connection with *liberty*. At the time of the French Revolution the working class and the bourgeoisie were allied in their opposition to the *Ancien Régime*—they were lumped together in the Third Estate—but conflicts between the two made it difficult for them to govern together. "An inner tension between the practical imperatives of capitalism and the moral claims of liberalism was there from the beginning" (Bronner 2004, 42). Indeed, a tension between the two factions has been a dominant feature of democratic regimes for over two centuries, a history that is relevant for our understanding not only of the modern Left and Right but also of the Left and the IDMP. Many neoliberals and libertarians, like leftists, believe in a generous set of political rights. They tend to be progressive on social issues. At times still today, especially in multi-party democracies, the liberal and social democratic parties join forces in Parliament, forming so-called unity governments. But the tensions remain and these tend to be unstable.

The disagreement between neoliberals and leftists can be interpreted as competing ideas about the meaning of economic freedom. From a leftist perspective, neoliberalism comes down too heavily on the side of private property and "free market" capitalism, downplaying or ignoring reasonable claims for economic equality. Some have framed this in terms of positive and negative liberty. Liberals emphasize negative liberty—the right to be left alone to pursue one's interests—including rights like freedom of speech, association, and religion. Leftists agree with these but insist as well on the need for positive liberty—the ability or capacity to achieve particular objectives—which requires a certain level of material resources. Many neoliberals will defend, say, the right to abortion and gay marriage, but these pose no real threat to private property. When other claims for justice conflict with the privileges of property owners, the latter tend to be given priority by neoliberals. Leftists, on the other hand, while embracing political liberty, do not see capitalist property rights as a fundamental freedom like, say, the right to speech, association, and political office. Political freedom must be protected but should not become an excuse to ignore economic inequality and to reject redistribution. As one rhetorical resolution consider Franklin Roosevelt's Four Freedoms: Freedom of speech; freedom of worship; freedom from want; freedom from fear. We might also note that the *March on Washington for Jobs and Freedom* was the full title of the *March on Wash-*

ington in August 1963 where Martin Luther King Jr. delivered his "I Have a Dream" speech.

Given the two strands of thinking—the conservative and neoliberal—right-wing political positions can be justified on the grounds of either tradition or (weakly regulated) markets. Each is philosophically consistent but real people often adopt different, perhaps even contradictory, elements. Indeed, some combination of support for tradition and capitalism characterizes most who identify in the U.S. as Republican. It was the genius of the modern Republican Party to convince a great many Christians that they shared the economic interests of the wealthy. There is, of course, no necessary logical link between the belief in, say, the "traditional" family and support for a low rate of taxation on capital gains. Nonetheless a psychological—and ultimately political—connection was sold by the political-economic elite and bought by many voters. The Bible has not a single word against abortion, and has many passages on poverty and wealth that could easily be interpreted as leftist, yet many Christians pray for the unborn and do little for children born into poverty. Philosophical frameworks are actually divisible into smaller, discrete pieces that can be selected and combined in various ways. Whether the final ideological amalgamation hangs together in a logically rigorous manner seems not to be especially important in the real world of politics.

The leftist critique of the Identity, Diversity, and Multiculturalism Program is more concerned, however, with the other side of the partisan aisle. The Democratic Party has its own complex ideological mixture, with some leftism, neoliberalism, and even conservatism. We talk about the different "wings" of the Democratic Party as well as the divide between politicians and the voters. Although there are many in the grassroots who could be considered leftists, the "New Democrats" dominate the party apparatus, certainly in terms of resources. Most of the Democratic elite lean to the left on social issues, that is, they often support a decent set of civil liberties, but are solidly neoliberal on economic policies. Still, this does not imply a uniformity of thought. While all neoliberals agree that capitalism should be the dominant mode through which resources are distributed there is some debate among Democrats about the degree to which the state can regulate the economy. The level of social security benefits or the rate of the minimum wage, for example, are open for consideration. The range of options, however, never threatens the position of the market as the dominant social institution nor the political dominance of those who have the most market power.

The inability to address our current economic problems is a clear illustration of the supremacy of neoliberalism in both major parties. The two leading causes of the economic crisis that began in 2008 were growing economic inequality, thus weak demand, and financial deregulation, thus banking as a

Ponzi scheme (Foster and Magdoff 2009; Scheer 2010). Economic inequality increased under every administration since Gerald Ford in the 1970s.[8] Financial deregulation was steadily promoted since the 1980s and received a significant boost when President Bill Clinton repealed the Glass-Steagall Act. Yet despite the worst economic crisis since the Great Depression neither Bush nor Obama nor Trump made any attempts to reverse economic inequality or to break up big banks and investment firms, or even to impose strong regulations on the financial sector. Financial giants were bailed out by the taxpayers, rewarding and even reinforcing too-big-to-fail, while wages were allowed to stagnate for the middle class.

Despite the evidence, many still believe that Obama was a leftist who did the best he could, and not a neoliberal defender of the bipartisan status quo. An excellent progressive case against Obama, and against those who believe him to be progressive, can be found in Bill Press's 2016 book, *Buyer's Remorse*. Not only did Obama fail to implement any serious structural reforms to prevent another repeat of the last financial collapse, he chose to pursue a rather tepid policy of fiscal expansion to address the short-run unemployment crisis. Obama most definitely did *not* try to do as much as possible only to get thwarted by Republicans. No, in his negotiations with Congress the starting point for the size of the economic stimulus was already too modest given the scale of the problem. And it could only go down from there, a compromise he seemed more than happy to make.

Despite the continuing weakness in the economy, by 2010 Obama had already changed direction and was pushing for deficit reduction, even though contractionary policy is exactly the wrong approach to generating jobs and thus boosting wages. Keeping the size of the government in check, even during times of economic stagnation and genuine human suffering, known as *austerity*, is a quintessential neoliberal preoccupation. From a political perspective, the genius of Obama was minimizing his responsibility for failure rather than achieving anything progressive on the economy. He created the Simpson-Bowles Commission, more formally the National Commission on Fiscal Responsibility and Reform, as a politically safe way of making cuts to popular programs. Although the findings of the commission were never fully enacted, the framework created by the commission led to deficit reduction during the weak recovery and the practice of budget sequestration. Yet austerity, of course, must largely be borne by the working and middle classes. The so-called Bush tax cuts, which largely benefitted the top 2 percent, were originally scheduled to expire in 2010 but were extended under Obama. Here Obama faced the central fiscal contradiction of neoliberalism: how to keep taxes low on the wealthy while chasing (vainly) a balanced budget. The solution: cut social programs. Obama followed the neoliberal script, calling for freezes on discretionary spending and even for cuts to very popular programs like Medicare and Medicaid.

In short, Obama's handling of the economy was far from progressive. According to Press, "On the economy, filling his team with ex-Clintonites was Obama's first big mistake. Putting forth a half-baked stimulus was the second. Shifting priorities from growing the economy to cutting the deficit was mistake number three. And naming the Simpson-Bowles Commission was big mistake number four" (2016, 43). Some progressives do recognize President Obama's failure to deal with Wall Street and to address the problems of unemployment and wages, even though they may not recognize the degree to which Obama was as culpable as Republicans (and other neoliberal Democrats). But many are willing to give him a pass not only because they don't want to criticize the first black president but also because of his eponymous achievement: Obamacare. Even a leftist critic will recognize that the number of people without health insurance did indeed decrease. Nonetheless, Obama's reform had two major problems. First, it was not universal. Tens of millions of people did not receive health coverage. Second, it was not single-payer, that is, government funded. While the law had many components, the key to Obamacare was the government mandate that Americans purchase private health insurance. Yet the law gave the government very little power over the prices that private actors could charge. In reality, the Affordable Care Act can be seen as another example of corporate welfare.

Defenders of Obama again maintain that he fought for the best (that is, most progressive) plan and unfortunately had to compromise with Congress. Such is the nature of politics, or so the story goes. But this story does not conform to the facts. Almost immediately *President* Obama contradicted presidential *candidate* Obama, coming out against a single-payer system as "hugely disruptive" (Press 2016, 27). The timing is important because it shows that Obama gave up on his campaign promise without a fight. Why? Perhaps universal single-payer healthcare was not worth the expenditure of political capital. That would have been odd, because this reform has been at the top of the list for progressives since the Truman administration. There could scarcely be a worthier place to spend political capital, at least for leftists. It seems more likely that Obama personally endorsed a modest reform that maintained the dominant role of private insurance and pharmaceutical companies. Either way, at the end of the day, Obama along with the neoliberal Democrats who controlled Congress did nothing to threaten the profits of the most powerful actors in the healthcare field.

In reality, both major parties are overwhelmingly neoliberal, that is, right-wing on economic issues. The most significant difference between the two parties is the degree of conservatism. Republicans tend to promote traditional and Christian values more than Democrats. And Republicans tend to be more hawkish on foreign policy, or neoconservative, than Democrats. But these are matters of degree. Obama continued an aggressive foreign policy, escalating a program of illegal drone assassinations, and supported authoritarian regimes. Obama spied on Americans and prosecuted whistleblowers. Even on social issues it was the previous Democratic president, Bill Clinton, who gave us the Defense of Marriage Act. Obama was better on this issue but nonetheless insisted that the Democratic Party platform make reference to *God*. In any case, a neoliberal governing philosophy tends to trump both social conservatism and neoconservatism inside the political establishment. Plutocrats need votes from Main Street, and conservatism is an ideological tool to get some of them, but ultimately Wall Street runs the show.

I offer this conceptualization of right-wing principles, with particular attention on the neoliberal branch, not as criticism of the Right, something that can be taken as given in this work. Nor is the point to criticize Obama or the neoliberal entity that is Democratic Party. This too can be taken as given. It's not my fight (at least in these pages), and others like Press and Thomas Frank have largely settled the record. My objective is to offer a leftist critique of the IDMP, specifically the tenet of *Diversity as Justice*. This background is necessary because I intend to argue that *Diversity as Justice* conforms more closely to a Democratic-Party version of neoliberalism than it does to actual leftist principles. *Diversity as Justice* calls for ending inequality and privilege on the grounds of race. As we will see below, this is not the same as the leftist call for equality and will do little to change the overall distribution of resources. The Program can perhaps position itself *to the left* of Republicans but not as actually *on the Left*, just as neither Bill Clinton nor Barack Obama could call himself a leftist. Second, it has a conservatism that functions to maintain the status quo, one that obviously serves the interests of the elite. The traditional tribal divisions it encourages, with race as the leading instance, confuse and divide the working and middle classes and thus facilitate the expansion of neoliberal policies. "One of the reasons for the success of these attacks on the welfare state . . . is the rise of doctrinaire forms of identity politics and their ideological justifications for fragmentation that have generally been accepted by the left in the name of promoting 'difference'" (Bronner 2004, 156).

We have made some progress in developing the conceptual tools we need for a leftist critique of the IDMP. I will argue that *Diversity as Justice* is simply too far from anything even close to the Rawlsian principles of justice to be considered leftist. Put into historical perspective, the Program is one strand of right-wing thought that is part of the cycle between leftist reason and romantic reaction. The class-based politics of the middle part of the twentieth century have given way to the romantic, identity-based politics in our time.

Part of its cleverness lies in the support it has among many progressives, despite its reactionary nature. But this insidiousness is not as unusual as it may seem. Classical liberals, who were part of the Enlightenment and fought the feudal order, replaced it with another exploitative system. In the post-war period Horkheimer and Adorno (1969) offered a supposedly radical reaction against the Enlightenment, going so far as to implicate it in the atrocities of the twentieth century. The twenty-first century now gives us the Identity, Diversity, and Multiculturalism Program. Yet another illustration of Marx's witticism that history twice repeats itself, once as tragedy, the other as farce. But to fully appreciate how *Diversity as Justice* diverges from the leftist path we must first define a few more concepts, starting with the notion of racism.

THE TRIPARTITE CONCEPTUALIZATION OF RACISM

Upon reflection one recognizes that human experience can be organized along three independent dimensions: ideas, actions, and outcomes. We think, we act, and certain things occur (or don't, as the case may be). These three spheres of human existence cannot be reduced to each other, at least not easily and perhaps not at all. This is the meaning of independence. An idea is understood here as any process of cognition. For example, the belief in god, feelings of compassion, or preference for a certain politician. An action involves use of the body in order to move itself, including speaking, and to interact with other objects. Reduced to the most basic level of physics, our bodies are machines that convert energy from food into work (and heat) via contracting muscles. This should not be taken as a reductionist insult. The vast number of distinct individual actions, aided by objects which are the result of previous human actions, provides the basis for an exceedingly complex social system. Finally, outcomes are descriptions of any state in time, including the physical objects that reflect human existence; that is, *objects* are *objective* proof of human existence, not our fleeting thoughts and momentary actions. Buildings, machines, paper money, and so on. We could also categorize the three dimensions by reference to physical space: ideas occur within the brain (or mind); actions are done by the body; and outcomes have an existence outside us, even though they were the result of prior actions and ideas. I suggest that the phenomena that social scientists want to understand are specific instances that fall into the three big categories of ideas, actions, and outcomes. For our purposes now I suggest that this tripartite division provides a useful means to think about the different types of the phenomenon of racism. Thus, in this work, I intend to employ the following tripartite conceptualization of racism:

- Racist ideas (or beliefs)
- Racist actions (or behaviors)
- Racist outcomes

Racist ideas are present when there is some type of negative cognitive evaluation of, or psychological reaction to, individuals or groups due to their racial identification. Negative evaluations and reactions would involve either the notion that some races are intrinsically inferior to others or hostile feelings including fear or animosity toward some races. Negative evaluations and reactions will vary in type and intensity, from strong hatred of another race to a milder preference for one's own race, and those holding racist beliefs may or may not admit to them or act on them or even be fully aware of them. We risk some conceptual confusion because we will at times speak of as racist an idea itself, that is, abstracted from any person who might hold it, and at other times speak of the person who holds the belief as racist. In any case, we call racist both the notion that, say, blacks are innately less intelligent than whites as well as those who hold that belief.

The second type of racism, racist actions, are behaviors that cause harm to members of a certain race because of their race. Here I follow quite closely the definition of individual racism by Robert C. Smith (1995): "when an individual or group *overtly* takes into account the race of another individual or group and takes action *intended* to subordinate that individual or group" (33, emphasis in original). As a definition, this seems well-formulated and fairly precise. At the same time, the identification of racist actions could be difficult in practice, especially under cultural or legal conditions that discourage any admission of racist intent. Furthermore, given the complexity of human cognition and multifaceted nature of decision-making, how might we know whether the poor treatment was due to race and not something else?

This is a challenge, but it is not unsurmountable. One way to determine the presence of individual intent is to consider outcomes at the group level, and then work backwards to individual-level behavior. As a general strategy, when dealing with a causal process involving many possible factors, we assess the effect of one factor by holding constant all the others. When only one variable is permitted to vary, then any change in the outcome should be due to that one variable. This is the heart of the experimental method. Or *ceteris paribus*, as the economists like to put it. As a thought experiment, let's consider a large group of individuals who are identical on all characteristics except race, where half are black and half are white. If we compare the outcomes for this group of identical and identically situated whites and blacks and find that blacks fared worse than whites, then we can conclude that racist behavior was involved somewhere along the way.[9] We should not lose sight of the fact that racist actions are committed by individuals, even though we observe the outcome at the group level. We are making an inference about individual behavior—when an employer doesn't hire somebody because of race, or a landlord doesn't rent to somebody, or a cop abuses a citizen, and so on—using group data. Individual actions will show up as average group differences, *ceteris paribus*.

By racist outcomes, the third type of racism, I mean the disproportionate subordination itself. To be subordinated is to possess fewer resources, that is, to have less or fewer of the things we value. Not every difference between racial groups should be considered a sign of subordination because it is possible that different groups may differ in their preferences and notions of value. Yet when the people in the groups recognize the difference as representing inferior and superior positions we can safely speak of subordination. Applying a leftist perspective, we can identify things like political liberty, personal freedom, income, and wealth to be important examples of resources but we could include other types of resources where relevant. We are looking for a pattern in the aggregate, not for every member of a race to be in a subordinate position.

I must emphasize a very important contrast between racist outcomes and racist actions, according to the conceptualization proposed here. Unlike racist actions, there is no *ceteris paribus* clause in the identification of racist outcomes. That is, we do not require other factors to be the same to claim evidence of a racist outcome. We must simply find an overall racial pattern to subordination, regardless of whether the individuals have similar or dissimilar characteristics. For example, the higher incarceration rate of blacks is a racist outcome, even if there are other differences between blacks and whites. On the one hand, it is racist *behavior* (discrimination) when police or judges treat differently blacks and whites who are alike in their behavior; on the other hand, it is a racist *outcome* to have more blacks in prison regardless of any differences in group characteristics. We have racism in the form of a racist outcome whenever one race has an average income that falls below the overall average even if there are other differences between the groups like education and training. This distinction between behaviors and outcomes will be crucial for the analysis that follows. In fact, the strength of the tripartite conception of racism is the clarity it lends to our understanding of causal processes.

The tripartite conceptualization can be compared to other usages of the term *racism*. I maintain that a good deal of the contention around Identity, Diversity, and Multiculturalism follows from conceptual misunderstandings. This is encouraging because it suggests a relatively simple (albeit incomplete) resolution to the conflict. Antagonists are not aware that the same word means different things or that different words might mean the same thing. In some cases, including academic treatises, the term *racism* is not even defined, certainly not explicitly, even when it might be central to the analysis. While it is not possible to claim that any definition is objectively true, in particular contexts some might be more useful than others, and in almost every case the strength of an argument cannot be assessed without a clear understanding of the meaning of key terms.

In popular usage, racism is sometimes equated with negative beliefs about a race or members of a race. This seems to be what people usually mean when they call somebody a racist. Some prefer to refer to this as racial prejudice. I will use the term *racist beliefs* in order to avoid confusion. But the same word, *racism*, is also used to describe the ways in which individuals behave toward other individuals. In this case racism occurs not when there are negative opinions but rather when people treat others poorly on the grounds of race. Delgado and Stefancic (2012) in *Critical Race Theory* define racism as "any program or practice of discrimination, segregation, persecution, or mistreatment based on membership in a race or ethnic group" (171). This seems quite close to my meaning of racist actions.

Finally, we can find usage of the term that roughly corresponds to my sense of racist outcomes. In *Racial Formation in the United States*, Omi and Winant (1994) propose that "a racial project can be defined as *racist* if and only if it *creates or reproduces structures of domination based on essentialist categories of race*" (71, emphasis in original). A structure of domination would produce, I believe, something like the disproportionate subordination I use to define racist outcomes.

Confusion is unavoidable and understandable when the same word, *racism*, can mean all these things. To minimize this threat (but at the risk of tapping the reader's sufferance for the academic proclivity for conceptualization), we should define a few more terms—institutional racism, systemic racism, and structural racism—and relate them to the tripartite conceptualization. In both popular and academic usage, *institutional racism* is rather broad, posing a risk that it might be used so expansively that it has no analytical value. James Jones (1997) gives the following definition:

> (1) It is the institutional extension of individual racist beliefs, consisting primarily of using and manipulating duly constituted institutions so as to maintain a racist advantage over others. (2) It is the byproduct of certain institutional practices that operate to restrict—on a racial basis—the choices, rights, mobility, and access of groups of individuals. These unequal consequences need not be intended, but they are no less real for being simply de facto. (14)

Jones includes terms like "using and manipulating," "byproduct," and "consequences" in his definition, suggesting certain types of racist actions and outcomes. In contrast, I will use *institutional racism* to denote any of the three types of racism—beliefs, behaviors, or outcomes—that occur inside important social institutions. I will use the term to emphasize the *site* at which racism is located, that is, in particular institutions, not the *type* of the racism. For example, by referring to institutional racism in policing we could mean that some officers have racist beliefs, that similarly situated whites and blacks are often treated differently, and/or that blacks have a higher rate of harassment and arrest. Or we could speak of institutional racism in employment, schooling, and housing, again meaning any combination of racist beliefs, actions, and outcomes at these sites.

According to Joe Feagin (2014) in *Racist America* "systemic racism includes a diverse assortment of racist practices: the unjustly gained economic and political power of whites; the continuing resource inequalities; the rationalization of white racist frame; and the major institutions create to preserve white advantage and power" (9). One problem with the definition is the identification of all the things after the colon—power, inequalities, the rationalizing frame, and institutions—as "practices" but we could probably find a different word to fix that. A more serious issue is the breadth of the concept. Indeed, Feagin goes on to add "some key aspects of systemic racism":

1. the patterns of unjust impoverishment and unjust enrichment and their transmission over time;
2. the resulting vested group interests and the alienating racist relations;
3. the costs and burdens of racism;
4. the important role of white elites;
5. the rationalization of white oppression in a white-racist framing; and
6. the continuing resistance to racism. (11)

These are reasonable topics to include in an analysis of racism but the list of "aspects" is simply too expansive to be of much use as a guide for a definition for this work. The root problem lies in making a concept so broad as to include the concept itself, its causes, and its consequences. Such a definition leads to logically valid but thoroughly unsatisfactory statements like *racism is caused by racism*. As such, I will avoid using the term *systemic* racism and instead refer to more specific types of racism.

Finally, *structural* racism is likewise too elastic to be of much value in our subsequent analysis. The adjectival modifier obviously references a structure, indicating that racism is part of or is due to the structure of society. Often the social structure is defined by sociologists as the patterns or regularities in social relationships and individual behavior. The term *structural racism* is not, however, always used in accordance with this sociological meaning and, in any case, the concept of the social structure itself is overly broad for most analytical purposes, including ours here. For some, structural racism "refers to the accumulation over centuries of the effects of a racialized society" (Grassroots Policy Project, n.d., 15). In this case I would use the term *racist outcomes*. But racism as a property of the social structure has also been defined to include "ethnic prejudices" and "discriminatory actions of persons as dominant group members" (van Dijk 1989, 28) and thus would correspond to both *racist beliefs* and *racist actions*. Again, I will refer to racism according to the three dimensions—beliefs, behaviors, and outcomes—or to the institutional site at which it occurs.

We are now equipped with a definition of racism sufficient for the analysis that follows. The tripartite conceptualization agrees with and adds precision to our intuitive understanding that racism is a multidimensional social phenomenon. It is no wonder that the word *racism* has come to take on multiple and varied meanings. All the definitions and all the related terms, like systemic racism and structural racism, may have utility in other contexts but the tripartite conceptualization is adopted here to make my exposition clearer. The distinction between racist actions and racist outcomes will play the most important role in that analysis. The tripartite conceptualization illuminates the ways in which neoliberalism perpetuates and exacerbates racist outcomes, and points to the inability of the Identity, Diversity, and Multiculturalism Program to solve the problems.

RACISM, NEOLIBERALISM, AND THE NEW JIM CROW

Alongside economic inequality there is perhaps no issue as important as the injustice in our criminal justice system, which poses a paramount threat to freedom. Michelle Alexander (2012) in her work, *The New Jim Crow*, has helped to substantially raise national attention regarding the atrocity that is mass incarceration in the U.S. The moral imperative she conveys is buttressed by her deep knowledge of the law and her detailed documentation of the harms caused by the criminal justice system. At the same time, however, the work is undermined by a questionable interpretative framework, specifically, the claim that mass incarceration *is* the new Jim Crow. The argument, I believe, would have benefitted from something like a tripartite conceptualization of race.

Jim Crow refers to the era after the brief period of Reconstruction following the Civil War, when discrimination on the basis of race was legally permissible. The *Plessy v. Ferguson* case of 1896 asserted the legal doctrine of "separate but equal," a precedent that would last until the judicial and legislative victories in the 1950s and 1960s repealed and obviated that decision. Since that time, the era of Civil Rights (or post-Civil Rights, as the contemporary period is also called), discrimination on the grounds of race in almost all aspects of life is legally prohibited. It is clear, however, that many outcomes for blacks are still much worse on average than they are for whites. In fact, for Alexander, mass incarceration of blacks in this era of *Civil Rights* is the *new Jim Crow*. While she admits the comparison is imperfect, Alexander maintains that "the similarities between these systems of control overwhelm the differences" (15). But is that actually a reasonable claim? I want to investigate this question by comparing the two systems according to our three dimensions of racism—beliefs, actions, and outcomes.

The closest correspondence between the two periods, Jim Crow and Civil Rights, is the continuation of racist outcomes. In a number of areas many blacks are still subordinated today much as they were before the Civil Rights victories. The similarities include not only the loss of physical freedom (i.e., incarceration) but also restricted voting rights, lower educational achievement, economic hardships, and so on. The documenting of these outcomes is the strength of Alexander's work, and the reality is indeed morally appalling. We have more than two million people incarcerated and another five million under community supervision—a larger percentage than South Africa under apartheid. Furthermore, "more than half of all young black men in many large American cities are currently under the control of the criminal justice system" (16). She documents the militarization of our police: "By the early 1980s, there were three thousand annual SWAT deployments, by 1996 there were thirty thousand, and by 2001 there were forty thousand" (75). One cannot walk away from this work without recognizing the scale and scope of the problems in the criminal justice system for blacks in America. As Cornel West puts it in the preface: "Once you read it, you have crossed the Rubicon and there is no return to sleepwalking. You are now awakened to a dark and ugly reality" (x).

Nevertheless, acknowledging these racist outcomes should not lead us to overlook some striking differences between Jim Crow and the era of Civil Rights. Let's start by considering the dimension of racist beliefs. Here we need to compare two groups: (1) those in power who write the laws that define the political system and (2) the majority of people who live under it. We have a pretty good understanding of both of these groups under Jim Crow. First, Jim Crow was intentionally designed by those in power to subordinate blacks, despite the legal cloak of "separate but equal." Second, many or perhaps most of the white people who lived under the regime held negative views of blacks and supported the system of discrimination. For whites, the ontological category of race itself helped to obfuscate the moral contradictions and to justify their social and economic advantages. Most blacks, on the other hand, recognized the hypocrisy and injustice of "separate-but-equal" in a society that professed equality as a core value.

Today beliefs have improved but they are also more complicated and harder to discern for both groups. While some whites still hold negative views of blacks, the empirical data indicate that racist beliefs are far less common today than during Jim Crow. The skeptic maintains that people lie to pollsters about their racist opinions, and there is some truth to this, but certainly not enough to dismiss the genuine and substantial progress that has been made with regards to attitudes. Alexander acknowledges this and notes the new "public consensus that explicit race discrimination is an affront to American values" (119). Furthermore, although Alexander does not discuss this point, many more people today recognize the idea of separate human races as pseudo-science.

The beliefs and motivations of decision-makers have also changed, but likewise remain mixed. Few on the Left would deny that many policies in the Civil Rights era have had the consequence of disproportionately harming the life-chances of blacks. There were cuts in federal grants for cities at the same time money was spent on transportation projects that favored suburbs. Cuts to welfare, job training, and public housing. And, of course, the wars on drugs and crime that led to the uniquely American phenomenon of mass incarceration. But these refer to policies and outcomes, not beliefs. We need to know, did elected officials intend to harm blacks with these policies? That is, were they motivated by racist beliefs?

William Julius Wilson (2010), perhaps with a bit of gallows humor, notes that in this area "the line between racial and nonracial is somewhat gray" (38). It's impossible to know exactly what motivates people (including, many times, even ourselves) but it seems almost certain that some people were motivated by racial animus and others were not. Furthermore, those motivated by racist beliefs may have had other motivations in play as well. What part was due to race and what part to something else? In any legislative body we might suppose some legislators have racist beliefs and some do not, and the racist beliefs vary in their intensity and the degree to which they compete with other motivations.

Furthermore, it is not unreasonable to suspect a certain amount of rational selfishness on the part of those in power. If fomenting racial division is in their interests, we should expect strategic racial maneuvers. Thus, voting restrictions that have a disproportionate impact on blacks (and the poor) must be at least partially intentional for many officials, and may or may not reflect a genuinely negative opinion of blacks, but rather a desire to win elections. One of the most effective restrictions utilizes the criminal justice system, especially in those states where a felony record removes the "right" to vote.

On the other hand, if the votes of blacks are important to the success of a political coalition, then we might see more friendly rhetoric and maybe even more favorable treatment.

It is interesting to note that, however strong their racist beliefs against blacks may have been, elected officials behind the push for mass incarceration were willing to sacrifice the well-being of millions of poor whites in order to get at millions of poor blacks. Prisons and jails hold a disproportionate number of blacks, but the greatest disproportionality involves income. Poor people of all colors are incarcerated at a much higher rate than anybody else. Blacks are disproportionately poor but in sheer numbers there are more poor whites than poor blacks. In other words, that is an awful lot of collateral damage if the intention of white politicians was to privilege their fellow whites and to subordinate blacks. Alexander recognizes the harm done to whites but discounts its importance in her analogy between Jim Crow and the current period. But it seems at least as plausible to consider that those with wealth and power desire to protect and augment their own positions of privilege and have little loyalty based on race or anything else.

Again, we can never fully understand what motivates people. In any case, we might think that the extent of actual racist behavior is more important than beliefs about race, and this puts us back into safer empirical territory. What of this dimension to the tripartite conceptualization? Do racist actions today look like those under Jim Crow? The crucial difference between contemporary mass incarceration and Jim Crow is the legal status of discriminatory behavior. Presumably there was more racist discrimination under Jim Crow than today but the distinction I want to emphasize is categorical, not quantitative. Under Jim Crow discrimination and segregation on the basis of race was not only widespread but it was also perfectly legal. In this era of mass incarceration, legal discrimination is based instead on a criminal record. Discrimination and segregation on the grounds of race today is illegal. Alexander is misleading on this point. In "mapping the parallels" she states that, "the most obvious parallel between Jim Crow and mass incarceration is legalized discrimination." What she means by this is that "many of the forms of discrimination that relegated African Americans to an inferior caste during Jim Crow continue to apply to huge segments of the black population today—*provided they are first labeled felons*" (192, emphasis added). This is a rather important proviso. The existence of legal discrimination on the grounds of race is simply not the same as legal discrimination on the grounds of a criminal record. It is, of course, correct to speak of continuing racial bias and *illegal*—as opposed to legal—discrimination on the grounds of race. But it's not correct to suggest *legalized* discrimination according to different mechanisms are all the same thing.

It is hard to overstate the importance of the role of the law in the characterization of a social system. Indeed, it is generally the legal rules of a society
that define it. A capitalist society has capitalist property rights, that is, laws. A
communist society has a different set of laws. Thus we should not say that the
oligarchy in Russia today is new Soviet Union. Despite a similar set of outcomes—a small political-economic elite and a large, poor working-class—we
know that the rules of society are different because the laws have changed,
in particular the property rights have shifted from communist to capitalist.
Thus it is not the *outcome* that defines the social system but rather the legal
mechanisms through which the outcomes are produced. Almost every society
since the Bronze Age has had a small elite, on the one hand, and a large group
at or near subsistence, on the other. We do not say that early capitalism was
the new feudalism. Or that feudalism was the new Roman Empire. Or that
Jim Crow was the new slavery. Or at least we shouldn't say these things if
our goal is to analyze the nature and functioning of the systems. They have
all had similar outcomes, but mechanisms matter.

An important task of social science is understanding how different social
systems produce their effects, even if the effects are quite similar. Alexander
actually recognizes these distinctions, noting that the "valiant efforts to abol-
ish slavery and Jim Crow and to achieve greater racial equality have brought
about significant changes in the legal framework of American society—new
'rules of the game,' so to speak" (21). She observes that "the 'negative cre-
dential' associated with a criminal record represents a *unique* mechanism of
state-sponsored stratification" (151, emphasis added). *Unique* implies that
our current system follows a logic different from Jim Crow. It is the rules
of the game, not who wins, that defines the game. Even if I lose the same
amount of money at poker and then at blackjack, the rules and the games differ. The money lost refers to the outcome but that doesn't define the game—
indeed the house always wins—but I wouldn't call blackjack the new poker
when I moved from one table to the next and kept losing.

So, instead of calling it the new Jim Crow, how should we identify the system under which we currently live? Above all, it is a *neoliberal plutocracy* (or
simply neoliberalism), that is, a system in which the wealthy effectively rule
the polity, regulating the economy in ways that overwhelmingly prioritize the
interest of the wealthy thereby generating extreme inequality. The ideology
of neoliberalism borrows from the somewhat more popular libertarianism,
speaking of things like freedom and free markets and fiscal responsibility, but
the actual policies benefit the largest corporations and the small percentage of
the population who own the vast majority of stocks and other financial assets.

If the outcomes are the same, why does it matter whether we call it the
new Jim Crow or neoliberalism? First, there is the academic matter of proper

social-scientific analysis. But more practically, legal mechanisms matter if we are serious about political solutions. If we correctly identify the nature of the system of oppression then we are better equipped to change it, in part because we will better recognize our allies and our enemies. If we live under a new Jim Crow system, we would be suspicious of many or most whites. After all, many of them probably have racist beliefs, or so we might suppose. Appeals to justice as fairness or universal human rights will fall flat except for a few. We would believe that they benefit in various ways from the current arrangement—their white privilege—and so we could not make appeals to their self-interest to change it. On the other hand, if we actually live under a neoliberal regime we should be suspicious of the economic elite and most political leaders, not of people with different skin color. Everybody in the working class and the majority in the middle class who are economically threatened, regardless of race, could potentially join a movement not simply out of an appeal to justice as fairness but also out of self-interest.

Whether we believe we live under one system or the other will suggest very different political strategies. After diagnosing our current situation as the new Jim Crow, Alexander tells us that "there is another path. Rather than shaming and condemning an already deeply stigmatized group, we, collectively, can embrace them" (176). A call for greater empathy and altruism is always appropriate but she adds "this is not mere platitude; it is a prescription for liberation. It we had actually learned to show care, compassion, and concern across racial lines during the Civil Rights Movement—rather than go colorblind—mass incarceration would not exist today" (177). Here is the key fault in the analysis, the one that does great damage to the all the other virtues in the work: the inability to pinpoint neoliberalism as the main organizing principle of our political-economy. The misidentification of the system leads to a misidentification of the root cause of our problem as colorblindness. Yes, neoliberalism can be colorblind, that is, neoliberalism is perfectly compatible with colorblindness. But one cannot pick a trait that is compatible with neoliberalism and blame it for the problems caused by the policies of neoliberalism. Neoliberalism is compatible with women's suffrage. Perhaps that is the culprit. Neoliberalism is compatible with free speech. Or gay marriage. And so on. It is neoliberalism, not colorblindness or these other things, that worsened inequality and perpetuated the black underclass.

Furthermore, a Rawlsian-inspired Social Democracy (Kenworthy 2014) or Democratic Socialism (Nove 1991) is also compatible with colorblindness. In a genuinely democratic society with little inequality and no underclass it is hard to imagine the possibility of mass incarceration. Whom would they lock up? Presumably a small number of the most violent people. There is no reason to assume, as Alexander must, that we are less able to care for our fellow humans if we see them simply as fellow humans, not as people with a color. Indeed, she echoes the Romantic expression of the Counter-Enlightenment; Enlightenment values suggest that religion, race, nation, all these things make it more difficult to adopt a universal humanism. Ultimately, colorblindness is neither necessary nor sufficient as a cause of mass incarceration. The framing of mass incarceration as the new Jim Crow encourages this race-based analysis and downplays the other mechanisms. Conceptualization is not the same as politics but our words shape our perception of reality. And perception is part of the framing that is crucial for building a broad and ultimately successful social movement. Blaming colorblindness instead of neoliberalism distracts the Left and only enables the status quo. We need the broadest possible coalition of people motivated on the grounds of a universal equality if we hope to change the system. Calling for love and caring across racial lines is fine but not really a political program. The problem with Barack Obama, Bill Clinton, and Hillary Clinton is not whether they are colorblind or not, it's that they recklessly promoted the interests of corporations and the wealthy. Even if some in the IDMP don't care about poor whites, or care more about helping poor blacks than poor whites, the metaphor of Jim Crow and the hostility toward colorblindness is actually contrary to the objective of improving the lives of poor and middle-class blacks.

Finally, for those who worry that the term *neoliberalism* does not have the same rhetorical punch as the *new Jim Crow*, and thus perhaps softens the moral condemnation, I would respond that a correct identification of the system does nothing to minimize our evaluation of the racist outcomes it produces. As a historical comparison, one of the goals of Marx's analysis of capitalism was to show how it produced exploitation that was in many ways akin to that found under feudalism, despite the move to an ostensibly voluntarist system built upon markets. But Marx did not call his magnum opus *Der Neue Feudalismus*, and the contempt of Marxists for capitalism is in no way diminished. Quite the contrary. The same could be true now. The task is to show how blacks are disproportionately oppressed under conditions of neoliberalism, and to fight the continuing discrimination on the grounds of race. The analogy with Jim Crow impedes that task and sends us looking in the wrong places.[10] Neoliberalism is its own thing, working according to its own logic.

The point of this discussion is not to minimize the important issues raised in Alexander's work, whose empirical points and moral condemnation I fully accept, but rather to sharpen the conceptual tools we need for a leftist critique of the Identity, Diversity, and Multiculturalism Program. My leftist critique does not seek to downplay these problems. It is important precisely because I am concerned with police repression and mass incarceration as a fundamental threat to our freedom and as a policy which disproportionately harms blacks.

RACIST DISCRIMINATION IN THE LABOR MARKET

We are ready to finalize the main objective of the chapter, namely, a left-ist critique of the first tenet of the Identity, Diversity, and Multiculturalism Program. *Diversity as Justice* maintains that the most important struggle for justice today is the fight to increase representation and to end discrimination on the grounds of race, gender, sexual orientation, and similar characteristics. The leftist critique of this tenet will depend in an important way on the distinction we have made between racist actions and racist outcomes.

I will approach the task by analyzing the problem in a very important social context: racist discrimination in the labor market, which occurs when an employer hires a white applicant over a comparable black candidate while taking the difference in race into account. Only a few employers will admit to racist discrimination but we have good evidence that it occurs by means of natural experiments involving resumes submitted by applicants of different races that are otherwise identical.[11] Both leftists and IDMP supporters will agree that this type of behavior is manifestly unjust. After that agreement, however, the matter quickly gets more complicated. What about other cases when employers hire white applicants with more experience, education, or skills? In these scenarios we could not conclude anything about racist discrimination. Racist discrimination in the labor market, as a type of racist behavior, requires that other relevant factors are equal: an employer must choose a white applicant instead of an equally (or better) qualified black applicant. For an employer to discriminate of the grounds of race it must be the case that the employer did not discriminate on some other, legal basis.

How could we tell whether the discrimination occurred on the grounds of race or something more palatable like education? Recalling our discussion from earlier, we would form groups of applicants according to similar levels of relevant labor market characteristics. We could place, say, all workers with a high school degree and five to ten years of work experience into one group. Another group could be college graduates with no experience. We could include other characteristics as well. In order to get at the effect of racist discrimination we should include all the other variables that employers would consider in their hiring decisions. Employers often try to learn something perhaps via contacts and references about qualities that are more difficult to assess at an interview: work ethic, team skills, etc. Whatever relevant labor market characteristics are chosen, we put everybody who has the same traits into the same group. Now, everybody in each group so defined should have, in a world without racist discrimination, the same overall chance of success in the labor market. We accept that people in different groups might have very different prospects. The group with a master's degree, twenty or more years of experience, and no criminal record will fare much better on average than the group that did not finish high school, has no experience, and has multiple felonies. We can make no inference about racist discrimination when those in the first group do better because other things are not equal. Comparisons must take place within each group, not between groups.

To assess the extent of racist discrimination we would make a further division *within* each group according to race. So within the group of, say, recent college graduates with no work experience we further distinguish between whites, blacks, Asians, and as many other racial categories we might please. The absence of racist discrimination would be observed when every race on average does as well as every other race *within* that same group. If the unemployment rate for white college graduates with degrees in mathematics is 1 percent it should be 1 percent for correspondingly educated blacks, Asians, Hispanics, and so on. Racist discrimination means that differences exist between the races *within* the same groups. If racist discrimination exists we will find some races doing better on average than other races in their same group. Again, comparisons *across* different groups are not relevant. Of course we do not need to find discrimination in every category. It is possible, for example, that black Ph.D.'s do just as well as or better than white Ph.D.'s. in the academic labor market, but these represent a small percentage of all jobs so the general finding of racist discrimination against blacks would not be invalidated.

I take as given, and I assume most in the IDMP would agree, that there are differences both across groups—those with more education and other similar traits will do better—and within groups—blacks will often do worse than whites even controlling for the relevant group characteristics. Empirical data would help to establish the relative strength of factors like education and race if we were interested in comparing across-group and within-group effects. But I do not need to enter this discussion because the strength of discrimination on the grounds of education or race is irrelevant for a leftist critique of *Diversity as Justice*. The real issue here is that ending racist discrimination, regardless of its magnitude, is not sufficient to achieve equality of opportunity. We agree that there must be an end to racist discrimination. Genuine equality of opportunity is much more than that. The focus on the within-group effect of race blinds the supporters of the Program to the more general problems of racist subordination and inequality.

EQUALITY OF OPPORTUNITY

The reader may have already recognized the problem with *Diversity as Justice* and the limits to focusing on race-based discrimination: it does not obligate us to make morally meaningful comparisons *between* groups defined according to characteristics like education and experience. Comparisons *within* the same hiring group based on race are the only meaningful comparisons from the framework of *Diversity as Justice*. Yet this is far too limiting to permit a leftist moral evaluation of economic outcomes. Legitimate characteristics from the perspective of the employer in the labor market may not be legitimate when considered from the standpoint of a just society. As a thought experiment consider a society that has rid itself of racist discrimination in employment so that within each hiring group we find that race is irrelevant. But we also find that children born into poverty have four times the rate of poverty as adults because, among other things, they are unable to get the same level of education as more privileged children. Whether black or white, those in the group with the lowest level of education simply do not fare as well in the labor market. Leftists should find such a situation unacceptable according to the principle of equal opportunity but the Diversity supporter would have no grounds according to the logic of *Diversity as Justice* to find fault with this situation. Blacks and whites are treated equally within every hiring group and, if our concern is racist discrimination and white privilege, we can make moral evaluations only within the relevant groups. *Diversity as Justice* gives us no moral basis to criticize discrimination by educational credentials because these differences exist between, not within, groups. I suggest that if supporters of the IDMP do object to this situation—and I hope many do—then they are tapping into their leftist moral intuition instead of *Diversity as Justice*.

A society can be said to provide *equality of opportunity* to its citizens when economic and social mobility satisfy certain criteria. If equal opportunity truly meant equality regardless of anything else, then it would be rather easy to define and assess. If we considered the top, say, 10 percent of the income distribution as rich then everybody should have a 10 percent chance of becoming rich. Similarly, if we considered poor to be the bottom 20 percent then everybody should have a 20 percent chance of becoming poor. This is not the correct approach, however, because an equal chance does not need to exist for all members of society but only within the proper groupings. Again we must construct groups of similar individuals—not this time from the perspective of the employer—but rather from our principle of equality of opportunity. The fundamental question is this: what are the legitimate grounds for differences in the rates of social and economic mobility? The Rawlsian response offers only two: our inborn talents and our willingness to develop and use them.[12] There is nothing in our leftist values that objects to those who are innately talented or those who work harder and more fully develop their talents from having higher rates of upward mobility than the rest of us. Those avenues to economic success are morally acceptable.

But we must be careful in the interpretation and application of this idea, lest it become an apologia for any observed inequality. The talents must indeed be inborn and could not include skills later developed as a result of better access to education and training. Justice is not bothered by the fact that it is easier to become a professional basketball player if you are taller than seven feet than if you are shorter than six. On the other hand, our sense of fairness is violated when children of the rich receive advantages from private schools that children of the poor cannot obtain in many public schools.

The contrast between equality of opportunity and simply ending racist discrimination as called for by *Diversity as Justice* can be seen by forming relevant groups. To make the presentation analytically tractable I will grossly simplify and categorize individuals as either innately talented or not, and as either hard-working or not. Thus from the perspective of equality of opportunity there are four groups in society:

1. Innately talented and hard-working individuals
2. Innately talented but not hard-working individuals
3. Not innately talented but hard-working individuals
4. Not innately talented and not hard-working individuals

Equality of opportunity exists when everybody *within* a particular group has the same rate of mobility. Differences *across* the groups are not relevant from the standpoint of equal opportunity (yet might be according to the Difference Principle) and will likely exist. Those who are innately talented and hard-working (group 1) should have a higher rate of upward mobility than those who are not innately talented and who do not work hard (group 4). In our simplified approach with only four types of people we would expect to observe four different rates of mobility. As shown in table 1.1 I assume that the group of individuals with the most talent and effort, in the top left, has the highest chance of getting the best economic positions. Those in the bottom right should have the lowest chance on average. The intermediate cases are high on one dimension and low on the other and will have rates of mobility somewhere between the other two cases.

DIVERSITY AS JUSTICE:
MISCONSTRUING EQUALITY OF OPPORTUNITY

For the IDMP, the problem of economic inequality reduces largely to inadequate representation based on categories like race and gender, and discrimination on these same grounds. The Left, too, objects to such discrimination but

Table 1.1.   The Pattern of Economic Mobility Consistent with Equality of Opportunity.

		Level of Innate Talent	
		High	Low
Degree of Effort	High	Highest Probability of Earning Highest Income (Blacks & whites same probability within group)	Moderate Probability of Earning Highest Income (Blacks & whites same probability within group)
	Low	Moderate Probability of Earning Highest Income (Blacks & whites same probability within group)	Lowest Probability of Earning Highest Income (Blacks & whites same probability within group)

insists that this stance does not go nearly far enough. Within every grouping according to inborn talents and work ethic, everybody—including blacks and whites, men and women, gays and straights, Christians and Muslims, and so on—must have the same probability of success. This is made explicit in table 1.1 where the rates of mobility for whites are equal to the rates for blacks within each cell. Thus a society with equal opportunity could obviously not have racist discrimination. But—here is the problem with *Diversity as Justice*—the converse is not true. A society without racist discrimination could easily violate equal opportunity. Furthermore, that violation of equal opportunity, even without racist and sexist discrimination, could still lead to subordination according to race, gender, sexual orientation, and so on. The failing of the IDMP from a leftist perspective lies either in ignoring genuine equality of opportunity or else confusing it with ending certain types of discrimination. Racist discrimination does indeed prevent equality of opportunity but the elimination of racist discrimination would not bring about equality of opportunity.

Simply put, the Identity, Diversity, and Multiculturalism Program is too tepid to be leftist. It does not call for the level of economic redistribution or regulation necessary to ensure that all those who fall within the same grouping based on talent and effort actually have the same rate of mobility. Consider two black children, equally innately talented and equally hard-working. One was the child of a millionaire (or maybe the president), attended private schools, received tutoring, ate well, played soccer, had health insurance, visited museums, and traveled the world. The other was the child of a single parent working for the minimum wage, attended an inner-city public school, had no tutoring, alternated between food insecurity and fast food, lacked healthcare, and never left the city of his birth. The first child attended college, received an MBA, got an interview via connections of his parents, and landed a great job. During the application process he was treated the same as white candidates. The second child graduated high school and found part-time work at Walmart. He too was treated the same as white applicants.

From the standpoint of *Diversity as Justice*, that is, coming from an opposition to racist discrimination and white privilege, these scenarios are perfectly acceptable. As long as the first person was treated the same as white MBAs and the second person was treated the same as white high school graduates, the Diversity supporter has no intellectual tools to criticize the outcome. The crucial point: *there is no difference here between the Identity, Diversity, and Multiculturalism Program and neoliberalism*. One response might be to insist that there must have been racist discrimination somewhere. When the only tool one has is a hammer, everything looks like a nail. Perhaps the poorer black child was discriminated against in school? This might be common enough but let us assume, even if it is not the typical case, that the poor black child was treated the same as the white children in the low-income school, which probably means neither received adequate instruction. The other response is to subconsciously leave behind the framework of *Diversity as Justice* and to adopt a moral perspective from which this situation can be properly analyzed and critiqued. Without recognizing the shift, the IDMP supporter will have actually abandoned *Diversity as Justice* in favor of a set of more robust moral principles—those from the Left.

DIVERSITY AS JUSTICE:
AVOIDING EQUALITY OF OUTCOME

The fulfillment of the leftist demand for equality of opportunity would necessitate a high level of equality of outcome. Starting from our current level of inequality we would need to redistribute resources until all children with the same levels of talent and effort would have equal rates of economic mobility regardless of the income and wealth of their parents. The ratio between the richest and the poorest families, which today is on the order of 1,000 to 1, would almost certainly have to be under 10 to 1 if we wanted to create fair competition for the children on the lower end.[13] *Diversity as Justice* is too weak to demand equality of opportunity because discrimination based on economic grounds—mainly the income of one's parents—is perfectly compatible with an end to racist discrimination. It is true that supporters of Identity, Diversity, and Multiculturalism do refer to inequality of opportunity, even if they use the term incorrectly. On the other hand, the program hardly acknowledges the other type of inequality: inequality of outcome. An end to racist discrimination and white privilege has no implications whatsoever for the overall amount of inequality of outcome tolerated in society. Leftist principles, on the other hand, demand very high levels of equality of outcome.

According to the Rawlsian Difference Principle, inequality of outcome must be to the greatest advantage of the least advantaged group. That is, only when inequality—generated through such mechanisms as incentives for education and work effort—improves the lives of the poorest can it be justified. Although I have taken the Rawlsian principles of justice as the exemplar of the Left, one does not need to wholly adopt the Difference Principle. Some nearby positions will suffice. A just society for a leftist cannot tolerate poverty or hunger or homelessness. It must provide education and healthcare to all. The crucial issue for leftists is the support for a substantial reduction in inequality of outcome via a massive redistribution of income and wealth, requiring ongoing and robust economic regulations to maintain the desired level of equality.

The main goal of *Diversity as Justice*—an end to racist discrimination and white privilege—is consistent with virtually any amount of income inequality. The moral problem for *Diversity as Justice* is not the existence of the rich and the poor but simply that too few of the rich are black and too many blacks are poor. *Diversity as Justice* can demand nothing more than that the rate of black millionaires equals the rate of white millionaires, on the one hand, and that the rate of blacks in poverty equal the rate for whites, on the other. A leftist, on the other hand, asserts that a just society cannot have millionaires at the same time that the average household income is around $50,000 and the official rate of poverty is above 10 percent (and the true rate, if we used a better method to measure it, probably much higher).

The political-economist Albert Hirschman observed two general responses to objectionable collective outcomes: Exit and voice. Those adopting the exit strategy simply leave their current organization, group, school, or town in search of better performing alternatives. It is thus the dominant mechanism in consumer-goods markets. Those exercising voice, on the other hand, attempt to improve the collectivity they currently inhabit. According to Hirschman, blacks eschewed the exit strategy when facing their common economic problems, instead maintaining group solidarity and insisting upon shared success:

> The novelty of the black power movement on the American scene consists in the rejection of this traditional pattern of upward social mobility as unworkable and undesirable for the most depressed group in our society. Significantly, it combines scorn for individual penetration of a few selected blacks into white society with a strong commitment to "collective stimulation" of blacks as a group and to the improvement of the black ghetto as a place to live. (1970, 109)

What's most remarkable about the statement is just how wrong it is as a description of political-economic activism by blacks today. No longer do we see anything like a Civil Rights movement that seeks collective uplift. Blacks, like just about everybody else in America, have adopted the strategy of Exit rather than Voice with regard to their economic situation. The goal is to leave poverty and poor neighborhoods behind, and scarcely look back. It's seen in the flight to suburbs, private schools, and gated communities. Our pop culture is heavily propagandized with such success stories. "Get rich or die tryin'," declares 50 Cent. The idea that we should all move up together, which requires group solidarity—or what Hirschman referred to as voice—is a leftist orientation, not a value of Diversity, which is fully satisfied via the tokenism of Exit.

> Success—or what amounts to the same thing, upward social mobility—has long been conceived in terms of evolutionary individualism. The successful individual who starts at a low rung of the social ladder, necessarily leaves his own group behind as he rises; he "passes" into, or is "accepted" by, the next higher group. He takes his immediate family along, but hardly anyone else. (1970, 108)

I'm not claiming that Hirschman—one of the keenest minds of the twentieth century—was wrong in his characterization of black activism, but rather than the ideology of neoliberalism has been adopted by blacks along with most who promote Diversity since he made his observations in the 1960s. The decline of black solidarity coincided precisely with the rise of Diversity. Neoliberalism and Diversity are perfectly compatible ideologies. Because the end to white privilege does not threaten the overall amount of wealth that can be held by those at the top of the distribution, they have no reason to fight Diversity. Indeed, Diversity is the ideal obfuscator: it fools progressives into serving the interests of the wealthy.

DIVERSITY AS JUSTICE: THE EQUITY EVASION

Some Diversity supporters might insist that they do call for something very much like equality of opportunity and even equality of outcome. Many Diversity Statements speak to *equity* or *equitable* outcomes. In discussions with supporters one will quite often hear concern expressed for equity. There are at least two problems, however, in trying to substitute equity for something like a leftist notion of equality. First, equity has no clear meaning. Equity seems to be a rough synonym for fairness but the content is never given precision as it is in Rawls's theory of justice as fairness. We never see anything remotely like the Difference Principle, which argues for maximizing the position of the least advantaged group. Given such imprecision it is quite easy to justify almost any action or outcome as fair or equitable. A libertarian believes that perfect markets produce fair or equitable outcomes; a neoliberal believes that loosely regulated capitalism is fair or equitable. A Director of Equity and Inclusion at any corporation or college in the country could justify a salary of $250,000 at the same time that the average worker in the organization faces a pay freeze and benefit cuts. Without much greater specificity the notion of equity can be used for almost any purpose.

Second, if we attempt to impute a more specific meaning to equity by looking at the recommendations and plans coming out of the program then we find two possibilities, neither of which comes close to a leftist response to the problem. One is to equate equity with an end to exclusion. IDMP supporters often treat economic inequality like cultural differences. We simply need to hire or admit more poor people. This, of course, does nothing to change the overall distribution of income in society or the economic forces that produce inequality but simply rearranges the winners and losers. A variation of this approach treats poverty like a culture that can be celebrated: We need to see the value in all types of economic circumstances, including poverty. This is nonsense. A leftist does not want to celebrate the excessive spread in income by calling it "diversity" but rather to reduce it and indeed to completely eliminate the existence of poverty.

Another approach to promoting equity involves takings steps to prevent poorer folks from getting their feelings hurt. I refer to this as "Don't rub their noses in it!" At a committee meeting I heard a report on Diversity followed by some discussion on how to make sure that incoming students with modest means do not feel bad when encountering conspicuous displays of purchasing power by some of their wealthier classmates. Not only does this leave the underlying inequality unchallenged but it's rather silly to think that poorer students have somehow gone through about 18 years of life without recognizing their position in the economic scheme of things. Poverty should neither be celebrated like some exotic foreign tribe nor be hushed up or ignored like a fart in polite company, but rather exposed for the evil it is and actively combatted.

Here's the crucial difference: Leftist principles of justice demand *less diversity* of income in society; *equity* does not. Our culture is not impoverished by eliminating poverty. Or if it is, so much the worse for culture. Cheap talk about equity only serves to obfuscate the issue, making it possible for supporters to see the Program as leftist while abetting our neoliberal drift.

SUMMARY AND CONCLUSION

The objective of the first tenet, *Diversity as Justice*, is increased representation of previously marginalized groups by ending their related types of discrimination. IDMP supporters are correct to demand an end to white, male privilege; indeed, the leftist principle of equal opportunity states that nothing should matter for economic mobility except talent and work ethic. Yet the end to racism, sexism, and other forms of discrimination based on identity would not be sufficient to bring about equality of opportunity and would be consistent with a level of inequality of outcome similar to what we see today in the United States. Our extreme inequality of income and wealth is largely avoided in Diversity talk or else diluted to irrelevance by vague palaver about equity.

Believers in the Program have used *Diversity as Justice* to promote a right-wing (neoliberal and conservative) agenda and as a cudgel to attack the Left whenever they push back. Politico celebrates, without any irony, the fact that "women took over the military-industrial complex," informing us that "it's a watershed for what has always been a male-dominated bastion" (Brown 2019). These female defense-industry executives and high-ranking officers in the military provide the "different perspectives [needed] to confront a host of highly complex global challenges on the horizon." Heather Wilson, the Secretary of the Air Force, tells us, "If I ask everyone in this room to think about the most protective person you know in your life, someone who would do anything to keep you safe, half the people in this room would think about their moms . . . We are the protectors; that's what the military does. We serve to protect the rest of you, and that's a very natural place for a woman to be." The CIA, presumably another protective institution, is led by Gina Haspel, the first woman to hold the post. Her nomination by President Trump was controversial because she oversaw a CIA black-site facility which employed waterboarding among other torture techniques (J. E. Barnes and Scott 2018). In response to the criticism, Sarah Sanders, the (also female) press secretary, tweeted "There is no one more qualified to be the first woman to lead the CIA than 30+ year CIA veteran Gina Haspel. Any Democrat who claims to support women's empowerment and our national security but opposes her nomination is a total hypocrite" (May 5, 2018).

In the introduction, we discussed the importance of *Diversity as Justice* in the liberal evaluation of the presidency of Barack Obama and the presidential campaign of Hillary Clinton. They are not, of course, the only beneficiaries. Nancy Pelosi became the Speaker of House after the Democrats won a majority in the 2018 elections but, for a brief moment, her position seemed uncertain as she faced some criticism of her record from progressives. One can already guess the defense offered by the establishment. "I think it would look ridiculous if we win back the House . . . we have a pink wave with women who have brought back the House, then you're going to not elect the leader who led the way?" said Representative Lois Frankel (Bade 2018). The argument in her favor was that "she'll prioritize legislation empowering women on issues ranging from equal pay to anti-harassment legislation." The organization *Feminist Majority* described her as "a selfless feminist dedicated to equality." Their definition of equality must be something like *Diversity as Justice* because Pelosi's record includes a vote to repeal the Glass-Steagall regulation of Wall Street and opposition to universal health coverage.

In short, *Diversity as Justice* is consistent with neoliberalism and can be used to promote (neo)conservatism. I'm not claiming that the IDMP caused neoliberalism (the latter preceded the former), simply that it's consistent with it, and furthermore that neoliberals have embraced Diversity because it lets them ignore economic inequality while simultaneously appearing progressive, thus placating much of the activist base. Perhaps some in the Program feel no need to have a strong position on equality of opportunity and equality of outcome. This is unacceptable because economic inequality is a fundamental moral consideration for the Left. Neutrality or agnosticism on a matter of such importance would itself violate leftist values. If promoters of Diversity are satisfied with simply being centrists—politically and philosophically—then let's be honest about it. The Identity, Diversity, and Multiculturalism Program is not a radical movement for justice but rather something far tamer. The demand for an end to racist discrimination and segregation was indeed courageous at a certain point in our history. So too was the fight to end slavery or to give women the vote. These positions are now mainstream, virtually universal, and no longer signify a commitment to anything stronger. It parallels the neoliberal Democrats who tout their opposition to Trump as sufficient evidence of their progressive credentials. The IDMP is closer to the *College Democrats* than to *Occupy Wall Street*. Safe, very safe. The interests of the political and economic elite are in no way threatened. They have happily embraced the rhetoric of Identity, Diversity, and Multiculturalism, and now use it as a way to push back against claims for social and economic justice.

The supporters who do make a fundamental critique of economic inequality have probably intuitively adopted a genuinely leftist perspective. The critique of *Diversity as Justice* in this chapter should move those leftist values out of one's vague intuition and bring them into the front of one's consciousness. Identity, Diversity, and Multiculturalism does not share our leftist principles of economic justice.

NOTES

1. For a statement, if p, then q, the contrapositive is, if not q, then not p. In this context the original statement is, if one is a leftist, then one supports the Identity, Diversity, and Multiculturalism Program. The contrapositive: If one does not support the IDMP, then one is not a leftist.

2. From Kant's article, *Beantwortung der Frage, Was ist Aufklärung?* (Answering the Question, What is Enlightenment?) published by the Berlinische Monatsschrift (1784). "Wenn denn nun gefragt wird: Leben wir jetzt in einem aufgeklärten Zeitalter? so ist die Antwort: Nein, aber wohl in einem Zeitalter der Aufklärung." ("If it were asked: Do we now live in an enlightened age? The answer is: No, but rather in an age of enlightenment.")

3. Rene Descartes's Meditations clearly reflect this confidence—some might say hubris—in the power of the human intellect to discover the truth. His most famous quote is *cogito ergo sum* but the passage at the conclusion of the *Fourth Meditation* more clearly reveals his confident spirit of inquiry: "I have not only learnt today what I must avoid in order to escape error, but also what I must do in order to arrive at knowledge of the truth. For certainly I shall reach truth if I fix my attention sufficiently on all the things I conceive perfectly, and if I separate them from others which I apprehend only confusedly and obscurely, which, from now on, I shall take great care to do" (1968, 141).

4. Some might respond by saying it was a capitalist revolution, not a democratic one. True, but in France of the eighteenth century I see no necessary contradiction between the two. The bourgeois fought against the powers of the king and church—some as a simple matter of self-interest, others for perhaps more noble objectives, and for many as a complicated mixture. In any case, the Left of the French Revolution is an ancestor of the modern Left. We can leave debates over the "true nature" of the French Revolution as work for historians.

5. The actual creation of capitalism out of feudalism is another matter. The centuries-long process of tearing serfs from the land, and thus their means of survival, was the source of immense suffering. Marx's chapter, *On Primitive Accumulation*, from volume I of *Capital* (1977) is a classic reading on the state-sponsored violence behind the making of a labor market. Karl Polanyi's *The Great Transformation* (2001) continues the story up through the triumph of capitalism in the West after the industrial revolution.

6. http://www.iep.utm.edu/rawls/#H3.

7. Moral philosophers typically interpret social contract theory in a slightly different manner. A social contract should in principle be agreeable to *everybody*. According to Rawls, "political power is legitimate only when it is exercised in accordance with a constitution (written or unwritten) the essentials of which all citizens, as reasonable and rational, can endorse in the light of their common human reason" (2001, 41). As a sociological matter that seems unlikely, so for our purposes we define leftists to be those individuals whose moral philosophy puts them in the neighborhood of the Rawlsian principles. That is, Leftists will accept these principles but others will disagree.

8. Look at the time series data in appendix A-2 of the most recent edition of the Census Bureau's *Income and Poverty in the United States*. The Gini index, for example, increased fairly steadily from 0.386 in 1968 to 0.481 in 2016.

9. As an empirical matter it is nearly impossible to find equality across many factors except the one of interest but throughout the social sciences and legal studies this is approximated via statistical control. The natural sciences also follow this approach, including much medical research, but can more often obtain experimental control, a more robust method not generally available in the social sciences. Regression analysis is one way to obtain statistical control.

10. As a historical analogy for the scientific importance of simple terminology consider the development of the branch of mathematics known as analysis. Both Isaac Newton and Gottfried Leibniz are credited with the invention of calculus in the 1660s or 1670s. Indeed, the timing of the discovery was a source of great controversy and determining who got there first spilled over into a nationalistic quarrel with the British claiming Newton and the Germans defending Leibniz. One consequence was that subsequent British mathematicians followed Newton's terminology for calculus while Germans (and indeed most continental Europeans) followed Leibniz. Looking back it is clear that Liebniz's notation, while ultimately conveying more or less the same key ideas about calculus as Newton's, was superior in suggesting further developments in differential equations and other topics in mathematical analysis. Thus simple terminology is seen as one reason for the superiority of continental mathematics in subsequent centuries. Today Liebniz's notation is standard practice everywhere, even England.

11. Good research in this area is being done by Devah Pager, Bruce Western, and Bart Bonikowski. See, for example, Pager, Western, and Bonikowski (2009) and Pager and Western (2005) available at http://scholar.harvard.edu/files/pager/files/race_at_work.pdf. They found that the white job testers received a positive response (callback or job offer) twice as frequently as the black testers (31.0 percent vs. 15.2 percent). Even when the applicants had a criminal record listed on the application, the white testers received a positive response 17.2 percent of the time compared to only 13.0 percent for the black testers.

12. Rawls's theory of Justice as Fairness generated a large reaction in philosophy and the social sciences. Some of it was strongly critical, like the libertarian response by Robert Nozick (2013) but even more can be seen as friendly criticism, like Amartya Sen, Ronald Dworkin, G. A. Cohen, and John Roemer, to take a few of the important figures. Despite the disagreements (with Rawls and with each other) I assume a leftist would favor something in the neighborhood of the Rawlsian approach to equality. The Identity, Diversity, and Multiculturalism Program fails not only the Rawlsian standard, but any similarly strong statement of equality.

13. Take $10,000,000 as the income at the upper end and $10,000 as the income on the lower end to arrive at this ratio. As for wealth, since the poor have essentially none, the ratio here is infinite.

Chapter Two

A Model of Economic Inequality

The critique of *Diversity as Justice* in the previous chapter was both conceptual and philosophical. Conceptually we needed to understand what was meant by terms like racism and equality of opportunity. Philosophically we needed to understand the moral imperatives of the Left and of the Identity, Diversity, and Multiculturalism Program (IDMP). Yet behind that discussion were assumptions about the way the world works. In this chapter, I build a model where I make explicit the causal mechanisms that I believe are responsible for economic inequality. The model accounts for the intergenerational correlation in income and thereby explains the perpetuation of racist outcomes.[1] The model strengthens the argument against *Diversity as Justice* from the previous chapter and is essential for the critique of the tenet of *Colorblindness as Racism* in the next.

Although we might find some disagreements between those coming from an Identity, Diversity, and Multiculturalism background and others with a leftist orientation I believe the explanatory framework offered here should be acceptable to both. After all, most in the Identity, Diversity, and Multiculturalism Program identify as progressive, leftist, or even radical. In this context, the conflict between the Left and the Program has less to do with competing views over the way the world actually operates and more to do with (1) what a just world would look like and (2) how best to get there. In other words, the conflict involves values and policy, not theory. The agreement between the Left and the IDMP regarding the proper explanation of inequality puts into sharper relief the disagreements on the other two aspects.

The model of inequality will combine political-economic and race-based mechanisms of stratification. Leftists agree that the causal factor emphasized by those in the Identity, Diversity, and Multiculturalism tradition—racist discrimination[2]—is present. It must be placed, however, in a fuller explanatory framework. The purpose of the model is to explain *earned* income, that is, the compensation received by individuals in exchange for labor. For most of us, our economic standing is overwhelmingly determined by the paycheck we receive from our job. Thus I want to explain the variation in individual outcomes in the labor market.[3] We can approach the question by considering a young adult just entering the workforce in search of a career, or at least a job. The explanation involves moving backwards over time—involving childhood and adolescent experiences—and outwards over space—from the family, to the neighborhood, and even to the entire society—to identify the factors behind the individual's outcome in the labor market.

EMBODIED CAPITAL AS PROXIMATE
CAUSE OF INEQUALITY

Why do some people get the high-paying jobs and others have to settle for less? The answer will become more complex as our discussion progresses but it is easiest to first consider the supply side of the labor market. On this side, we can start with the educational level of an individual, an important element of what is referred to by economists and other social scientists as human capital. The evidence is clear that a substantial pay gap exists between those with and without educational degrees.[4] While educational training may or may not indicate a specific occupational skill it certainly is taken as a favorable signal in the labor market. It might indicate that the worker is able to learn what the employer wishes to teach, certainly a valuable trait from the perspective of the employer. Whatever the fundamental reasons for the relationship, any model of inequality or stratification will predict that workers with more human capital will earn a higher wage on average in the labor market.

Human capital is one type of a broader set of characteristics known as *embodied capital*. Unlike financial capital—a type of *disembodied* capital— human capital cannot be (directly) exchanged from one person to another. Embodied capital becomes a characteristic of the individual like, for example, being a college graduate. Here I follow the usage of French sociologist Pierre Bourdieu (1986) and consider two other types of embodied capital: *social capital* and *cultural capital*. Social capital refers to the resources that result from one's position in a social network, which include obligations and expectations along with access to information. Cultural capital is a bit fuzzier but potentially no less important. Capital in a generic sense is an asset, making cultural capital those particular elements of culture that bring an advantage in the labor market (among other places). Different individuals can be part of the same culture but still differ from each other across many distinct components of their common culture. At its foundation a culture requires a common meaning system: members of the same culture should be able to communicate with each other. For example, if you don't speak a word of Japanese then you cannot claim to be a part of Japanese culture: You couldn't talk to a Japanese person in Japanese! But language skills even among those who ostensibly speak the same language vary considerably. The styles of speech that are more highly valued by employers would be considered one aspect of cultural capital. We can go beyond language to include other learned manners and mannerisms that bring an advantage on the job or at a job interview.

All three of these types of capital belong on the *supply side* of the market. They are traits of the agent that is selling, or *supplying*, the commodity on the market. In this case, the commodity is the ability to spend time doing work and the market is the labor market. This is only half the story. We must add the *demand side* of the labor market, which captures the behavior of the employer. We can conceive of the demand side as the amounts of different types of labor desired by employers and the rates they are willing to pay. It is true that labor market demand is affected by the overall level of economic activity—(almost) all demand curves shift outward when the economy is strong—but for now we focus on the variation among workers and not on the overall level of unemployment (Keynesian issues about the overall state of the economy will be added below).

The causal diagram of the model of inequality is presented in figure 2.1. Causation goes from left to right but for the exposition we will work backwards from right to left. The dependent variable is the *Labor Market Outcome* of an individual. We begin with the most proximate factors: *Embodied Capital* and *Employers*. The diagram displays the idea that supply and demand factors interact on the labor market, leading to whatever earned income we observe. Essentially, people with different skills and traits are competing with each other in the eyes of employers. The model predicts that workers who supply more embodied capital will on average obtain better labor market outcomes, that is, earn more income.

Even within this simple model we can say something about the perpetuation of racist outcomes that should be acceptable to both leftists and IDMP supporters, at least the majority of the latter who identify as on the Left. If, due to previous racist behaviors, the current distribution of the three types of embodied capital exhibits a racial pattern (a racist outcome) such that blacks start with less capital than whites, then the labor market outcome will necessarily reflect these differences. This is true even if we suppose an absence of current discriminatory racist behavior on the demand side. In this scenario the problem would be located in the unequal distribution of embodied capital on the supply side and not in any inappropriate racist behavior on the part

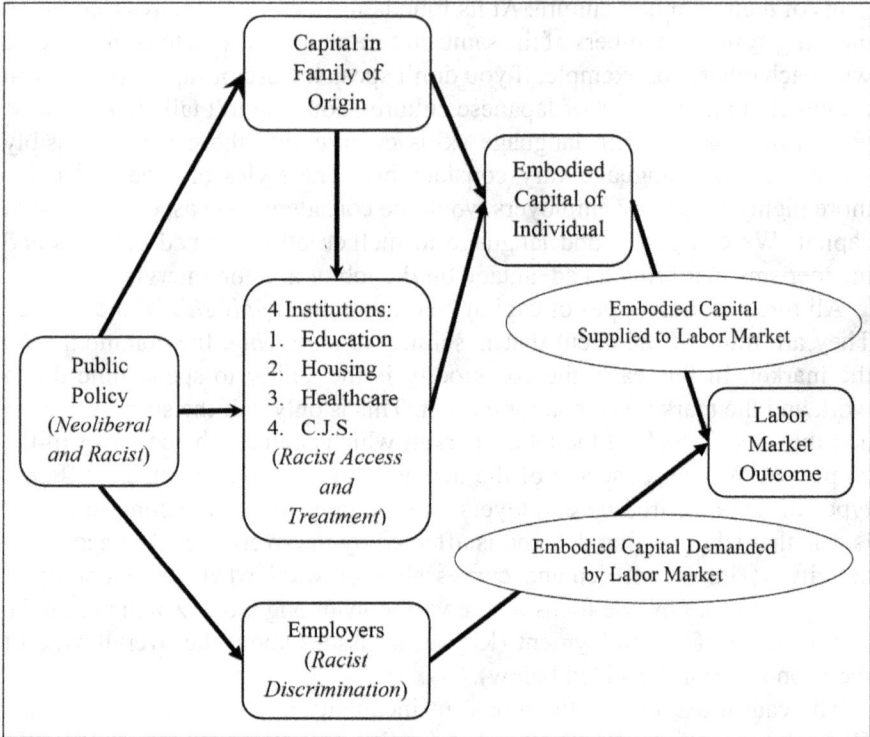

Figure 2.1. Model of Labor Market Outcomes with Political-Economic and Racist Mechanisms

of employers on the demand side. Within this framework we conclude that it is possible for racism as an outcome to persist, at least for a certain period of time, without racism as ongoing demand-side behavior. Adding racist discrimination on the part of employers, as I do in the model, only worsens the problem.

THE INSTITUTIONAL REPRODUCTION OF INEQUALITY

I refer to embodied capital as a *proximate* factor of inequality because it would not suffice to end the explanatory story here. It is important to explore the reasons for the variation in embodied capital among workers. Human capital, social capital, and cultural capital are all *economically conditioned phenomena* (Weber 1949, 65), meaning that resources in the family can be converted to a greater or lesser degree into all three. According to this approach, it is not only financial capital that can be transformed into embodied capital. The social, cultural, and human capital of parents helps to form the embodied capital of their children.

The reproduction of the various types of capital across the generations is a process that occurs not only within the family but is also substantially mediated by other social institutions, by which I mean those parts of society recognized as possessing logically related and patterned sets of behavior. To keep the model manageable, I include four institutions that seem to be of the greatest importance: (1) education; (2) housing; (3) healthcare; and (4) the criminal justice system. As mediating variables these social institutions have two properties. First, the quality of the contact with the institution varies directly with the level of capital in the family of origin, specifically, the more capital at home, the better the experience with the different institutions. Second, participation in the social institutions is related to the level of embodied capital developed by the worker, that is, the better the treatment in the institution, the higher the level of embodied capital at the time when the worker enters the labor market.

Working backwards from *Embodied Capital* in figure 2.1 are the factors of *Capital in Family of Origin* and the *4 Institutions*. The direct link between family capital and embodied capital captures several relationships or causal mechanisms. Primary socialization tends to produce children with traits similar to their parents. Speech patterns, a key ingredient in cultural capital, are largely instilled by parents even before the child enters formal schooling.[5] The social capital of a young adult depends greatly, at least at first, on the social network of the parents. In all these cases variation due to the accident of one's birth leads directly, after 18 or so years of familial interaction, to labor market consequences. The correlations may vary in magnitude, of course, but they are all positive: higher levels of capital (financial, social, cultural, or human) in the family of origin are associated with more embodied capital for the offspring.

Over and above the embodied capital that parents instill into their children inside the home, opportunities to develop embodied capital can be purchased on the educational, housing, and healthcare markets. That is, embodied capital is institutionally mediated, as depicted by the lines into and out of the four institutions in figure 2.1. Private schools constitute one dramatic instance of such conversion of disembodied resources (i.e., money) into embodied capital but even in the public K-12 system the relationship between economic resources and educational quality is mediated through the neighborhood. The institution of housing, which is clearly economically conditioned, is thereby connected to the production of human capital. The degree of housing segregation by income has actually increased in recent decades, meaning that an ever higher share of poor households lives in majority poor neighborhoods, and the same is true at higher income levels (Taylor and Fry 2012). Thus the contrast is not only, or not even primarily, between underfunded public schools serving a disproportionate number of poor children and well-funded private schools serving mainly the well-to-do, but also among public schools in very different economic environments. Indeed, there are a great many public schools that successfully educate our children; however, most of those children do not come from poverty.

Healthcare is the third institution that links capital in the family of origin to embodied capital of the offspring. Researchers have established clear links between family capital and childhood health, on the one hand, and childhood health and economic mobility, on the other, thereby making healthcare another important mediator in the model. In a review of the large literature on the subject, Janet Currie (2009) concludes that there is substantial evidence behind both claims. First, poorer children tend to fare worse on a long list of maladies ranging from respiratory problems, mental problems, hearing and vision problems, and ADHD. The causes include such factors as fetal health and low birth weight, poor nutrition, and toxic exposures. On the other side of the relationship, the evidence suggests that the correlation between health in childhood, on the one hand, and education and income in adulthood, on the other, reflects a genuine causal connection. As we might expect, health problems do indeed limit life chances and outcomes.

The fourth institution in the model, the criminal justice system, is one where typically less is more, in contrast to the other three. The goal for most children and their parents is to avoid contact with the system, and failing that, to avoid an arrest record, conviction, and incarceration. Again there are two sides to the causal chain. On the one hand, more family capital is associated with less contact and, when contact with the criminal justice system does occur, more lenient dispositions (Reiman and Leighton 2016). On the other hand, coming out with a criminal record or time spent in jail directly hampers one's ability to develop human, social, and cultural capital, and is regarded as a liability by many employers.

The model with this institutional mediation predicts that inequality in family capital works through socialization in the home and through participation in social institutions to produce young adults who possess varying amounts of embodied capital when they face the labor market. Therefore the model predicts that the inequality between families at the beginning of the period will to some degree be perpetuated in their offspring (Mazumder 2005).[6] Poorer children develop less embodied capital and end up with lower-paying jobs. *Mutatis mutandis* for richer kids. This model of labor-market inequality is clearly leftist in orientation but should be acceptable as well to those who support the Identity, Diversity, and Multiculturalism Program. Because the original distribution of family capital has a racial pattern—given previous racial oppression and white privilege, black families on average start with less capital than whites—the model predicts that whites will have better institutional experiences and ultimately more embodied capital as they enter the labor market. Dalton Conley (2010) found that the racial difference in family wealth—white families had on average 15 times the net worth of black families—was a strong predictor of the wages of the offspring (see, especially, the regressions in table A4.3). Again it is important to note that, so far, we have not yet discussed racist discrimination by any actors. Employers (legally) discriminate only on the grounds of embodied capital and that institutions largely discriminate on the grounds of a family's ability to pay. Racist outcomes can be perpetuated without racist discrimination in a society where parents are able to convert their capital into the capital of their offspring. The U.S. neoliberal political-economy is this society, par excellence.

THE POLITICAL ECONOMY OF INEQUALITY

We still need to explicitly discuss the forms of racist behavior in this model but there is one more step before that task. Our capitalist economy is not, of course, a completely "free" market. Every capitalist economy is regulated to varying degrees by the state, and the labor market probably more than any other.[7] The institution of the state therefore deserves a prominent place in our analysis because it is involved—or at least has the potential to be involved— in virtually all economic phenomena. In other words, our model must reflect the fact that the economy is actually a *political-economy*. The coercive power of the state creates the background rules in which voluntary action—whether self-interested or otherwise—occurs. The next element in the model is therefore public policy, which will be the center of our attention in the next chapter when we deal with the debate on colorblindness. The model explicitly links, directly or indirectly, the variables already considered to public policies. In figure 2.1, the arrows indicate where *Public Policy* affects *Capital in Family of Origin*; (2) the *4 Institutions*; and (3) *Employers*.

Consider the top arrow on the far left running from policies to family capital. This captures redistribution that occurs via income (and wealth) taxation and transfer payments. The more progressive the tax system, the bigger the share taken from higher income levels thereby reducing, other things equal, the inequality in the distribution of resources across families. Less progressive systems do less to alter the market-based distribution of income. Transfer payments have similar distributional implications. Social spending like that seen in European social democracies improves equality but heavy spending on the military-prison complex or corporate welfare as in the United States seems to do little good (Blanden, Gregg, and Machin 2005).[8] *Neoliberal* as a modifier of *Public Policies* in the diagram is meant to highlight the limited efforts taken by the U.S. to reduce income inequality.

Next consider the influence of public policies on other social institutions. The state funds many and regulates all social institutions. Because two of the four leading institutions—education and criminal justice—are primarily public, state policies heavily impact the experiences of the individuals who participate in them. The other two institutions—healthcare and housing—are delivered privately for the most part but do not fall outside the scope of public regulation. The two arrows pointing into the institutions indicate that the extent and quality of an individual's experience in an institution results from an interaction of resources in the family of origin and the public regulation of the institution. Seen from a broader perspective, institutions mediate the development of embodied capital not only for the family but also for society at large, where the level of embodied capital of the citizenry can be seen as a public *desideratum*. *Neoliberal* in this context refers to the absence of universal healthcare and inadequate support for public education alongside a bloated criminal justice system, which is needed in large part to manage the problems that follow from economic inequality.

The final arrow leaving public policy points to the demand side of the labor market. The most important labor market regulations affect the unemployment rate and wage level. Taking a Keynesian view of the economy, one that should be acceptable to leftists as well as most IDMP supporters, I claim that the government has the power to strongly modify both unemployment and wages. The federal government establishes the minimum wage and many state governments have set their own higher standards. The impact of fiscal policy is felt most strongly during economic downturns but deficit spending in general stimulates economic growth. The state directly employs millions of workers and indirectly contributes to the employment of millions more through the multiplier effect. I will have more to say about Keynesian policies in the next chapter but here I want to note that a neoliberal approach to the labor market means that the state does not aggressively use its tools to encourage full employment at high wages.

One key point to take from the discussion so far is that the neoliberal approach in the United States largely reproduces the market inequality inherited at the start. Richer families contribute too small of a share of their income to the commonweal, meaning the state has less revenue to spend on social institutions. The rich, however, can purchase better institutional participation for their children, ultimately giving their offspring higher levels of embodied capital. Because the inequality exhibits a racial character at the beginning of the period, we would expect to see racial inequality at the end. A disproportionate number of black households start with less capital and therefore their children tend to have worse experiences in social institutions, develop lower levels of embodied capital, and end up in lower paying jobs. Although capable of redistributing income, strengthening social institutions, and promoting employment, as would be consistent with a leftist view of justice, policies in the U.S. largely leave intact the enormous disparities created by the capitalist economy (Moller et al. 2003).[9] The uneven ability of different households to develop embodied capital perpetuates existing inequality.

INCORPORATING RACIST MECHANISMS

Having identified the main political-economic mechanisms behind the reproduction of inequality, we now have a good foundation to discuss the racist components to the model. The political-economic mechanisms discussed so far do not preclude the role of racism. On the contrary, they clearly reveal where and how to incorporate racism. I suggest this approach is analytically superior to the vaguer but more popular discourse about things like *intersectionality* and *lived experiences*.

The behavior of employers is modified to include the presence of racist discrimination, which, as discussed in chapter 1, occurs when an employer selects a white candidate over a black candidate when other relevant factors are held constant. From the perspective of the model this means that if we compare whites and blacks with identical levels of embodied capital, whites will be hired more often or at a higher wage. An economist would say that there are different demand curves; the curve for whites is located farther out and higher up than the curve for non-whites. The best evidence for such discrimination comes from studies of matched applicants, which find that whites are more likely to receive job offers than blacks (Pager and Western 2005; Pager, Western, and Bonikowski 2009).

Next consider racism in the four institutions. Racist discrimination can occur in two ways, identified as *racist access* and *racist treatment*. Racist access means that blacks have a lower (or higher, in the case of the criminal justice system) rate of acceptance into institutions than whites with the same level of family resources. Discrimination at the site of institutional access can be seen as the reversal of discrimination in the labor market. In the labor market discrimination occurs on the demand side: employers do not want to buy from blacks what they want to sell (their ability to labor). In institutions, on the other hand, the problem occurs on the supply side: agents in the institutions do not want to sell to blacks what they have the money to buy. For example, when homeowners, real estate agents, or mortgage lenders do not give blacks the same opportunity to purchase or rent real estate as they do to whites. Racist discrimination is also present when private schools or healthcare facilities refuse to admit blacks at the same rate as whites, assuming in all cases that everything else is equal, particularly that everybody has the same ability to pay. The criminal justice system, however, is unique among our selected institutions. Although the criminal justice system does not sell a service it is nevertheless possible to convert resources into the *avoidance* of access. Racism at this site means that blacks are scrutinized, stopped, or arrested more often than comparable whites.[10] For these reasons blacks participate disproportionately in an institution that almost everybody seeks to avoid.

The other type of racism here occurs when blacks receive worse treatment than whites when comparably placed. For example, when black students are placed incorrectly into lower tracks more often than whites with the same academic ability in the same schools. Even when placed in the same classroom black students might receive inferior instruction from teachers. Or when black patients receive worse healthcare than whites by the same doctors and nurses. And blacks who end up in the criminal justice system tend to receive worse treatment than whites, up to and including the highest form of punishment, the death penalty. In general, the model includes any type of mistreatment within institutions such that blacks develop less embodied capital than whites who are similarly positioned.

Moving from institutions to the level of the state, the nature of racism changes. The three dimensions of racism—beliefs, behaviors, and outcomes—help give precision to the notion of racist policies. I propose that a racist policy must involve both racist outcomes and racist beliefs. First, the policy must produce a racist outcome, that is, it must tend to put blacks into subordinate positions. Second, it must have been passed with racist intent, that is, the lawmakers must have been influenced, at least in part but not necessarily entirely, by racist beliefs. Such acts (with the dual meaning of both behaviors and laws) by legislators can be designated as racist public policies or racist laws. It is possible for policies to be partially racist if we believe that at least some of the motivation of some legislators comes from a desire to give preferential treatment to whites.

The requirement of racist beliefs makes it more difficult to prove that policies are racist because even conservative lawmakers are unlikely to admit such biases. Nonetheless we can certainly find some plausible legislative and administrative examples. *White flight* was abetted by a shift in public spending priorities away from urban toward suburban areas, including the massive direct and indirect subsidies for highways and for driving in general. It is difficult to imagine anything other than racist beliefs as a motivator for at least part of the war on drugs and particularly for the unequal sentencing for different types of cocaine. And as recently as 2010 it was easy to find racist arguments in the opposition to healthcare reform particularly within the so-called Tea Party. In many cases, however, it becomes difficult to separate class conflict and its concomitant attack on the working and middle classes from the desire to subordinate blacks. Given the disproportionate number of blacks in poverty it turns out that either motive will suffice.

One final point about racial inequality. We have largely taken as given the preexisting distribution of resources in society. That is, the model assumes an economic situation like the one we find ourselves in today, fifty or more years after the Civil Rights Era. That does not mean that there is no explanation for the inherited distribution of family capital, a distribution which exhibits racial inequality. It simply means that this model does not explain it. It would be possible to provide a historical explanation for the racial disparities in the distribution of family capital and to bring in other manifestations of racism. The model in figure 2.1 explains the *perpetuation* of inequality, not the *origination* of inequality. To some extent this is a necessary simplification when dealing with such a complex system—some elements are necessarily excluded—but there is another sociological and political rationale. The model can be interpreted as applying to the post-Civil Rights Era where *de jure* separate but equal has been rejected. Racial inequality over the previous centuries—spanning slavery to Jim Crow—clearly involved legally coercive racist mechanisms. The model takes for granted that prior to the current regime coercive behavior was substantially responsible for the racial component to the original distribution of family capital. The model, however, intends to capture the key mechanisms of inequality under our current neoliberal political-economic system and therefore emphasizes the modern labor market, social institutions, and state policies, factors that are far subtler than *Plessy v. Ferguson*.

MODELING WHITE PRIVILEGE AND RESOURCE PRIVILEGE

The model of labor market outcomes with political-economic and racist mechanisms in figure 2.1 can be used to explore the notion of white privilege, a key concept in the Identity, Diversity, and Multiculturalism Program and indeed the foundation for *Diversity as Justice*, the tenet analyzed and critiqued in the previous chapter. Two observations follow from the explanatory model. First, higher levels of capital in the family of origin lead directly or indirectly to higher levels of embodied capital for the offspring. Second, racism in institutions—whether through access or treatment—makes the relationship between family capital and embodied capital more favorable for whites than for blacks. In the context of economic mobility and inequality, the first observation can be considered a statement of *resource privilege*, the second, a statement of *white privilege*.

I know that many in the IDMP will object to this framing of white privilege as crude and mechanistic, as insensitive to the subtle or even invisible aspects of the phenomenon. After all, economic inequality is merely one expression of subordination or oppression. Despite this limitation I maintain that economic inequality and poverty are important enough aspects of our life chances to deserve our analytical attention. Furthermore, analysis of income differences does not preclude investigations of other phenomena, including those that might be more difficult to measure or even to define.

The claim that both race and class of origin are important factors might be recast by many in the Program as a statement of *intersectionality*. This term, however, is unacceptably imprecise and obfuscates an important asymmetry in the way the types of privilege operate. Not only are family capital and race distinct concepts, as are all variables, but they are two different *types* of variables. Race is a categorical variable; there are a limited number of different categories of races. Family capital, taking, for example, family income as a measure of financial capital, is a quantitative variable; it could be arranged on a number line spanning a wide range.

Observe further that the dependent variable, embodied capital, is also quantitative (again there are suitable empirical proxies, like years of education for human capital). The relationship between the *categorical* independent variable (race) and the *quantitative* dependent variable (embodied capital) must necessarily be different from the relationship between the *quantitative* independent variable (family capital) and the *quantitative* dependent variable (embodied capital). An example of these different relationships is presented in figure 2.2 (in principle there could be a distinct line for each race but we will pursue the argument with just two). The horizontal axis is the level of family income. The vertical axis, embodied capital, is a quantitative index of the three different types. (Or we could simply take years of education if an index cannot be constructed.)

Race, the categorical variable, is used to split the population into blacks and whites. For each race we could estimate the best linear relationship between family income, the independent quantitative variable, and embodied capital, the dependent quantitative variable. The two general parameters of a line—the slope and intercept—have important real-world interpretations. Resource privilege exists if the lines have a positive slope. White privilege exists if the line for whites lies above the line for blacks. The lines as drawn in figure 2.2 thus depict both resource privilege and white privilege.[11] I do not believe the notion of intersectionality, which conjures images of overlapping circles in a Venn diagram, captures these privileges as effectively as the algebraic and geometric approach here.

The representation of resource privilege and white privilege in figure 2.2 is implied by the model of inequality with political-economic and racist mechanisms shown in figure 2.1. If the latter model is acceptable to both sides, then so should be the linear representation in figure 2.2. A disagreement between the two camps might arise, however, as soon as some specific magnitudes get attached. Even so, the disagreement could be expressed within this model in terms of the slopes and intercepts of the two lines. The greater the vertical distance between the lines for whites and blacks the stronger white privilege. As the lines converge, that is, as the intercepts move closer together, white privilege declines. The steeper the slopes of the lines, the stronger the resource privilege.

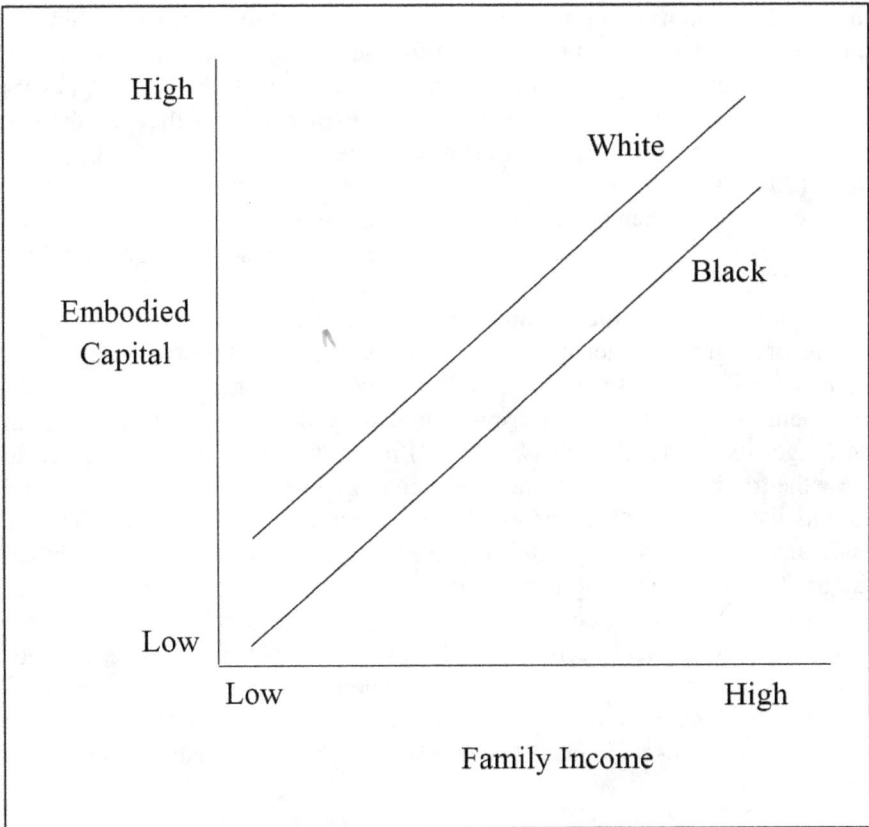

Figure 2.2.   Embodied Capital as a Function of Race and Family Income

A sometimes heated debate in this area has formed around William Julius Wilson's hypothesis of the declining significance of race (1980). His claim is that over time, as we move further away from the era of Jim Crow racism, political-economic mechanisms become more important determinants of our life chances (labor market outcome, in our discussion here) relative to racist mechanisms.

> [A]s the influence of race on minority class-stratification decreases, then, of course, class takes on greater importance in determining the life chances of minority individuals. The clear and growing class divisions among blacks today constitute a case in point. It is difficult to speak of a uniform black experience when the black population can be meaningfully stratified into groups whose members range from those who are affluent to those who are impoverished. (x)

In other words, the outcomes for black children born into money come to look more like the outcomes for white children born into money than they do like black children born into poverty. Those opposed to Wilson fault him for downplaying racism as an explanation for the economic condition of blacks, or at least certain segments of the black population. Robert Smith (1995) asserts that "Wilson dismisses racism as an explanation of the 'recent' rise of the ghetto underclass as 'indiscriminate' and 'worn-out' talk" (105). Tim Wise (2010) is even stronger is his language, asserting "the rhetoric of racial transcendence," which he links to Wilson, among others, "is dishonest, in that it obscures the power of racism and its impact on present-day communities of color" (71).

Despite the sometimes strong language, the differences are actually a matter of degree. (Academics have occasionally been known to engage in such rhetorical excesses.) While Wilson may see racism as less powerful than some of his critics, like Smith, he clearly does not claim that racism no longer exists. Indeed, Wilson (1980) notes "it would be shortsighted to view the traditional forms of racial segregation and discrimination as having essentially disappeared in contemporary America" (2). Thirty years later he maintained his position that racism persists alongside economic and political factors that are to varying degrees independent of race (Wilson 2010). For example, "racial bias or concerns about race influenced but were not the sole inspiration for political decisions, such as the fiscal policies of the New Federalism, which resulted in drastic cuts in federal aid to cities whose populations had become more brown and black" (38). For Wilson, downplaying the importance of non-racist factors would actually be a disservice to the cause.

> Many social observers who are sensitive to and often outraged by the direct forces of racism, such as discrimination and segregation, have paid far less at-

tention to those political and economic forces that *indirectly* contribute to racial inequality . . . economic changes and political decisions may have a greater adverse impact on some groups than on others simply because the former are more vulnerable as a consequence of their position in the social stratification system. These indirect structural forces are often so massive in their impact on the social position and experiences of people of color that they deserve full consideration in any attempt to understand the factors leading to differential outcomes along racial lines. (5–6, emphasis in original)

The model here provides a framework that could be used to empirically assess the hypothesis of the declining significance of race. We could track the time trend of the various parameters. If the gap is constant or expanding, then we would reject Wilson's hypothesis. We might also want to consider over time the ratio of the slope to the difference in the intercepts. But an empirical estimate of the relative effects of race and class is precisely what I want to avoid. Such an exercise would almost naturally lead to the conclusion that my critique of the Identity, Diversity, and Multiculturalism Program somehow hinges either on class being stronger than race or on the declining significance of racism. It does not. As long as (1) the slopes are positive and (2) there is *some* gap in the intercepts, then we can proceed by means of the model of inequality in figure 2.1. My critique does not require that the intercepts are converging. For the argument presented here it simply does not matter whether Wilson is correct. My critique is conceptual, theoretical, and moral—not empirical, at least not at such a fine-grained level.

REVISITING THE LEFTIST CRITIQUE
OF DIVERSITY AS JUSTICE

The model of inequality developed here should not be especially controversial, certainly not in its main features, to those on the Left or to those in the Program. The intellectual and moral challenge is to accept the conclusions that necessarily follow. Using the model, we can graphically restate part of the leftist critique of *Diversity as Justice* from the previous chapter. Let's start with a few hypothetical examples before moving to a more general representation. Consider a white child born into a family with a certain family income, I_1, shown on the horizontal axis in figure 2.3. Because the child is white we use the higher line to predict that the child will develop C_2 amount of embodied capital; this is point x on the diagram. A black child born into the same level of family income is predicted to have an amount of embodied capital of C_1 (point y). The distance between C_1 and C_2, which is a difference in the amount of embodied capital, can be taken as the amount of white privilege in this particular context. It says that, for the same level of family capital, the white child has a higher predicted level of embodied capital than the black child, presumably due to some combination of differences in access and treatment in institutions.

Finally, consider a black child born into I_2 resources. Here we predict embodied capital C_2 (point z). Note that this black child has a resource privilege over the children born into I_1 resources. We can further observe that the resource privilege of the black child at point z over the black child at point y is exactly equal to the white privilege of the white child at point x over the black child at point y. The difference in embodied capital is C_2-C_1 in both cases. Note further that black children born into families with resources above point I_2 are predicted to have embodied capital greater than C_2 and white children born into families with resources below I_1 are predicted to have less embod-

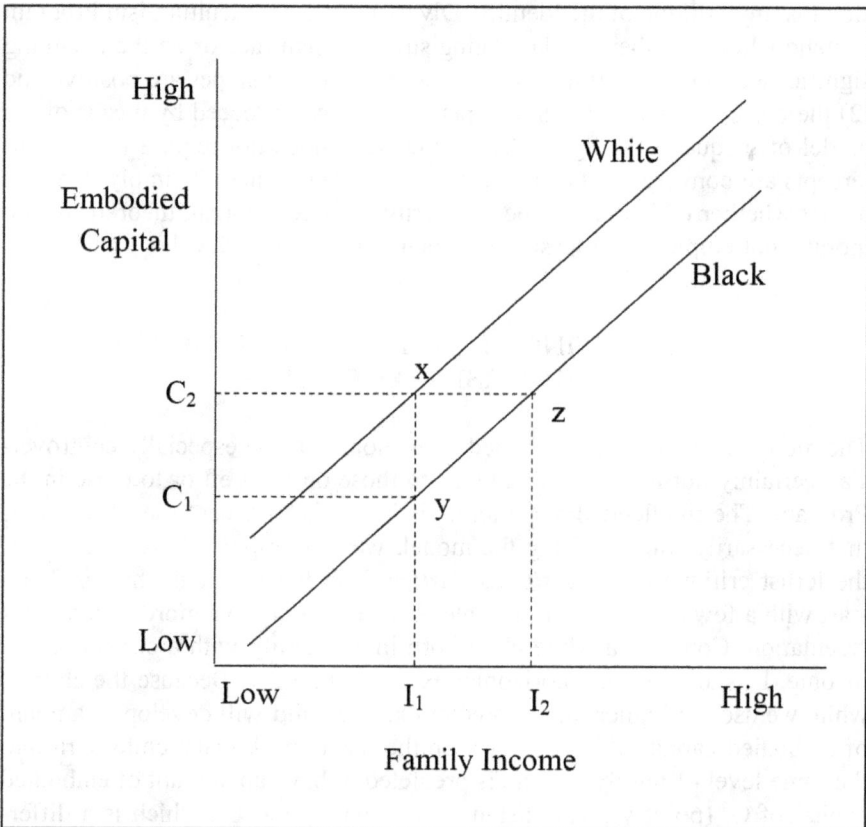

Figure 2.3.   White Privilege and Resource Privilege for Three Cases

ied capital than C_2. The difference, I_2-I_1, is thus the amount of family capital needed by blacks in order for resource privilege to compensate for white privilege. For specific cases—a poorer white child and a richer black child—we could predict which child would have the higher level of embodied capital.

Diversity as Justice demands an end to white privilege. In this context it means that a black child and a white child at the same level of family capital must have the same predicted level of embodied capital. This will occur only if the line for whites and the line for blacks converge, that is, only if they have the same intercept and the same slope. This convergence is depicted in figure 2.4: white privilege no longer exists, at least in the context of the institutional development of embodied capital. *Diversity as Justice* would be satisfied.

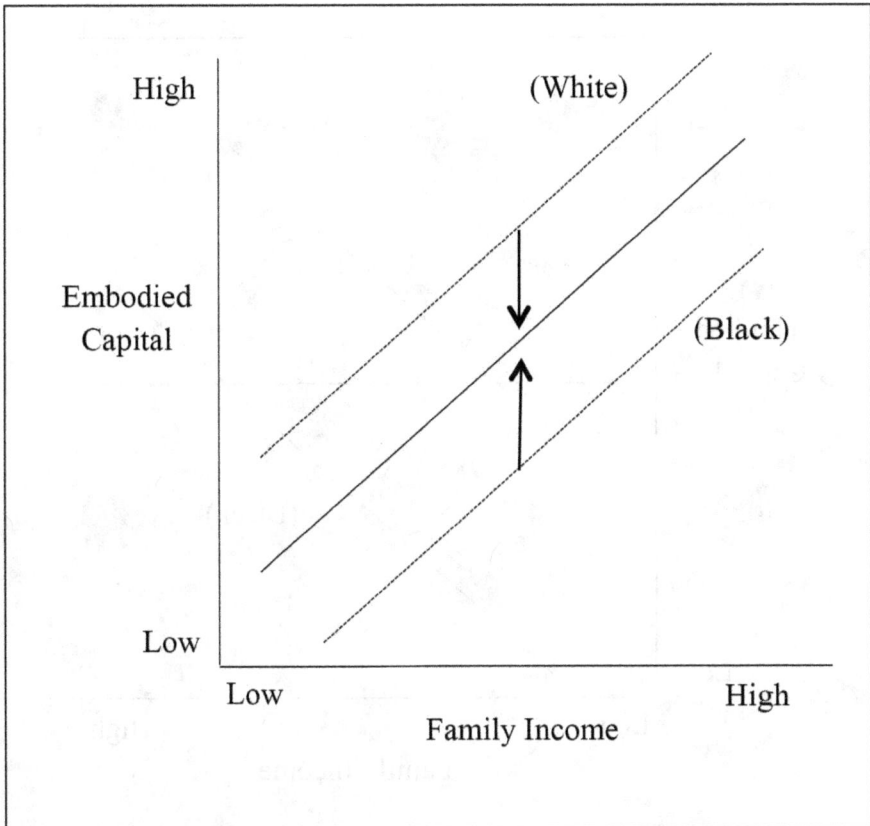

Figure 2.4. **Elimination of White Privilege in the Institutional Development of Embodied Capital**

The leftist demand for equality of opportunity goes well beyond the IDMP demand to end white privilege. The Left requires not simply that blacks and whites *at the same level of family income* be treated equally but rather that the link between family income and embodied capital be completely severed, at least if we adopt the strong, Rawlsian position of complete equality of opportunity. Resource privilege is reflected not by the intercepts of the lines but by their upward slopes. Only a relationship that does not vary according to either race or family capital is acceptable. The elimination of white privilege is depicted by convergence to a *single* (but upward-sloping) line; the elimination of resource privilege is depicted by a *flat* line. Putting these together we arrive at the horizontal line shown in figure 2.5.

The single, flat line does not mean that everybody has the same level of embodied capital but rather that family capital and race are not predictors.

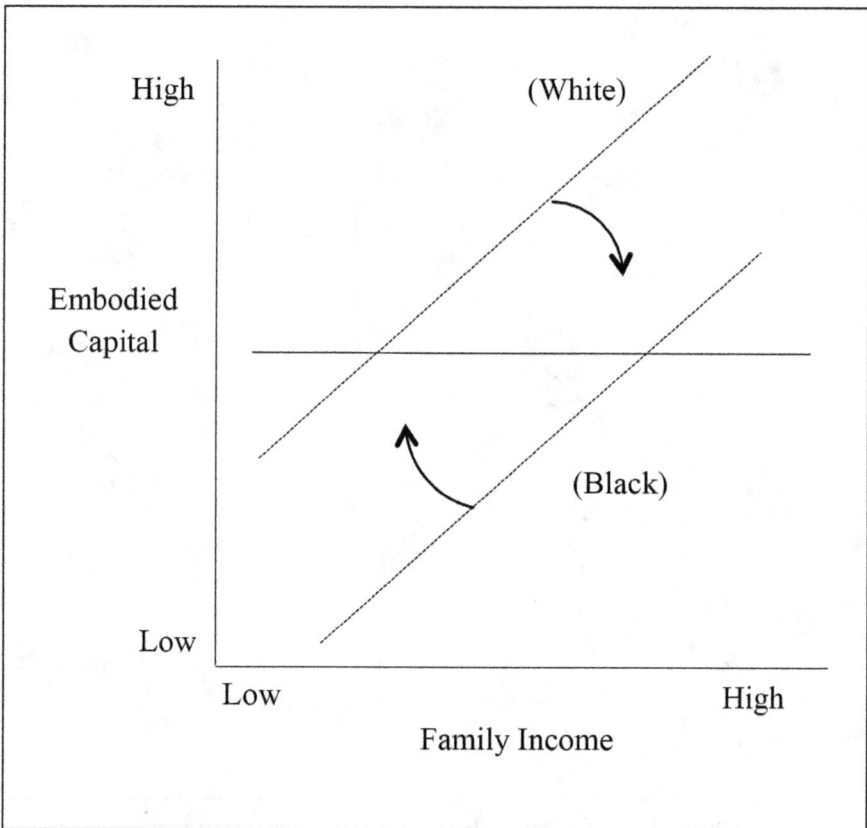

Figure 2.5.   Elimination of White Privilege and Resource Privilege

Recalling our discussion from chapter 1 we know that equality of opportunity means that individual outcomes should be determined by innate talent and effort, and nothing else. Thus a world consistent with leftist principles would look like a series of flat lines in this two-dimensional space, as shown in figure 2.6, where those with more effort and inborn talent have higher predicted embodied capital than those with lower levels. There would, of course, be more than three (flat) lines; we could make as many different groupings of effort and talent as we wished. But neither race nor family income would matter in any of them.

The contrast between figures 2.4 and 2.6 provides an alternative representation of the critique of *Diversity as Justice* from the standpoint of a leftist commitment to equality of opportunity. Just as Diversity cannot, according to the logic of its own principles, criticize a high rate of poverty for blacks but

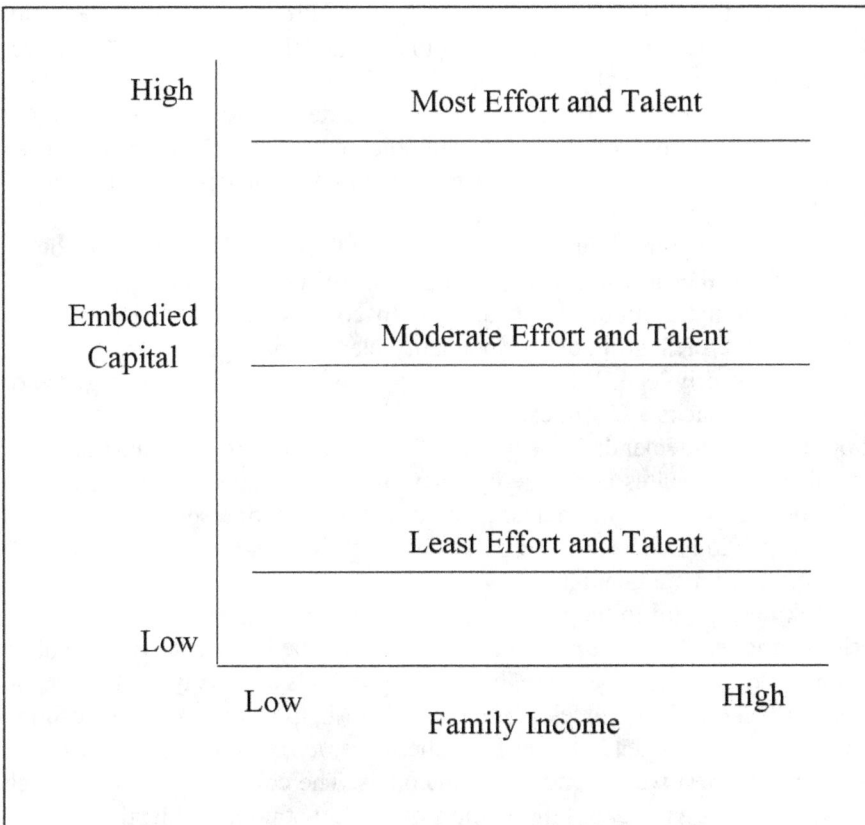

Figure 2.6. Equality of Opportunity in the Development of Embodied Capital

rather only a higher rate of poverty for blacks than whites, it is similarly unable to criticize the positive relationship (upward sloping line) between family capital and embodied capital. I have not seen a single Diversity Statement ever call for an end to resource privilege, that is, institutional discrimination on the grounds of family income. The concern is white privilege and racist discrimination. The end to white privilege implies merely that poor black children, just like their poor white playmates, will not have the same chances as rich children of any skin color.

SUMMARY AND CONCLUSION

Let us take stock of the leftist critique of the IDMP so far. In the previous chapter I critiqued *Diversity as Justice* and found it too soft on inequality to be considered leftist. The critique involved a moral principle, that is, a statement about the way the world *should be*. The presentation in this chapter suggests that the conflict is not related to any fundamental disagreement over the way the world actually *is*. The model in figure 2.1 should be acceptable to both sides. Almost all leftists and IDMP supporters believe that more family capital can be converted into more embodied capital for the offspring. They would further agree that racist discrimination makes the terms of that conversion better in general for whites than blacks.

The graphical representation in figure 2.2 of white privilege and resource privilege in the institutional development of embodied capital follows logically from the model of inequality. In contrast to the intersectionality approach, the present model of inequality clearly distinguishes between the two types of privilege. Whereas Diversity calls only for the convergence of the lines for blacks and whites, that is, an equal intercept (assuming the same slope), the Left demands full equality of opportunity. Not only must the lines for blacks and whites converge but they must also flatten. Children can receive neither privilege nor punishment for the amount of resources into which they happen to have been born. Different (flat) lines can exist on the grounds of effort and innate talent alone.

Looking forward to the next chapter, I will use the model of inequality to critique the tenet of *Colorblindness as Racism*. The key issue will be public policy, that is, the link between the way the world is and the type of world we want to make it. The model of inequality will help to reveal that colorblind policies are not, in general, racist. Furthermore, *leftist* colorblind policies are probably the best way to end racist outcomes. The color-conscious approach of the Program will again fall far short of the leftist notion of justice.

NOTES

1. In chapter 1 three meanings or types of racism were offered: racist beliefs, racist behaviors, and racist outcomes.

2. I again offer the caveat that the discussion will continue to focus on race instead of other characteristics like gender, sexual orientation, and age because the Identity, Diversity, and Multiculturalism Program talks about race more than other factors. Furthermore, the presentation will be far cleaner. This should not be taken as a denial of the significance of these other factors. The reader will see where other factors can be incorporated into the approach.

3. I therefore exclude one source of inequality: financial wealth. Leftists certainly recognize the importance of inherited wealth as a mechanism for the perpetuation of income inequality—and would tax unearned income at a far higher rate than earned income—but I focus on the labor market simply because most people earn their living by working for a paycheck. In other words, I limit the model to explaining the variation in wages, not the difference between wages and profits. A trade-off between tractability and complexity is unavoidable in all modeling.

4. The literature on the returns to human capital is quite extensive but see, for example, Michael Hout (2012), Christopher Tamborini, ChangHwan Kim, and Arthur Sakamoto (2015), ChangHwan Kim, Christopher Tamborini, and Arthur Sakamoto (2015).

5. Linguistic skills continue to be developed, of course, in the educational system but the cultural capital learned at home may put students on different tracks at an early grade. See, for example, Annette Lareau and Elliot Weininger (2003), who provide a good summary of different approaches to the concept of cultural capital and argue for a definition that is consistent with Bourdieu's.

6. Mazumder argues that the correlation in earnings between fathers and sons in the U.S. could be as high as 0.6.

7. Drawing attention to its distinctive nature, Karl Polanyi (2001) in *The Great Transformation* referred to labor as a *fictitious commodity*. Land and money fall into the same category. Our language confirms the peculiarity of these *fictitious commodities* by referring their respective prices as wages, rent, and interest.

8. According to Blanden et al. (2005) the United States has the highest intergenerational correlation in earnings. In other words, the U.S. has the lowest levels of mobility.

9. Moller et al. (2003) find that the U.S. has the worst performance among advanced capitalist democracies in reducing relative poverty through taxes and transfers. The rate is reduced by only 12.1 percent. At the other extreme is Belgium where taxes and transfers reduce poverty by 78.8 percent. The mean reduction in poverty among the 14 countries is 49.1 percent.

10. To give some sense of the idea of *comparable* we might accept that youth are more likely to offend than elderly, that men are more likely to offend than women, that poor are more likely to offend than rich, considering only "street-level" crimes, of course. Thus young, poor men might justifiably receive more scrutiny than old,

rich women. But young, poor, white men and young, poor, black men, for example, would be comparable.

11. I have made the two lines parallel thereby making the gap between whites and blacks constant along the entire distribution of family capital. This need not be the case. Modifying this simplifying assumption, however, would not alter the general conclusion. If the lines were not parallel there would be more white privilege at one end of the distribution of family capital and less white privilege at the other, assuming the line for blacks stays below the line for whites for all relevant values of family capital.

Chapter Three

A Leftist Critique of
Colorblindness as Racism

The model of inequality developed in the previous chapter will now be put to good use as we return to our main objective, namely, a leftist critique of the Identity, Diversity, and Multiculturalism Program (IDMP). In this chapter I consider and critique the tenet of *Colorblindness as Racism*: Race-neutral solutions to the problems caused by racism are harmful to blacks. The belief in *Colorblindness as Racism* will be criticized from a leftist standpoint in two ways. First, as a simple matter of logic the claim is wrong because it is a gross overgeneralization. It is true that *some* colorblind policies are harmful to blacks but the general claim that colorblind policies, *ipso facto*, are racist cannot be substantiated. Second, we can push the point further by arguing that leftist colorblind policies, which promote a high degree of equality throughout society, would in fact solve the problems of racial inequality. Indeed, it is the color-conscious policies of the Identity, Diversity, and Multiculturalism Program, not those of the Left, that are perfectly compatible with the high levels of inequality generated in a neoliberal political-economy. In reality, there are colorblind and color-conscious ways of producing racial inequality, but *leftist* colorblind policies would solve the problems of racism because they entail extensive and equal civil liberties as well as high levels of economic equality.

Before getting into the heart of the critique of the second tenet we need to have a fuller appreciation of the concept of colorblindness. As it turns out, the meaning is more complex and multifaceted than recognized in most of the discussion on the topic. Furthermore, most types of colorblindness are fully defensible from a leftist standpoint. We will also review our leftist principles, particularly in light of the model of inequality presented in chapter 2, and contrast them with the far more modest claims of the IDMP. Once equipped with the proper tools—conceptual, theoretical, and moral—we can then better understand the tenet of *Colorblindness as Racism* and recognize its fundamental flaws.

A GENERAL TYPOLOGY OF COLORBLINDNESS

The intuitive sense of colorblindness reflects the idea that race does not or should not matter. This general notion must be sharpened by identifying the appropriate contexts where race does not or should not matter. We could potentially carve the world into a great many pieces but, in practice, we can identify four contexts or spheres that often get implicated where colorblindness is concerned: political, societal, interpersonal, and biological. They go from the social structure to micro-level personal interactions and include the natural sphere of biology. As a first approximation these contexts would lead to four statements about colorblindness:

- *Political Colorblindness*: Race does not or should not matter in the law or policies.
- *Societal Colorblindness*: Race does not or should not matter in society.
- *Interpersonal Colorblindness*: Race does not or should not matter in individual interactions.
- *Biological Colorblindness*: Race does not matter in biology.

The use of both *does* and *should* indicates that these statements actually contain a second dimension, one built upon mode (or mood), that is, the attitude taken toward the statement. Grammatically, the former is the indicative mood while the latter is the subjunctive, which we can implement with the modal verb, *should*. Making this explicit, I will separate the statements that race *does* not matter from the beliefs that race *should* not matter. For the three social contexts (that is, excluding biological colorblindness) we can take colorblindness to express either a statement about the current condition of the world or about a potential, desirable state of the world. Of course, the real debate is not a matter of grammar. The underlying issue depends on whether we believe in colorblindness *in fact* or colorblindness *in principle*.

The final issue is the clarification of what it means to *matter*. This is not, however, especially difficult, at least in a broad sense. The political context is about laws and policies. The societal and interpersonal, which are distinguished by macroscopic and microscopic levels of analysis, respectively, are both concerned with reactions and behaviors. The biological context deals with a genetic taxonomy. The combination of these four contexts with the two modes leads to seven types of colorblindness, as shown in table 3.1. (Because the subjunctive mood does not apply to the biological sphere we obtain seven, instead of eight, types.)

Some explicatory notes are in order. For grammatical completeness, we can consider whether the tense or timing of colorblindness figures in the con-

Table 3.1. Seven Types of Colorblindness Derived from Four Contexts and Two Modes.

Context	Mode	
	In Fact	*In Principle*
Political Colorblindness	Laws and policies ignore race.	Laws and policies should ignore race.
Societal Colorblindness	People in society ignore race (thus racist behaviors do not occur).	People in society should ignore race.
Interpersonal Colorblindness	One ignores race in interpersonal relationships.	One should ignore race in interpersonal relationships.
Biological Colorblindness	Race is not a meaningful biological division among humans.	(Not a meaningful category)

ceptualization. While in principle it would be possible to discuss other time periods, the claims regarding racism we address in this work have bite only when applied to the present. We are concerned about colorblindness as racism in the contemporary, post-Civil Rights United States. The historical record of racism is not really a sticking point for those who may find themselves taking opposite sides regarding colorblindness today. That is, those who believe colorblindness to be racist and those who do not may agree on exactly the same set of historical facts. Regarding the future, both may take the optimistic view that someday race will not matter. The real question is whether that day has arrived. Thus, while we could perhaps talk about colorblindness in the past or in the future, those discussions hardly matter for today's debate over colorblindness as racism. Claims about colorblindness are in the present.

The three forms of colorblindness that apply *in principle* are statements about values. They follow from personal and political moral philosophies, even if not fully and rationally appreciated. As such, they are empirically non-falsifiable statements. We would defend or attack them using philosophical arguments, although empirical facts about reality will likely play a part in our reasoning, especially if we adopt utilitarian instead of deontological ethics. The forms that apply *in fact* may or may not be empirically true statements. Indeed, the veracity of those propositions may be important to the evaluation of colorblindness as racism. At the same time, however, the claims about reality are not absolute. Colorblindness in fact is actually a matter of degree.

Take, for example, political colorblindness in fact. The statement is largely, although not wholly, accurate. It is not true that the law never refers to race, but those situations represent the exception, not the rule. The legal trend is to eliminate the consideration of race in institutional settings like employment, education, and housing. Furthermore, race-based inequality is scarcely ameliorated by extant laws that explicitly include reference to race. This is not just my position; the critics of colorblindness believe that America is, for the most part, politically colorblind. Indeed, critical race theorists object precisely to that colorblindness. Law professor Gary Peller (2011) argues that the Supreme Court's decision in *Parents Involved in Community Schools v. Seattle School District* in 2007 marked "the contemporary triumph of the colorblindness principle over racial integration in American law" (90). Leslie Carr (1997), author of *"Color-Blind" Racism*, maintains that "the conservatives are essentially correct, the Constitution is color-blind" which only exposes the "racism inherent in the Constitution" (x).

Therefore, the disagreement between supporters and opponents does not involve political colorblindness in fact but rather the other mode—colorblindness in principle. That debate is the focus of this chapter and is framed by the second tenet of the Identity, Diversity, and Multiculturalism Program. Those who oppose political colorblindness are saying that the law *should* consider race as it seeks to ameliorate racist outcomes. That is, they recognize the empirical veracity of political colorblindness in fact yet morally oppose political colorblindness in principle. I, too, acknowledge the reality of political colorblindness but want to defend political colorblindness in principle. But before engaging that discussion, let's briefly consider the remaining types of colorblindness.

At the interpersonal level, different individuals will take race into account to different degrees. Those who attempt to ignore race will not be equally successful. Yet if an individual can mostly ignore race for most interactions, we will take this as interpersonal colorblindness in fact for that particular person. As an empirical matter, complete interpersonal colorblindness in fact must be nearly impossible for many people. In a culture that has created the notion of race, and where that construction has served a crucial role in the manifest system of oppression and stratification, it takes either a very unusual upbringing or a monumental act of intellectual will to completely ignore race. Still, there is no reason to deny the very possibility that some few souls are able to do this. Furthermore, there's again the matter of degree. Many people might be quite good at downplaying race to a large degree in many interactions.

Of course, there must be some people who claim to ignore race and who are not, in fact, able to do so. They are guilty either of misrepresenting their true position or of simply misunderstanding their cognitive abilities. It is not clear, however, whether this should be seen as any type of racism, even if they are lying (which we might condemn on other grounds). If they are simply wrong, then what they might be saying is that they believe they *should* ignore race in their dealings with others. The fact that they fail in their attempt seems to be far less important than their belief that they should. In other words, the important moral issue involves interpersonal colorblindness in principle. I will not spend much time on this debate here. It will come back, however, in a slightly reformulated version for the third and especially fourth tenets of the IDMP. Opposition to interpersonal colorblindness in principle follows from the belief that blacks and whites come from different cultures and that cultures *should* be respected and celebrated.

Next, consider colorblindness at the societal level. In part, this is a matter of scaling up from the interpersonal level. If we believe that all individuals should be colorblind, then we believe in societal colorblindness in principle. If enough individuals are, in fact, colorblind in their interactions, then the society is colorblind in fact. Yet some interesting consequences follow from this ostensibly quantitative move. Eduardo Bonilla-Silva (2010) argues that "color-blind racism is the ideology of the 'new racism' era" (173). He writes, "the new racial ideology is still about justifying the various social arrangements and practices that maintain white privilege" (211). Bonilla-Silva decomposes the colorblind ideology into four distinct frames: abstract liberalism, naturalization, cultural racism, and minimization of racism.

> The frame of abstract liberalism involves using ideas associated with political liberalism . . . and economic liberalism . . . in an abstract manner to explain racial matters . . . Naturalization is a frame that allows whites to explain away racial phenomena by suggesting they are natural occurrences . . . Cultural racism is a frame that relies on culturally based arguments such as "Mexicans do not put much emphasis on education" or "blacks have too many babies" to explain the standing of minorities in society . . . Minimization of racism is a frame that suggests that discrimination is no longer a central factor affecting minorities' life chances. (28–29)

The first, abstract liberalism, is the "most important, as it constitutes the foundation of the new racial ideology" (26). This frame "necessitates ignoring the fact that people of color are severely underrepresented in most good jobs, schools, and universities and, hence, it is an abstract utilization of the idea of 'equal opportunity'" (28). Furthermore, the "claim requires ignoring the multiple institutional and state-sponsored practices behind segregation and being unconcerned about these practices' negative consequences for minorities."

The key idea is that colorblindness means "ignoring the . . . practices behind segregation." According to my typology, Bonilla-Silva has an issue with societal colorblindness in fact. He argues, correctly, that as an empirical matter American society does not ignore race and that racist behaviors still occur. Furthermore—and this is the main point of his work—the pretense that societal colorblindness in fact is valid is used as an ideological justification to block redistributive policies that would favor blacks. It is this ideological function that makes (societal) colorblindness the "new racism" for Bonilla-Silva. I have no quarrel with him on this point. The typology makes clear that we are talking about different things. The tenet of *Colorblindness as Racism*—race-neutral solutions to the problems caused by racism are harmful to blacks—refers to *political colorblindness in principle* whereas Bonilla-Silva is attacking the premise and consequences of *societal colorblindness in fact*. They are distinct ideas and must be treated independently. The failure to do so, a problem I consider below, is the source of considerable confusion about colorblindness.

Finally, take biological colorblindness in fact. It turns out that biological colorblindness is a scientific fact, that is, it is supported by a consensus in genomics, the relevant research community. "Not only are the relevant genetic data absent, but the distribution of polygenic phenotypes does not suggest that race is a useful category" (Cooper, Kaufman, and Ward 2003, 1168). Given that this biological state is immutable, it is not racist to simply accept the fact as true. The squeamishness of some to this statement probably reflects a desire to maintain that race is "real" as a social construction, which is also true. Because they exist in completely different substrates, the existence of race as a social construction is in no way threatened by its meaninglessness in biology. Indeed, we might note that Paul Gilroy's (2001) starting point for his "nonracial humanism" in *Against Race* is the acceptance of this biological fact. He observes that the "proponents of the idea of 'race' are further from ever from being able to answer the basic question that has confounded them since the dawn of raciology: if 'race' is a useful way of classifying people, then how many 'races' are there? It is rare nowadays to encounter talk of a 'Mongoloid race'" (37). The dismantling of racism will be aided by embracing the biological truth. To the squeamish we simply need say something like, "Some people believe that race is real, as in objectively real. They are wrong, but the false belief in race has, of course, motivated people to act. And those actions have had real and disastrous consequences."

TWO VIEWS OF JUSTICE

A critique of the tenet of *Colorblindness as Racism*, which from the discussion above we could now call (were it not too wordy) the tenet of *Political Colorblindness in Principle as Racism*, necessarily involves a discussion of policy, that is, the means by which we can collectively transform the world as it currently is into something closer to what we would like it to be. A complete understanding of policy thus requires an understanding of both the "is" and the "ought." We must know which variables cause inequality and the ways in which we can manipulate them via public regulation. The model of inequality presented in the previous chapter will aid us in that regard. I argued that leftists as well as defenders of Diversity should accept, more or less, a model of inequality with political-economic and racist mechanisms like that presented in figure 2.1 in chapter 2.

If the two sides can indeed agree, and thus share a similar outlook on the way the world actually operates, then any disagreements in policy should largely reflect disagreements in the outcomes favored by the Left and by the IDMP. Of course, many people have not been introduced to an explicit model of inequality. Leading concepts in the discourse, like *intersectionality* and *lived experiences*, do little to explain either the way the world actually works or what a just world would look like. Yet for those who accept an explanation similar to that modelled in figure 2.1 and who still support the tenet of *Colorblindness as Racism*, it seems that their values must differ from those of the Left, at least as I conceptualized the term in chapter 1.

The main moral objective contained in the tenet of *Diversity as Justice* is the elimination of discrimination and white privilege.[1] The model in figure 2.1 depicts racism in several sites. It identifies employment discrimination in the labor market and discrimination in four other important social institutions: education, housing, healthcare, and the criminal justice system (CJS). The comment in the box for the four institutions notes both racist access and racist treatment. Racist access controls for the level of resources; whites have more or better access than blacks who come from the same level of household capital. Racist treatment controls for institutional placement; blacks receive worse treatment and therefore develop lower levels of embodied capital when placed in the same site as whites. Racist discrimination in the labor market means that, controlling for embodied capital of their applicants (and other relevant variables), employers tend to hire whites over blacks. The final type of racism in the model is racist public policies, which have the potential to reach every other variable.

The ideal world reflected in *Diversity as Justice* is one in which the racist components have been eliminated. Thus the just world according to Identity, Diversity, and Multiculturalism can be depicted as in figure 3.1. At the four institutions, an end to white privilege would mean that individuals with the same resources have the same access to institutions and that blacks and whites are treated identically when occupying identical institutional sites. In the labor market, employers would make no distinction on the grounds of race among workers with equal amounts of embodied capital. Finally, the racist intent behind state policies would disappear.

In other words, the end to white privilege means that blacks and whites would be treated equally, *ceteris paribus*, by institutions, the labor market,

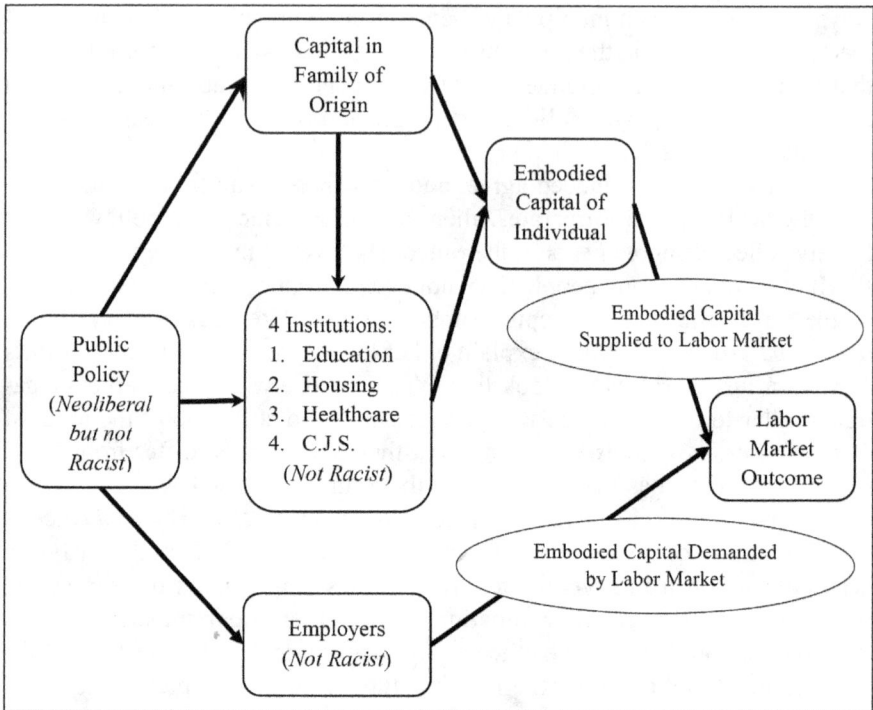

Figure 3.1. Just Determinants of Labor Market Outcome for the IDMP

and the state. The changes called for by the Diversity approach might represent an improvement for blacks compared to the current level of inequality. It is possible, on the other hand, especially during this neoliberal regime, that greater equality between blacks and whites could be obtained by declining incomes for many whites and not by rising incomes for blacks, leading to an overall increase in economic inequality. Regardless, Diversity policies would not lead to a just outcome according to leftist principles. The leftist conception of equal opportunity demands not simply that blacks and whites *with the same economic resources* be treated identically—this is the problem with the *ceteris paribus* clause in the statements of the Program—but rather that resources be distributed in order to make economic mobility a function of only two factors: effort and innate talent. (Moreover, the Difference Principle calls for even greater redistribution: inequality of outcome must be to the greatest advantage of the least advantaged group.)

Realizing a leftist notion of justice would require substantial, indeed truly radical, changes in the way the world actually works. The general model of inequality consistent with this leftist vision is shown in figure 3.2, which should be compared with the IDMP approach of figure 3.1. In the leftist version, the links between family capital and the four institutions, on the one hand, and between family capital and individual embodied capital, on the other, have been completely severed (presented as dotted lines) in order to show that equal opportunity has been achieved. Furthermore, public policies are now designated as *Leftist*. This means that both in intent and effect they realize our goals of equal opportunity and a high level of equality of outcome (more on this below). Recall that a leftist approach does not object to all inequality of outcome; the objective is not (necessarily) an egalitarian distribution. We can permit variation in labor market outcomes if it is due to differences in individual effort and innate talent, operating either directly or indirectly through the mediating factors of institutions and embodied capital. No other determinants of inequality would be morally acceptable. It should be clear that this moral demand goes well beyond anything contained in the principles of the Identity, Diversity, and Multiculturalism Program, which sidesteps the stronger claims for equal opportunity and equality of outcome with fuzzy and toothless talk about "equity."

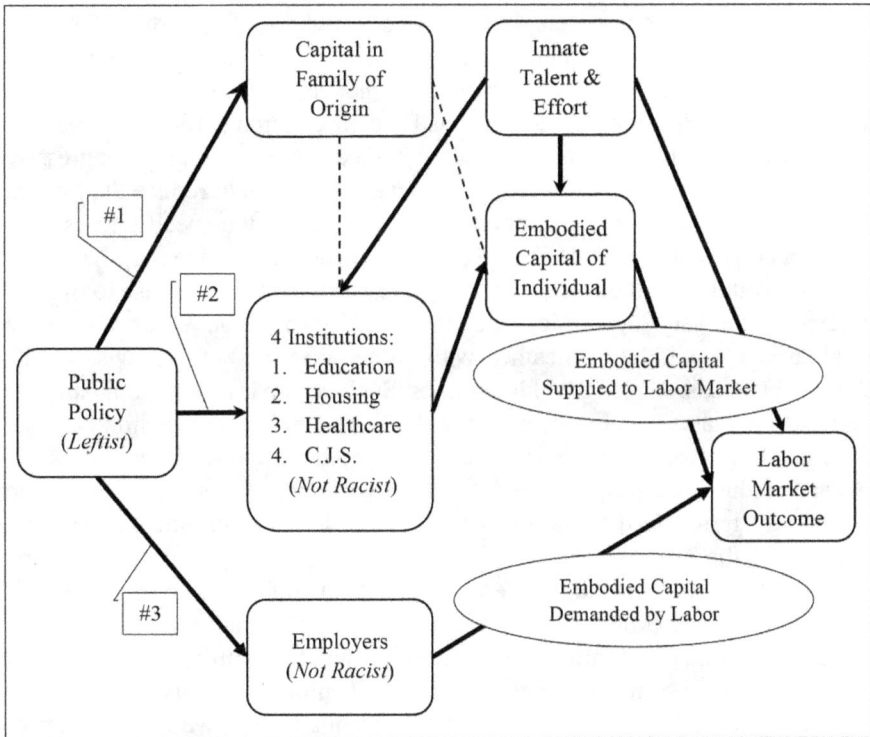

Figure 3.2. Just Determinants of Labor Market Outcome for the Left

LEFTIST COLORBLIND POLICIES

Leftist policies are the means by which we could transform the world as it is into a world that matches our leftist principles of justice. Viewed schematically, the policies would change the determinants in the model of inequality in figure 2.1 (chapter 2) into those of figure 3.2. Public policies rely upon government expenditures and the coercive powers of the state to effect changes in the economy. Ultimately the state moves resources around and establishes constraints for voluntary action. In order to achieve a just society, the state must use, as shown by the numbered lines in figure 3.2, its various powers to regulate three other sites: (1) *Capital in Family of Origin* (financial capital, for the most part, in this instance), (2) the *4 Institutions*, and (3) *Employers*. These three categories guide our subsequent discussion.

(1) Family Capital

The top arrow in the left of the diagram connecting (leftist) public policy with family capital depicts, above all, redistribution—taxation and public spending—up to the point at which we realize both equality of opportunity and the Difference Principle (or something nearby). The spread in income must be reduced to such an extent that parents on the higher end of the income distribution cannot purchase institutional advantages for their children sufficient to reestablish a link between family capital and embodied capital. A highly progressive income tax and an even more progressive wealth tax would reduce the ratio of the resources of the richest to poorest families. While the specific rates need not (and could not) be established except in practice, I imagine that the rate of taxation would be null on the lowest levels of income but would rise to over 90 percent on the very highest levels of income. *A fortiori* for wealth. Perhaps a small amount could be bequeathed with limited taxation but otherwise wealth should not be passed along within families. Such wealth is morally unjustifiable because it violates equality of opportunity: there is no necessary link between the talent and effort of the recipient and the amount of money inherited.

Part of the revenue generated by means of progressive taxation would be directly transferred to families with lower income, producing far more equality in the post-tax than the pre-tax distribution of income in society. Transfer payments can take several forms. A guaranteed minimum income for all citizens, also known as a basic income, could be maintained (Parijs and Vanderborght 2017). Similar to but stronger than the family allowances that currently exist in some European countries, the more generous and universal payments would largely obviate the stingy, means-tested "welfare" programs in the United States. The exact degree of redistribution would be monitored and adjusted so as to maintain the fulfillment of the leftist objectives of equal opportunity and something like the Difference Principle. Regardless of the specific rates and payments, the key point for the critique of *Colorblindness as Racism* is that the race of both the taxpayers and the transfer recipients would be irrelevant: these are *leftist* and *colorblind* policies.

(2) Four Institutions

A second purpose for the revenue generated through progressive taxation would be proper support for public institutions. In a just society the state would create, fund, and regulate institutions in order to achieve equality of opportunity (among other motivations like protecting individual liberties). These moves by the state—redistribution and institutional support—would be pursued up to the point where family capital no longer influenced the embodied capital of the children. The links from *Family Capital* to both *Institutional Participation* and *Embodied Capital* found in figure 3.1 have been eliminated in figure 3.2, leaving only talent and effort as the ultimate determinants. It is important to recognize how the two tools of redistribution and institutional support work together to eliminate the need for race-conscious policies within institutions.

For example, with the proper support public education could live up to its ideal as the great equalizer and would undermine any rationale for race-based affirmative action. First, redistribution of income (arrow #1 in figure 3.2) among families eliminates most of the distinctions now present between "good" and "bad" neighborhoods. It is difficult to empirically disentangle the separate effects of neighborhood, family capital, and schooling but James Ainsworth (2002) in *Why Does it Take a Village* argues that the effect of the neighborhood on educational outcomes is on par with those of the family and the school itself. Second, schools in the poorer neighborhoods would receive more public support (arrow #2) than those in richer neighborhoods in order to nullify whatever economic advantage still remains after redistribution.

Another important leftist policy is free, universal healthcare, a policy supported by most in the IDMP as well. Yet *universality* is, by definition, *colorblind*. Progressive taxation would fund healthcare for everybody. Healthcare becomes a right of citizenship (or maybe even a human right) and citizenship is independent of race. Of course, even in a just world there will still be the personal tragedies of disease and illness but such misfortunes will not fall disproportionately on the poor and uninsured. Housing, our third leading institution, would largely remain privately administered by means of the market. This does not directly threaten leftist principles, however, because the redistribution of family income (arrow #1) will necessarily produce more equality within and across neighborhoods. When the range of variation in income is limited in accordance with equality of opportunity and the Difference Principle, the range in housing prices must be correspondingly moderated. It would no longer be possible for some families to own multiple mansions just as it will become unnecessary for other families to rely upon subsidized rentals. Indeed, support for public housing can diminish in step with reductions in income disparities in the private market.

Our fourth institution of interest, the criminal justice system, is today colorblind in law but not in practice. The solution is not, however, to make the system color-conscious as the logic of the IDMP might suggest but rather to bring the behavior of police and courts into accordance with our current colorblind principles. Here again we see how all of the leftist policies work together to promote a just outcome. The reduction in income inequality across families and entire neighborhoods (arrow #1) changes both criminogenic factors as well as the response of the criminal justice system. Poverty and inequality are causes of certain types of crime and the reduction in the former will lead to a reduction in the latter.[2] Furthermore the current inequality across neighborhoods generates a targeted approach to policing. Police spend more of their time in neighborhoods with higher rates of poor and black people, where as a result they are disproportionately stopped and arrested. By eliminating poverty and shrinking the variability in average income levels across neighborhoods, the targeting by police of poor, racial minorities becomes impossible to maintain. When ghettos and slums do not exist the police will not patrol them. Unlike the institutions of education and healthcare, the criminal justice system would be dramatically reduced in scale and scope by leftist policies, from the number of police to the number of prisoners. Today our bloated *criminal* justice system speaks largely to the lack of actual *social* and *economic* justice.

The public regulation of institutions is to be guided by the objective of ensuring that the variation in embodied capital is due to the variation in inborn talents and the effort in developing them and, perhaps to a lesser degree, by the Difference Principle. As a complement to direct redistribution of income, the regulation of social institutions ensures that the state lives up to its commitment to equality of opportunity. Only then would the inequality in labor market outcomes be morally justifiable. This set of *leftist colorblind* policies would produce equality of opportunity and make it impossible for white privilege to persist. Furthermore, under a leftist system, *color-conscious* policies would have no place; they could only distort a just outcome.

(3) Employers

In contrast to the mainstream (neoclassical) model of economics,[3] which asserts that the pricing mechanism should produce full employment and thereby offers very little useful advice when we actually encounter unemployment in the real world, the Keynesian approach emphasizes the role of aggregate demand—the combined spending on commodities by consumers, businesses, and the government—on the level of economic activity.[4] The Keynesian approach predicts that the *laissez-faire* economy will tend to have a level of aggregate demand insufficient to produce full employment. Fortunately, there is a solution: the state can inject more demand into the economy via deficit spending. The added dollars recirculate in the private sector, a phenomenon known as the multiplier effect. In addition to deficit spending, known as fiscal policy, the state can use monetary policy as well. To expand the economy, the Federal Reserve Bank will lower the interest rate to encourage borrowing, and hence spending and demand.

Arrow #3 in figure 3.2 should be interpreted as depicting the Keynesian position that the unemployment rate largely depends on public policy; a state that wants to reduce unemployment has the power to do so. Such public spending helped to move the economy out of the Great Depression and has been used in every subsequent economic downturn. It was one of the great failures of the Obama Administration that it used these tools too cautiously, thus prolonging the human suffering of the financial crisis and Great Recession of 2008. In this regard Obama is no different from most of his neoliberal predecessors. While Keynesian tools have been used, they have been underutilized, as evidenced by the nearly permanent presence of unemployment, even though this violates the Full Employment Act of 1978.

In fact, the government has often used contractionary Keynesian policies. To weaken the economy, the government could reduce its deficit but, because this can be politically challenging, more commonly we see an increase in the interest rate by the Fed, an institution run by bankers and all but immune to democratic regulation. Either way, we might wonder why the state wants to generate unemployment. The neoliberal state, certainly the Federal Reserve, has the power and incentive to act on behalf of the capitalist class to weaken the bargaining position of workers in order to keep wages down. Although such concerns about the strength of the working class were temporarily dampened in the aftermath of the economic crisis of 2008 in more "normal" times the Federal Reserve typically steps in early to prevent the economy from "overheating," a favored term for low unemployment. While the problem will be identified as "potential inflationary pressures" in reality the threat will take the form of a working class with sufficient power to cut into profits. The bankers who operate the Fed will not tolerate such market "instability" and will wield the monetary power given to them by the state to promote their interests.

A leftist state, on the other hand, would use those same tools to maintain full employment. The economy is not a car and euphemisms like "overheating" are to be rejected as neoliberal propaganda. The real fear is not that we'll need to let the car cool down on the side of the road but rather that workers will earn a high wage—and this is exactly what leftists support. From a leftist perspective full employment has two positive features. First, it benefits workers at the margins, that is, those who are the last hired and the first fired. When aggregate demand is strong, businesses are able to sell the goods they put on the shelf and their biggest concern becomes letting production fall behind sales. Thus even workers with the lowest levels of embodied capital will be hired. Production requires the combination of physical capital and labor—employers cannot be overly choosy when sales are on the line. Perhaps they will need to spend more to train such marginal workers, that is, develop their embodied capital inside the firm. Again, leftists would find this perfectly acceptable. The second advantage to full employment accrues to all workers. With low unemployment workers become more difficult to replace and thus more capable of demanding wage increases. The ultimate objective is wage growth in line with overall productivity.

In sum, full unemployment means both more jobs and higher wages. Labor market regulations complement the other two leftist policies. The greater the level of equality achieved within the labor market itself (arrow #3), the lighter the task for redistribution and the other forms of public regulation (arrows #1 and #2). If the pre-tax distribution of income is already close to producing equal opportunity and the Difference Principle, then taxation and transfer spending can be minimized. I conclude by stating what should be obvious: full employment means full employment for all workers, regardless of race. Full employment for white workers alongside unemployment for blacks is not full employment. As with other leftist policies, the use of expansionary Keynesian fiscal and monetary tools in accordance with the leftist objective of equality is colorblind.

REJECTING COLORBLINDNESS AS RACISM

The previous discussion permits us to quickly dismiss the tenet of *Colorblindness as Racism*. It is easy to show that racism (whether beliefs, actions, or outcomes) does not necessarily follow from the premise of colorblindness. If it were true that colorblind policies in general were racist, then the leftist colorblind policies described above that regulate (1) family capital, (2) social institutions, and (3) the labor market would have to be harmful to blacks, that is, produce racist behaviors and racist outcomes.[5] It should be obvious that the set of leftist colorblind policies offered above would quickly eliminate—not exacerbate or even perpetuate—racist subordination. The level of redistribution necessary to achieve equal opportunity and the Difference Principle would move resources into many black households and would lift them out of poverty. The rate of poverty among blacks would fall from over 20 percent to nearly nothing. A truly awesome reduction in racist subordination. Healthcare would be free and universal. Public education would not only receive more funding but it would educate children who come from families freed from the handicap of material deprivation. Labor market demand would be stimulated through Keynesian policies until full employment was reached, thereby reducing black unemployment from double-digits to perhaps 2 percent.[6] The fact that poor whites would see similar improvements in their quality of life in no way means that colorblind policies would fail to end racist subordination.

Let us contrast the leftist colorblind policies with the color-conscious tackling of white privilege. Race-conscious remedies include giving black candidates more points on applications and establishing racial quotas. These policies would be implemented throughout society, in particular in education and the labor market. The reader should look closely again at the representation of a just world according to the Identity, Diversity, and Multiculturalism Program in figure 3.1. Upon inspection we see that it looks disturbingly similar to figure 2.1 in chapter 2: the political-economic model of inequality. In a world without racism and white privilege nothing prevents a neoliberal capitalist economy from sorting people out, and this system is consistent with almost any level of inequality. It is possible that color-conscious policies might help poor black children to be treated the same as poor white children but, given the lack of resource privilege that comes with being poor and white, that is not good enough for the Left. A great many poor black children will be poor black adults. Not because they are black, but because of endemic poverty and a lack of embodied capital.

It turns out that the notion that race-based problems require race-based solutions is simply specious. It has a sheen of plausibility as long as one does not probe beneath the surface to see what it truly implies. Upon deeper reflection the fallaciousness should not surprise us because it is not a logical truth that problems of type X require solutions of type X. The problems of crime and educational achievement might be best solved by economic remedies. Eating problems might be solved by better sleeping habits. Sleeping problems might be solved by exercise. Behavioral problems might be solved by drug treatments. Drug problems might be solved by yoga or mediation. The list of counterexamples could be quite long. Problems of type X might be solved by solutions of type X, Y, or Z.

The intellectual flimsiness of the claim for *Colorblindness as Racism* coupled with the intelligence of its proponents suggests that they may actually have something else in mind. I explore two other possibilities. First, IDMP supporters may have an alternative meaning for their claim that colorblindness is racist. Second, they may be referring to the messy world of political calculations and not to the ideal world of moral principles. I consider these possibilities in turn.

MISCONSTRUING AND MISREPRESENTING COLORBLINDNESS

While it is incorrect to claim that the problems caused by racism cannot be solved by a race-neutral approach—indeed the leftist, colorblind policies just described would doubtless be the best solution—there are other ways of linking the concepts of colorblindness and racism, and some of these might be valid assertions. The alternatives have no direct bearing on the validity of my leftist critique of *(Political) Colorblindness (in Principle) as Racism*—that is, the claim that race-neutral solutions to the problems caused by racism are harmful to blacks—but they may help to explain how this belief has become so widespread despite its rather weak intellectual foundation.

Alternative #1: Racists' preference for colorblind policies

If racists today face a choice between colorblind policies and policies that would give special aid to blacks, then it's clear they would prefer the former. Contemporary racists no longer have explicit discrimination against blacks as a legal option. It is easy to understand how alternative #1 might be confused among supporters of Diversity with our tenet of *Colorblindness as Racism*. At its most stripped-down, the tenet for *Colorblindness as Racism* looks like this:

If colorblind, then racist.

Alternative #1 is the converse of this:

If racist, then colorblind.

I suspect that many people in the Program began with Alternative #1 and then fell for the alluring fallacy of *affirming the consequent* in order to arrive at the notion of *Colorblindness as Racism* more generally. A brief review of logic will persuade them that *p implies q* does not mean that *q implies p*, as tempting as it might seem at first. While it is probably true that many racists prefer colorblind policies, we cannot infer that those who prefer colorblind policies are racist. Thus the validity of Alternative #1, which is simply the reality of racism given the legal foundation of the post Jim Crow era, does nothing to alter to the invalidity of the original tenet of *Colorblindness as Racism*.

Alternative #2: Neoliberal or conservative colorblind policies as racist

This claim differs from the previous in that it focuses on the outcomes of the policies not on the beliefs of the advocates. As we have already discussed, a regime with neoliberal policies allows a weakly regulated market to determine economic outcomes. Families are thus largely unrestricted in their ability to transform their resources into embodied capital of their offspring and as a result a neoliberal system will tend to perpetuate inequality. Thus the subordination of blacks—a racist outcome we have inherited—could continue for a very long time via market mechanisms. Conservative policies are similar to neoliberal ones in that they privilege the status quo but rely even more on punishments and criminal enforcement.

It should be clear that alternative #2 is irrelevant for our critique of *Colorblindness as Racism* because our position is leftist, not neoliberal. To designate all colorblind policies as racist is tantamount to claiming all policy is neoliberal, obviously a false statement. The substantial differences between a robust social democracy (or democratic socialism) and neoliberalism are rhetorically blurred when overly broad assaults on colorblind polices are made. It is not reasonable and perhaps even intellectually dishonest to lump together welfare "reform" with universal healthcare or, for that matter, Charles Murray with William Julius Wilson.

Alternative #3: All colorblindness as societal colorblindness in fact

Our conceptualization of colorblindness provides seven distinct types. Only one of them—societal colorblindness in fact—can be taken as racist, specifically as a racist ideology according to the argument made by Bonilla-Silva and others. None of the remaining six types of colorblindness—including political colorblindness in principle, as just argued above—can easily be construed as racist. Because most forms are not racist, the third strategy of attacking colorblindness is through portrayals, perhaps unwitting, of all colorblindness as societal in fact, the one type that no leftist would defend. Supporters of any type of colorblindness are called out as racists as if they supported societal colorblindness in fact. The root of the problem is the failure to acknowledge and identify the many forms of colorblindness. Once we properly appreciate the multifaceted nature of the concept, we recognize that their meanings and implications vary greatly and cannot be adjudged as a single thing. Let us consider some examples of this hasty generalization, what I refer to as a rhetorical sleight of hand.

Tim Wise (2010), author of *Colorblind: The Rise of Post-Racial Politics and the Retreat from Racial Equality*, asserts

[C]olorblindness, by discouraging discussions of racial matters and presuming
that the best practice is to ignore the realities of racism, makes it more difficult
to challenge those biases, and thus increases the likelihood of discrimination . . .
Encouraging individuals and institutions to downplay the role of race and racism
in the lives of the public will only impede the ability to respond to the needs of
that public . . . In the final analysis, the problem with colorblindness and post-
racial liberalism is that they ignore the different ways in which we experience
the society around us. (18–19)

Wise quotes with approval Julian Bond, a civil rights activist, Georgia state
senator, chairman of the NAACP, and president of the Southern Poverty Law
Center, who averred that "whether race is a burden or a benefit is all the same
to the race-neutral theorists; that is what they mean when they speak of being
colorblind. They are blind, all right—blind to the consequences of being the
wrong color in America today" (63).

These harsh characterizations would be appropriate only if the type of colorblindness is societal in fact. The error committed by the critics like Wise and
Bond is not the identification of societal colorblindness in fact as racist but
rather the insinuation that all colorblindness is of this type. It may be true that
some, even many, who consider themselves colorblind do indeed "ignore the
realities of racism," including all those who accept as valid societal colorblindness in fact. Yet we have no reason to believe that those who reject this variety
but accept other types of colorblindness are racists. The belief in societal or
interpersonal colorblindness *in principle*, for example, is perfectly compatible
with support for equal opportunity, and both may lead to a strong concern with
racist discrimination. Notice as well the rhetorical sleight of hand in the phrase
"downplay the role of race and racism." Race and racism are not—to state the
obvious—the same thing. Downplaying the former is asserting interpersonal
colorblindness in principle or biological colorblindness, perfectly reasonable
positions for leftists; downplaying the latter is societal colorblindness in fact,
which is factually wrong (for everybody) and not endorsed by the Left.

Leslie Carr, in a very different context, attempts to characterize all colorblindness as societal colorblindness in fact. In *"Color-Blind" Racism,* Carr
(1997) discusses the nineteenth-century conflict between English and Irish
workers based on nationalism, and a debate among Marxists as to the appropriate response to this division. According to Carr, one such English Marxist,
a Mr. Hales, "proposed that it be done in an Irish-blind manner, so to speak"
(55). Carr's interpretation of Hales's position is a good example of the rhetorical sleight of hand employed against colorblindness:

Mr. Hales . . . referred to "barriers that separated man from man." This is an
example of the "left-wing," "progressive" supremacist cloaking his nationalism

in a lofty, moralistic universalism. There are no English or Irish, only "men" said Hales. Thus, anything that even recognized the oppression that existed was itself a perpetuation of oppression. This is classic ideological inversion. It is precisely the same line of argument used today by the "color-blind" against affirmative action in the Unites States. The say that there is only one race, the human race—there are no White or African American people, just people. This is typically said with a glowing, religious-like expression of transcendent morality. This ideal universalism rises above the real world as a solution to real-world problems, while in that real world, people's eyes tell them that races exist and real problems exist between those races. (56)

Carr criticizes Hales for failing to recognize "the oppression that existed" and ignoring that "real problems exist between those races." If this is true, Hales expressed *societal colorblindness in fact* and for this he would deserve our criticism. But what else is Hales claiming according to Carr's interpretation? Hales (or a like-minded contemporary, which is the real message of the historical anecdote) upholds a universal morality, in other words, a belief in societal colorblindness *in principle*. He believes in one race, the human race, that is, a belief in *biological colorblindness*. While societal colorblindness in fact is indefensible, both in Hales's time and our own, the other two types of colorblindness are reasonable and morally defensible. Carr's sleight of hand obfuscates the reasonableness by characterizing it in disparaging language: Hales is a supremacist using a lofty, moralistic universalism, manifesting a glowing, religious-like expression of transcendent morality, rising above real-world problems.

In *Unpacking the Race Talk*, Pierre Orelus (2013) offers another example of the rhetorical sleight of hand:

[M]any individual Whites . . . and, ironically, some People of Color with a colonized mind, often say, "color does not matter to me" or "I believe there is only a human race." . . . If race does not matter, why is it then that Black, Brown, and biracial people have been denied housing, access to quality education, and economic opportunities; have been targeted at stores; and have been called names? . . . Moreover, if race does not matter, why is it, then, that people in powerful political and professional positions have been mostly Whites, particularly rich White males? (583)

After relaying instances of interpersonal colorblindness—"race does not matter to me"—and of biological colorblindness—"I believe there is only a human race"—Orelus proceeds to attack societal colorblindness in fact. This is unwarranted. Those who believe in the first two may reject the third. They would have no difficulty in pointing to racist discrimination as an explanation for inequalities in housing, education, and the economy. Furthermore, the first two types of colorblindness are reasonable and defensible.

For Williams and Land (2006) "[n]on-recognition of race reinforces and reproduces the flawed structure of society because it does not allow for the analysis of social inequality at the core of the problem" (580). As a general claim this is false. Most forms of colorblindness do allow for the analysis of social inequality. One may believe in biological colorblindness and practice interpersonal colorblindness, the two types of colorblindness suggested by the phrase, "non-recognition of race," yet comprehend that inequality due to race exists and support policies to redress it.

There are many others but let us return to Bonilla-Silva for some final examples of the rhetorical sleight of hand that associates colorblindness in general with societal colorblindness in fact. As an "archetype" of abstract liberalism, the most important of the four ideological frames for colorblindness, Bonilla-Silva (2010) offers the following quote from Sue, a university student:

> I don't think they [minority students] *should* be provided with unique opportunities. I think that they *should* have the opportunities as everyone else. You know, it's up to them to meet the standards and whatever that's required for entrance into universities or whatever. I don't think that just because they're a minority that they *should*, you know, not meet the requirements, you know. (31, emphasis added)

Bonilla-Silva offers an interpretation: "Sue, like most whites, ignored the effects of past and contemporary discrimination on the social, economic, and educational status of minorities." Here Bonilla-Silva conflates two distinct types of colorblindness. Sue expresses support for political colorblindness in principle: Simply look at the repeated use of the work "should." Minority students *should* not "be provided with unique opportunities"; they *should* "have the opportunities as everyone else." Bonilla-Silva accuses her of societal colorblindness in fact. Bonilla-Silva is claiming, in effect, that those who oppose race-based programs must necessarily deny racist actions and outcomes. It might be true for some, but it does not logically follow.

Bonilla-Silva offers Diane as another example of abstract liberalism. Diane explained her opposition to affirmative action:

> That's so hard. I still believe in merit, you know, I still believe in equality, you know. If you did have two people with the same qualifications, one's minority and one's not, you know, I'd want to interview them and just maybe a personality stands out that works with the job, I don't know. Just find something other than race to base it on, you know? Let that not be a factor if they qualify. (32)

Bonilla-Silva questions this: "How could Diane maintain these views and remain 'reasonable'?" And answers: "Diane could say these things and seem reasonable because she believes discrimination is not the reason why blacks are worse off than whites" (33). Diane, of course, never said that discrimination is not a problem for blacks. We have no reason to think she believes it. She is accused of believing in societal colorblindness in fact when she might instead favor political colorblindness in principle. Whereas the former is racist, the latter need not be.

I do not know Sue or Diane. It is possible that they believe in societal colorblindness in fact. It is possible they are racists, they may dislike blacks, or discriminate against them. Or that they wish to keep blacks subordinated and perpetuate racist outcomes. In any case, let us step back and examine the broader frame that they presumably represent. Abstract liberalism "involves using ideas associated with political liberalism" like "equal opportunity" (28). Since abstract liberalism is racist, the implied conclusion via a loose form of transitivity is that liberal ideals like equal opportunity are somehow tinged with racism as well. This is completely unfounded and indeed even contradictory. It is from a commitment to equal opportunity that we can derive an opposition to racist discrimination, along with an opposition to discrimination based on gender, sexual orientation, religion, and so on. Support for equal opportunity is the primitive moral principle behind our opposition to all of these forms of discrimination. The intimation that equal opportunity is somehow the problem should be rejected. All of this is quite clear if we keep in mind the distinction between societal colorblindness in fact and political colorblindness in principle. Support for equal opportunity is consistent with political colorblindness in principle. We reject societal colorblindness in fact because we know that we do not have equal opportunity.

It is an effective rhetorical move to portray all colorblindness as societal colorblindness in fact because only this one type is wholly indefensible. I do not doubt that some, perhaps many, of those accused by the critics are in fact guilty of this type of racism. I object to the language that implies universality of this type. This rhetorical sleight of hand leads, of course, to a fallacious conclusion via a hasty generalization. In none of the examples provided above do we find mention that other types of colorblindness might be debatable, or even exist. We find no qualifiers to suggest that in certain cases colorblindness might not be racist or that some portion of those who are colorblind may not be racist. The seven-part conceptualization of colorblindness reveals clearly that many of the allegations of racism are due to misattribution. In reality, nobody on the Left believes societal colorblindness in fact is valid for contemporary America. Certainly the approach presented here (see the model in chapter 2) explicitly includes racist discrimination and racist policies and thereby explicitly rejects the notion of societal colorblindness in fact. While many leftists recognize that race is socially constructed, that is, they accept biological colorblindness, no leftist believes that race is irrelevant in contemporary American society. Leftists recognize that most people in society act as if race were real, and that a great many race-based actions are harmful.

The plausible alternative #3 could be stated as *Societal Colorblindness in Fact as Racism*. Bonilla-Silva is correct to give attention to the concept of ideology, that is, a set of beliefs that benefits the interests of some group, in this case, those of whites by maintaining their privilege. Furthermore, it is quite reasonable to suppose that the denial or ignorance of a problem would impede working to solve the problem. If whites believe that blacks are already equal, then they would likely show less support for policies that explicitly benefit blacks. At the same time, however, the critique says nothing about the debate around colorblind policies. Bonilla-Silva and others are correct to talk about the role that race plays in that system but they are talking about something other than political colorblindness in principle as racism.

In sum, the original IDMP tenet of *Colorblindness as Racism* is false but it is easy to see how it might be confused with some other claims about colorblindness and racism. These other claims, at least the three considered here, should do nothing to undermine support for leftist and colorblind policies. Yet there is another possible reason for the hostility toward colorblindness among those in the Program, one which is bolstered by the success over the last several decades of the political establishment in lowering expectations about what is possible. We consider this pragmatic objection next.

PRAGMATIC CONSIDERATIONS ABOUT LEFTIST COLORBLIND POLICIES

I have argued that leftist colorblind policies would quickly end racist subordination. Some people in the Program might acknowledge this but may nonetheless prefer weaker measures on the grounds of political pragmatism. I understand that compromise may be a strategic necessity in the realm of politics but this does nothing to salvage the claim that race-neutral policies are harmful in general to blacks. True, a genuine leftist program has little chance of support in the U.S. in the present political environment. Many good ideas cannot be implemented under the current two-party regime, but that doesn't make them bad ideas. For example, policies to substantially reduce carbon dioxide emissions have little chance of support but we would never say that these proposals are actually harmful to the environment, simply because they cannot be implemented now given political realities. A reduction in carbon emissions is still the right thing to do. So are leftist colorblind policies.

Any policy can be viewed in (at least) two ways: first, by considering the likely consequences if implemented; second, by estimating the likelihood of implementation. These are distinct and the tenet of *Colorblindness as Racism* deals with the first issue. A discussion of the latter is reasonable—what can we realistically hope to implement now?—but IDMP supporters must recognize that the topic has changed. The claim is no longer that colorblind policies are racist but rather that leftist policies are unlikely. Although not strictly relevant to the leftist critique of *Colorblindness as Racism*, I will offer a few brief comments on the nature of these political calculations.

First, I suggest that one should not compromise on a principle *qua* principle even though one may have to compromise on a plan of action in order to get as close as possible to the realization of the principle. This is an important distinction. I maintain that compromising on a principle *as a belief* is the same as not holding the principle. Principles reside, so to speak, in our heads and there is no need to compromise with one's own beliefs. One supports equal opportunity or one does not. One believes that a certain level of poverty is acceptable or that it is unacceptable. One believes that healthcare is a right or that it is not. It is possible, of course, to not yet have figured out a position on some of these issues but this is not the same as supporting both a position and its negation. Compromise enters our considerations once we acknowledge that other individuals may not share our principles yet we must find some democratic *modus vivendi*. For example, a leftist will believe that healthcare is a universal human right but may have to compromise with people who do not in order to at least move in a better direction. The act of compromise does not diminish the belief in the principle of healthcare as a right.

Second, some people might have confused the positive form of an adjective with its comparative. To be *better* does not necessarily mean to be *good*. The weather might be warmer today than yesterday but that does not mean it is warm. A number of IDMP policies might be *to the left* of the status quo— they are *more left*—but they are not *left*. There is a clear analogy with party politics in the United States. The Democratic Party is not a party of the Left but it is at times to the left of the Republican Party. A leftist, for example, would argue in support of the minimum wage as a living wage but the debate between the two parties involves a small increase vs. no increase in the minimum wage. It would be fair to say that the Democrats are to the left of the Republicans but they are not, under any reasonable interpretation, on the Left. I believe that one of the most morally toxic effects of the Democratic Party, the party with which most IDMP supporters identify, has been the acceptance among liberals of our neoliberal trend alongside their maintenance of a progressive self-identification.

A third observation: the proper way to act in order to realize a moral principle involves all sorts of strategic calculations that might have little to do with moral principles. Left-leaning Americans have long been troubled by the nature of voting under a plurality system. Should one support a candidate from the Democratic Party who has a good chance of winning but who does not support leftist policies or should one support a candidate on the Left who does not have a realistic chance of winning? It is impossible to decide on the grounds of our moral principles. Even reason cannot adjudicate when there are several reasonable alternatives and when predictions about the future are little more than guesses. Individuals who hold the same principles may have different time horizons. Do we pursue immediate victory or do we accept social change as a process that takes generations, where the pay-off may not arrive until after our death? Do we look at voting strategically as a one-shot or as a repeated game? What short-run costs are we willing to accept for the promise of a long-run victory? Neither justice nor reason settles the issue. That is, people who share the same values may reasonably disagree on the best course of action. The difference between supporters of colorblind and color-conscious policies might to some extent reflect these considerations. Leftists can argue among themselves, including with progressive IDMP supporters, over the best strategy but care must be taken to sort out issues of values from those of strategy.

Finally, purely as a strategic decision, it is not at all clear that arguing for weaker, race-conscious policies is smarter than pushing for the stronger, colorblind policies of the Left. Given the dominance of the wealthy and the limitations of the two-party system (i.e., the absence of proportional representation), any movement toward the left in the U.S. will be difficult. From the perspective of the political sociologist William Domhoff (1990, 2013) the Left can win significant policy victories only during periods of social disruption. The Occupy Movement and other similar reactions to the economic crisis of 2008 had the potential for such disruption but they required even more people in the streets for even longer. As a strategic matter we should consider whether the set of leftist colorblind policies is a better way to rally supporters than the race-conscious Diversity approach. The latter approach not only makes a weak appeal to leftist values but it also carries the potential to racially divide the movement. It insists that whites recognize their white privilege and support policies that explicitly benefit blacks. But many poor whites—the unemployed or underemployed, those who have lost their houses and health insurance, and so on—might react negatively to the notion that they are privileged. And, in point of fact, poor whites do not have resource privilege. The potential to divide-and-conquer the movement should be obvious.

I suggest that the leftist message of solidarity among all workers would likely draw more support. Indeed, the framing of the movement as the 99 percent vs. the 1 percent points to the resource divide in America and not to the racial one. Thus, while leftist colorblind policies will be harder to implement because they are a bigger threat to the interests of the wealthy than the more timid race-conscious policies, they also have the potential for a much larger mass movement behind them. We face a trade-off and, while it is not obvious which is the best strategic move, it seems clear that neither should be labeled racist among those who want economic reform.

In sum, it is possible that when IDMP supporters allege that leftist color-blind policies are racist they really mean that they are politically impossible and therefore that we should try to get something more modest passed that might improve just a little bit the lives of black people. This is not an unreasonable position. At the same time, the leftist colorblind policies described above would improve the lives of black people—certainly those who are poor or middle class—more than the race-conscious policies offered by Diversity considerations. The fact that a weaker program might be more likely to succeed does not make the stronger program wrong. In the arena of politics, some leftists might support color-conscious affirmative action as presumably the only currently feasible improvement over the status quo but they should recognize the inability of those policies to bring about a truly just society.

SUMMARY AND CONCLUSION

In this chapter I critiqued from a leftist standpoint the second tenet of the Identity, Diversity, and Multiculturalism Program: *Colorblindness as Racism*. The Left believes as a matter of principle in policies that would realize equal opportunity and a high degree of equality of outcome. The leftist colorblind policies required to bring about the leftist conception of economic justice—redistribution of income and wealth, institutional support and regulation, and the pursuit of full employment through expansionary Keynesian policies—are clearly not racist because they would move blacks out of economic subordination. That is, they would eliminate racist outcomes. The IDMP, even if its policies were fully implemented, would do little to help the poorest blacks or even the threatened middle class. The program can demand little more than that poor black children be treated the same as poor white children. But poor white children are not treated terribly well in this land of inequality.

Thus the tenet of *Colorblindness as Racism* cannot be maintained. Opponents could make a reasonable, albeit obvious, alternative claim by limiting themselves to colorblind policies that are *conservative* or *neoliberal*. Other alternative ways of linking colorblindness and racism were considered, and whatever the merits of these alternative claims, they too do not validate the general assertion of *Colorblindness as Racism*. It is also possible that

IDMP supporters are speaking pragmatically and believe that more modest affirmative action policies have a better chance of political success. This may or may not be true but, in any case, has no bearing on the faults with the original tenet.

NOTES

1. Because the subject of the chapter is colorblindness there is little reason to refer to issues of sexism, heteronormativity, etc. The leftist policies discussed below are, in any case, general enough to deal with these other forms of inequality as well.

2. I say certain types of crimes because the greatest amount of harm is probably perpetrated by white collar offenders and corporations while street level crimes like assault and theft are more likely to be committed by the poor. See Terance Miethe et al. (2005) *Crime Profiles: The Anatomy of Dangerous Persons, Places, and Situations*. Unlike many criminological theories, which are overly broad, this approach differentiates according to type of crime and then investigates the characteristics of offender, victim, and situation.

3. The earliest (recognized) versions of the neoclassical model were developed by Stanley Jevons and Leon Walras (among others) in the 1870s but the mathematically complete formulation waited until Kenneth Arrow and Gerard Debreu's (1954) *Existence of an Equilibrium for a Competitive Economy*.

4. The foundational statement is John Maynard Keynes (1964) *The General Theory of Employment, Interest, and Money*. His approach led to the development of several non-neoclassical schools of thought. I recommend the Post Keynesian branch, which includes the work of Luigi Pasinetti, Alfred Eichner, Marc Lavoie, and Hyman Minsky. Much of the research conducted at The Levy Economics Institute at Bard College is Post Keynesian. My analysis of the economy draws upon this school.

5. The other type of racism—racist beliefs—is less relevant in the context of public policy. For example, the legalization of abortion is a policy that benefits women, an outcome which is not sexist. It may be true, however, that legalized abortion adds fuel to the sexist beliefs of some individuals. But we would not, therefore, favor the repeal of abortion rights simply to quell the sexist beliefs of some.

6. There might always be a bit of unemployment as workers move from declining industries and failing firms to growing industries and expanding firms. This is known as frictional unemployment. As long as workers find new jobs after a relatively brief search, all the while receiving adequate unemployment and retraining compensation, leftists would have no serious concerns.

Chapter Four

A Leftist Critique of Race as Culture

The first two tenets of the Identity, Diversity, and Multiculturalism Program (IDMP)—*Diversity as Justice* and *Colorblindness as Racism*—were political-economic in nature. With the two remaining tenets the focus shifts to the cultural side of the program. In this chapter, I critique the tenet of *Race as Culture*: Members of different races belong to different cultures.

In order to critique the cultural claims, we need to expand the leftist principles that were provided in the first chapter and applied to the critiques of the first two tenets. The previous approach could be regarded as leftist *political economy* and *political philosophy*. The analytical and moral framework adopted here and in the next chapter is best characterized as *existential sociology*.[1] Sociology, like all social science, ideally uses empirical evidence as the ultimate arbiter of competing claims about society. Of course, empiricism isn't everything. For many social issues, moral principles obviously have an important place as well. The Enlightenment values of liberty and especially of equality were the foundation for the critiques of *Diversity as Justice* and *Colorblindness as Racism*. Enlarging the leftist standpoint to now include existentialism we can praise human freedom or, seen from the other direction, we can condemn bad faith. From this standpoint I regard the study of society not simply as an interesting academic endeavor but rather as an important component in a project of human emancipation. We need to understand the machinery of oppression in order to free ourselves from it.

Drawing upon both moral and scientific arguments from the position of existential sociology I will make two distinct arguments against the tenet of *Race as Culture*. I refer to them as the *ontological critique* and the *empirical critique*. In the first section below I explicitly state how I incorporate existentialist principles into the leftist standpoint. After defining the concept of culture and sharpening the meaning of *Race as Culture,* I move to the ontological critique. This is considered first as it is the more fundamental of the two critiques because it challenges the very status of race itself. At its root, race is a conservative and pernicious lie. The standpoint of existential sociology exposes the bad faith and calls for a deconstruction of the very notion of race. Next I make an empirical critique of *Race as Culture*, which is independent of the first. Regardless of the ontological status of race, the evidence for cultural differences between those who self-identify as black and those who self-identify as white is quite weak. This is seen by reviewing survey data across various social indicators for blacks and whites. The data reveal that over many cultural variables blacks and whites can hardly be distinguished from each other.

THE LEFT AS EXISTENTIAL FREEDOM

The Rawlsian principles regarding equality used in the previous chapters to critique the political-economic tenets—*Diversity as Justice* and *Colorblindness as Racism*—come out of the social contract tradition in moral and political philosophy. Morality obligates us to design just social institutions, that is, the right types of state coercion and control. These ideas are less useful when dealing with cultural issues so we must shift into a second strain of leftist thinking—existentialism—in order to evaluate more personal behaviors. Social contract theory is inherently political, or political-economic, in nature. The prescriptions and proscriptions apply primarily to social institutions. A just society is one whose laws and institutions promote liberty and equality as citizens go about their own life-projects. As long as individuals stay within the boundaries established by just social institutions it would be difficult to offer any further moral evaluation of their behavior. We could say that those who violate the laws of a *just* society have behaved immorally but leftists looking only at the social contract would have a difficult time evaluating behavior that stayed within the rules of the game even if we observed considerable variation. In the social contract approach the idea of justice resides foremost at the level of the political structure, not individual behavior. Our intuition suggests, however, that some people are more virtuous than others even if everybody stays on the right side of the (just) law. Existentialism offers leftists a way to move forward on the issue of personal morality.

By comparison, conservatives do not face this same challenge with regard to personal morality. Most religions—Christianity, Judaism, and Islam, to take the dominant groups in the U.S.—are built around individual-level prohibitions, injunctions, and other god-given strictures. Yet, as Bronze Age and Iron Age constructions, they have little to say about designing a just social contract for industrialized, democratic societies. In contrast, the Left comes out of the Enlightenment and takes human reason—not a divine plan for the world—as the only tool we have for arranging our affairs. The existentialist tradition derives from the very same Enlightenment conception of human reason that gives us social contract thinking. An existentialist assumes that we were not made by somebody or something for some purpose but rather that we simply exist and must decide individually what to do about that existence. The personal rules we follow are the rules we make for ourselves.

An *essentialist* starts with the opposite assumption, maintaining that humans have some nature—whether it be from god or biology or somewhere else is of secondary importance—from which we can extract a purpose. The religious conservative, for example, supposes that a personal denial or rejection of god's plan for the world would lead to nihilistic immorality. This is a hasty conclusion. The implied virtue of the frightened believer is likewise a flawed supposition. What is true, however, is that the existentialist evaluates the morality of behavior quite differently from someone equipped with a set of sacred precepts. According to Sartre, we can morally criticize only bad faith (*mauvaise foi*), which is above all a rejection of the freedom rooted in the human condition and our capacity to reason. In other words, bad faith is the belief that we have been created for some purpose, and the use of that supposed essential nature as the explanation of our personal behavior. Bad faith thus "is a lie to oneself" (Sartre 1993, 89).

It is important to emphasize that freedom in an existential sense differs from the political liberty we take as part of a leftist social contract. Liberties like freedom of speech, assembly, and so on create a space where others cannot legitimately impede our projects. But these are legal limits coercing us to stay within certain bounds. In Isaiah Berlin's (1969) terminology they are *negative liberties*: "the area within which . . . a person . . . is or should be left to do or be what he is able to do or be, without inference by other person" (121–22). For an existentialist the legality of a behavior is largely irrelevant to our moral evaluation of it. There is no contradiction here. The social contract is neither so strict nor so narrow that it permits only one way to live. Furthermore, each of us must decide whether those bounds are just.

When we adopt the standpoint of the Left as existentialism we are able to criticize bad faith and praise authenticity. Thus as leftists we can condemn, for example, racist beliefs even if they happen to cause no harm to other members of society. When racism takes the form of exploitation or oppression we clearly have a violation of the social contract and will likely have legitimate grounds to use the coercive powers of the state to prevent or remedy the damage. An existentialist stance, on the other hand, is not used to justify the wielding of state power but instead to expose racist beliefs as bad faith.

Tribalism too is a form of essentialism, a belief not in a universal human condition but rather in a group-based distribution of different human natures. A Catholic who uses his religion as a reason to oppose either gay marriage or abortion is guilty of bad faith. On these issues the Catholic is above all a human and thus has a choice whether to support or oppose such laws. Neither the devil nor god can make us do anything. Either decision—support or opposition—would be fully protected as a political liberty, and either could be justified according to a set of personal values, but it would be bad faith to deny one's freedom to choose behind some identity like Catholicism, an identity which is, after all, also freely chosen.

This suggests that existentialism aligns better with an atheistic or agnostic outlook. Perhaps so, but we should not infer that religious believers cannot be existentialists. As Sartre (1975) observes, we bear the entire responsibility for the interpretation of signs from above (356–57). Only the madman hears god so clearly that no ambiguity remains. The real conflict with existentialism comes not from theism *per se* but rather from the denial of human freedom associated with any form of essentialism. Religion is neither a necessary cause of bad faith—an atheist might believe that DNA is destiny—nor a sufficient cause—a believer may accept that god gave us reason and freedom to choose. The sine qua non of existentialism is the affirmation of our responsibility to choose.

CONCEPTUALIZING CULTURE

Before we can critique *Race as Culture* we must understand what is meant by the terms *race* and *culture*. I conceptualize culture now but defer discussion of race until the ontological critique, the first of the two critiques. I hope to use the term *culture* in a way that is acceptable to most supporters of the Identity, Diversity, and Multiculturalism Program. If my definition is reasonable then the discussion can proceed to areas of disagreement. I think it is best to take a definition that falls in the middle between the broadest usage—where cultural is virtually synonymous with everything human—and the several narrower applications to norms and values, to "high" culture, or to organizational culture. According to the *Oxford Dictionary of Sociology* (1998) culture is "a general term for the symbolic and learned aspects of human society" (137). This is sensible but omits the explicitly comparative aspect that is crucial to discussions of Identity, Diversity, and Multiculturalism. If we add a comparative component we get something like the following definition:

Culture: A group of individuals with a set of learned and distinctive beliefs and practices.

This seems to capture the meaning of the term as used by supporters of the IDMP and remains consistent with a common sociological approach. We assume that members of one culture have learned a particular set of beliefs and practices, which can be used to distinguish them from members of another culture, where another set was learned. Central to the meaning of culture is the general idea of homogeneity of certain traits within a group and heterogeneity between groups. We seem to be on the right track but this definition, and other similar approaches, will face a serious problem once we try to apply it: How much homogeneity within and heterogeneity between must we observe? At the finest level of inspection, no two individuals share exactly the same beliefs and practices; there is no perfect homogeneity within even the smallest group. On the other side there are some elements that are universal or nearly so to all humans; there is no perfect heterogeneity between groups. There are some things we share due to the universal human condition.

The question is really one of cultural boundaries. If there is always some degree of difference within a group and some degree of sameness across groups, then how can we decide who is a member of a culture and who is not? Who is in and who is out? One theoretical and practical resolution is to privilege the substratum in which almost all human interaction resides: language. Anthropologists since Franz Boas, the founder of the modern discipline, have justifiably regarded language acquisition as the first step in understanding another society (Jakobson 1944). Although it is possible to form thoughts without language, say, as images or feelings, it is language that gives *Homo sapiens* the ability to form culture unlike anything that exists in the rest of the animal kingdom. For many analytical purposes it seems clear that language is the best way to define a cultural boundary. Those who speak German are part of a Germanic culture; those who speak Japanese are part of Japanese culture. Adopting this standard we could dismiss *Race as Culture* summarily because blacks and whites in the United States share a common language, English. To maintain some notion of *multi*-culturalism supporters must find another and almost certainly weaker cultural boundary between blacks and whites.

Let us proceed to search for other boundary criteria. We can divide cultural beliefs into two categories: those involving values and those involving real-world or empirical phenomena. Values are judgments that have no empirical or phenomenal basis. The main subtypes here are norms, ethics, and aesthetics, which refer respectively to beliefs about the proper, the good, and the beautiful. In contrast to values, which are judgments about the way the world *should be*, phenomenal or empirical beliefs are about the way the world actually *is*. Subtypes here include cognitive approaches to defining different settings as well as problem-solving or decision-making heuristics. In plainer language phenomenal beliefs tell us what is going on around us and values tell us the way things should go. Thus taken together cultural beliefs include three major categories: language, values, and phenomena. Because most blacks and whites can communicate with each other using the same language, the tenet of *Race as Culture* requires that they at least have substantially different values and phenomenal beliefs. Otherwise, why speak of *multi*culturalism?

The definition of culture refers to learned practices, the behavioral dimension to the human experience, as well as beliefs (language, values, and phenomenal schema). Members of a culture should act in distinctive ways, presumably even when they are in similar environmental situations. The reader may associate particular behavioral traits with different nationalities. There are behavioral stereotypes of, say, the Germans or Japanese and some of them may have some basis in reality. Within the U.S. *multi*culturalism would claim that blacks largely behave like each other and behave differently from whites. Ironically, therefore, both multiculturalists and racists need some racial stereotypes to be true.

The two critiques of *Race as Culture,* coming from the standpoint of existential sociology, will use the above conceptualization of culture. I intend to show that that blacks and whites are not distinct cultures as the term has been defined. The tenet for *Race as Culture* can be maintained only by excessively weakening the meaning of culture, or race (still to be defined), or both.

THE ONTOLOGICAL CRITIQUE OF *RACE AS CULTURE*

In order for the tenet of *Race as Culture* to make sense there must be some way to determine the race to which a person belongs. Furthermore, the determination of race must be prior to the analysis of culture. That is, we cannot first decide what it means to "act black" and "act white"—a cultural designation—and then use these behaviors to assign individuals to races. We must first determine who is racially black and who is racially white and then investigate the degree to which they form distinct cultures. The ontological critique challenges the notion of *Race as Culture* by focusing on the impossibility of the first task: the very classification of individuals into racial categories. Ontology speaks to the nature of reality; the ontological critique asserts that race is not real. The argument is quite simple. If we cannot make the initial racial categorization, then we will be unable to look for any cultural patterns (or anything else) based on race.

The ontological critique depends on the unsoundness of the notion of race, the fact that race has no objective, biological basis. Race is nothing more than a social construction. It is true that people have different biological traits, including the color of our skin. It is also true that many people believe that race is real. IDMP supporters typically use one or both of these as foundational for their belief in race. The ontological critique explains why neither is satisfactory. If race is defined as a biological trait, then it can be rejected on scientific grounds. If race is taken to be real because some people believe it is real, then it can be rejected as a misapplication of the notion of a social construction. I treat each of these positions in turn.

Race as a Biological Trait

For much of the last several centuries race has been generally accepted as a biological trait, one that varied among different peoples of the world. Skin color did not capture the full meaning of race but rather was a marker of the supposed deeper biological differences. It might help to remember that until relatively recently the microscopic and genetic foundations of biological processes were poorly understood. In its early years, biology was little more than an attempt to categorize species according to macroscopic features. Even the insights of Darwin in the middle of the nineteenth century preceded the development of modern microscopy by Köhler, which occurred around the end of that century. Indeed, the Darwinian paradigm provided a plausible biological rationale for race, one that was well-suited to the existing social and political inequality. A biological hierarchy built upon race is a story that legitimates social and economic oppression.

Although we cannot excuse racist propaganda we might understand how it was possible for nineteenth-century biology to be used in such a manner. But these inaccuracies—whether by racists or multiculturalists—can no longer be accepted in light of contemporary biology. Modern genetics provides clear evidence against race. There is simply no gene or even sequence of genes that corresponds to the conventional notion of race. It is true that biologists and anthropologists can find genetic markers that indicate evolutionary pathways. A certain sequence might indicate that some of one's ancestors were in northern Africa 5,000 years ago. Another might suggest that some of one's ancestors crossed from Asia into North America during the last Ice Age. Or that one has Scandinavian "blood." But nothing in the genetic markers of these various ancestral pathways leads to anything like the one-drop rule in the United States or any of the other various racial rules created in other societies. We now know that most of human history was spent in Africa. Even today the most genetic diversity still exists in Africa, further confounding the linking of the "black" race with African ancestry. Although we are all quite similar at the genetic level, an African and a European might have even more genetic similarity than two Africans.

Believers in *Race as Culture* thereby face the insurmountable problem of determining the racial category into which any particular individual belongs. If race had biological significance then we would be able to sort members of our species (*Homo sapiens sapiens*) into racial groups by means of some biological assessment, presumably by some genetic test. But because race is not a meaningful term in modern biology there is no way of assigning individuals to racial categories. When pressed, most Multiculturalists will admit that there are no biologically meaningful differences among human groups. It turns out that our human ancestors were not sufficiently isolated from each other for sufficiently long to produce sub-species. Even though most now accept the modern genetic thinking on race, some still maintain the contradictory position that blacks and whites differ at some fundamental, essentialist level.

In making the ontological critique, I do not simply state what should today be obvious—there is no gene for race—but also reject the subtler statements of biological essentialism. Some people hold a metaphysical conviction in race. Take, for example, the feeling that there exists a special, perhaps sacred relationship with long dead and even unknown ancestors. This has no more foundation in reality than the claim by some people that they actually talk to god.

In this regard blacks differ little from other groups. Americans with some Irish "blood" may speak of the potato famine as if it were somehow a living memory. Americans of Chinese descent may feel a strong connection to the building of the transcontinental railroad and the subsequent purges. But in reality a black child must learn about the Middle Passage the same way as a white child. Or not learn, as the case may be. The fiction of race brings no epistemological privilege. We carry no memories in our genes but instead must learn nearly everything—for better or worse—from our environment. The only plausible argument, then, is that different children learn different things, whether by means of an oral tradition or from the books they read. But this brings us a long way from any connection to biology. If some families talk more about slavery, or some talk more about *their* genocide, catastrophe, or other such historical calamity they may feel closer to their ancestors—real or imagined. And in many cases reality may disappoint the imagination. As Jim Sleeper notes, "while black American pilgrims to Africa were newly preoccupied with the significance of being 'black,' they found that the designation has no significance is most of Africa" (1997, 106). The feelings that come from racial self-identification are real (as feelings) but the concept of race itself is a social construct, and often misleading at that.

Again, most Multiculturalists will ultimately accede to the validity of modern biology and at least formerly disavow biological essentialism. This does not mean, however, that they give up on the reality of race. Instead the defense shifts to race as a social construction. Yet as I argue next this ultimately fails because it confounds laws in the natural world with those in the social world.

Race as a Social Construction

The belief in race as a biological fact can easily be dismissed as non-scientific and essentialist. The subsequent and stronger argument on behalf of race goes something like this:

> Race may not be real in the biological sense.
> But most people believe race is real.
> And people act on those beliefs.
> The actions have real consequences.
> The consequences generally lead to the subordination of blacks by whites.
> Race is therefore real in a practical sense.

Thus the revised argument supposes that the reality of a thing is determined not by its objective status as a thing-in-itself but rather by the reality of the consequences of the belief in it. This, however, is an invalid assertion. The issue is not whether some believe that race is real or even whether they act on that belief. That is true and nobody would deny it. The ontological question is about whether something is *objectively* real. The fundamental error in the IDMP argument is to conflate objectivity with inter-subjective agreement. An objectively real phenomenon can be repeatedly found by every observer (requiring perhaps the right instrumentation, say, a microscope or a genetic test). Such phenomena exist outside us, independently of our will. This is not to say that we can truly and fully understand the objective world. Each of us may have a different take on objective reality but our cognitive imperfections do not negate the existence of that reality; it indicates merely that we imperfectly understand a reality that is nonetheless real. Phenomena in the *natural* world are objectively real. The earth, moon, and sun are real regardless of our opinions about them or our different appreciations of them. Even if we all pretended the sun no longer existed or even if *Homo sapiens* suddenly disappeared, the hydrogen and helium in the sun would keep on fusing into heavier elements, and entropy would inexorably march forward.

Not so with things formed merely out of inter-subjective agreement among certain parties. They cannot be confirmed by *every* observer because they exist inside the mind of some observers and perhaps not inside others. The issue is not the biochemical processes in the brain responsible for the belief in something like race. Such processes are real enough. We are talking about the object of the belief: race as an objective trait. The object of the belief is not real even though the thought process is. If humans were to disappear we would take our intersubjectively created phenomena down with us. The belief in race is analogous to a belief in a flat earth or the belief in god. God is not an objective phenomenon (that is, there is no verifiable method for detecting the existence of such an entity) yet the belief in god strongly influences the behavior of many. Some people believe in angels and miracles. The fact that many people *believe* in such things—a fact accepted by every atheist—does not constitute objective proof of their existence. The same is true of race. Race is a fiction regardless of the degree of intersubjective agreement.

The process by which human-made concepts come to be seen as objectively real is known as reification. We thus say that race has been reified in American culture. Race does not have an objective existence but instead matters only to the extent that people in our culture believe it matters. As argued by Berger and Luckmann (1967) in *The Social Construction of Reality* much of this is accomplished through the use of language. While humans are not the only species with the ability to communicate, nothing else in the animal kingdom compares to the complexity of human language. When we communicate through language we are using words as symbols, that is, as things that represent other things. The word *chair* is not a chair but rather invokes a mental representation of a real chair. Many words stand in for real objects but—and this is the almost magical power—it is possible to create words that lack a counterpart in reality. Moreover, simply creating a word for a concept often can lead us to believe that whatever it represents must be real. The fact that we have a word for god makes it easier to suppose that the thing must really exist. The same is true of race. The word does not stand in for some real sequence in our genetic code but is simply a word, one that has tricked some into believing there must be a real object behind it.

The ontological critique alerts us to the genuine threat to human freedom in the cultural processes that fill our heads with ideas like god and race, yet at the same time it points to the liberating potential of these processes to transform the social world. Natural laws have an ontological status that differs from social "laws." The former operate everywhere. The latter are necessarily contingent in time and place. There is nothing that can be done if one has a problem with gravity, due perhaps to a parachute that did not open. Objective phenomena are independent of our beliefs. Our opinion about gravity is irrelevant to the acceleration it will give to a body. A great deal can be done, on the other hand, if our problem is with race or religion. Our opinions are ultimately the only thing that matters. The idea of social *construction* contains within it the potentially liberating notion of social *deconstruction* and *reconstruction*. We are not stuck with the ideas that happened to be in our culture at the time and place of our birth. In reality, culture is never completely static. The question is whether we want to be active participants or passive enablers.

Cultural Constructions and Legal Constructions

The reader may agree that race is a social construction but feel that I have gone too far toward the position that the social world is whatever we believe it to be. We do indeed need to be careful to navigate between the Scylla of reification and the Charybdis of solipsism. While language is at the root of all social constructions it manifests itself in different ways. I distinguish between two important types of social constructions in the modern period: *cultural constructions* and *political constructions*. The object of a cultural construction is believed to exist (or be real) by many individuals in a culture. Race is thus clearly a cultural construction. The object of a political construction, on the other hand, may also receive similar support through public opinion but the key characteristic is that its "facticity" is sanctioned in some way by the state. All laws, for example, are political constructions. Put differently, cultural constructions are enforced by informal sanctions—if they are enforced at all—and political constructions are enforced by formal sanctions, that is, by the coercive apparatus of the state.

Cultural and political constructions are related to each other but not identically, and the differences between the two can be quite significant. For a state to exist and for the law to carry weight a sizable number of people must believe in the state and its laws. The opinions of those who carry weapons on behalf of the current order, that is, the police and military might be particularly important, but without broad support from even ordinary citizens the entire state becomes unstable and liable to collapse. Social constructions that have both the coercive backing of state (political constructions) as well as the support of public opinion (cultural constructions) can be very hard to resist. Not only is resistance probably futile but it could come at quite a cost for the lone dissenter through formal and informal sanctions. There is a quantitative side to this as well—both formal and informal sanctions vary in their intensity. Murder is punished more severely than shoplifting. Burning a flag might receive a more serious, albeit informal, punishment by onlookers than the refusal to stand for the national anthem.

Let us apply these ideas to race. In the contemporary period, that is, the post-Civil Rights era, the foundations of the social construction called race are relatively weak. On the political side, there are no official punishments today for violating the convention, that is, for believing that race is not real or for refusing to adopt a racial identity. There may be some advantage with regard to college admission, financial aid, or employment by checking the right box on a form, but this can be performed strategically and insincerely. We have come a long way toward a political deconstruction of race. Prior to the victories of abolitionists and civil rights activists it was difficult to fight the system because race was both enforced by the coercive power of the state and backed by widespread popular opinion. A slave would have pointed in vain to the faulty science used to justify the racial system. A couple that rejected racial categorization may still have been prevented from marrying by anti-miscegenation laws. The social construction of race had a legal foundation and was enforced when necessary with lawful violence.

Today things are very different. The state is no longer in the business of enforcing racial categories.[2] The U.S. Census Bureau has changed its language and offers no real definition of *race*.[3] Individuals are free to self-identify as any race they select—or no race at all.[4] The racial categories that supported first slavery and then Jim Crow no longer exist as legally backed social constructions. The remaining basis is public opinion, so we must consider the degree to which there are informal means of control. Individuals could be shamed or ostracized for failing to acknowledge their "correct" racial identity.

While they are increasingly infrequent, social punishments are still meted out for racial transgressors like Rachel Dolezal. Dolezal (who has since changed her name to Nkechi Diallo) was the leader of the local chapter of the NAACP in Spokane, Washington, until it came out in the summer of 2015 that she was a white person pretending to be black, that is, Dolezal's biological parents identify as white yet she identities as black. She resigned her position after being criticized, much of it coming from academics in fields associated with Identity, Diversity, and Multiculturalism.

It was a sad incident not only for Dolezal, who seems to have been a good, progressive leader of the local chapter, but because it revealed that the IDMP now leads the charge to punish those who wish to break down the socially constructed barriers between the "races." The times have changed indeed. The maintenance of race, as a concept and a category, is in the interest of only a few groups in society, for example, conservative politicians who see it as electorally favorable to maintain racial divisions. Although the mainstream media framed it as a controversy about race in America, the Dolezal story had a remarkably short lifespan, which suggests that most people—those not trained in the Programmatic ways of thinking—did not really care all that much about the race Dolezal adopted. Even the national NAACP, to their credit, did not attack Dolezal or call for her removal. To the current generation of progressives schooled in the Program this might be taken as evidence that the NAACP, with its emphasis on equal treatment regardless of race, is passé.

Cultural constructions do have a second means of defense, one which is even stronger than outrage directed at transgressors like Dolezal's. Cultural hegemony is present when the degree of intersubjective agreement is so wide-spread that the belief requires no sanctioning because nobody can imagine an alternative. Here we can speak of a worldview that is completely taken for granted. Yet the idea of race is no longer hegemonic in our culture. Once questions can be asked of others and of oneself then things can unravel very quickly, especially when the answers are unsatisfactory. Even those who want to keep race alive acknowledge that it is a social construction. Ever fewer believe that race captures a meaningful biological difference among humans.

To further illuminate the point we can contrast the flagging cultural construction of race with the stronger political and cultural construction of class. The private ownership of capital and the prerogatives it affords capitalists, the foundation of our contemporary class system, are backed up by the coercive powers of the state. Workers are not free to simply pretend as if the factory belonged to them. A worker who is fired must vacate the premises or will be forcibly removed by the cops. Racial categorization, on the other hand, lacks the apparatus of legitimate coercion. Of course it was different in the past but the legal mechanisms behind the social system have changed. Under slavery blacks were a type of capital whose ownership was defended by the state, much like the capitalist factory is protected today.

Furthermore, capitalist property rights are so taken for granted that it rarely occurs to workers to even attempt to resist them. Class relations have a hegemonic status in the culture that race no longer does. What is the racial analog of a worker conceiving of an economic system without capitalists? A person conceiving of a social system without race. The latter thought, though not yet ubiquitous, is far more common than the former. Although it is premature, as Identity, Diversity, and Multiculturalism supporters correctly assert, to pronounce America a post-racial society, the fact that the issue is debated in the media and among everyday folks shows that the idea of race is not hegemonic. Holes in the dike have appeared and they are growing. On the other hand, the conversation about a move toward a post-capitalist economy is limited so far to a relatively small number of socialists and anarchists, and the majority of those are actually social democrats, who simply want a better regulated capitalist system. Our class-based economy is in a legal and cultural position far stronger than our race-based society.

While most in the IDMP acknowledge that race is a social construction, it's not clear whether they fully appreciate the substantial difference between the cultural and political variants. Their criticism of Dolezal sharply exposes their conceptual blinders. Linda Martín Alcoff, author of the *Future of Whiteness*, argued on a Democracy Now (2015) interview:

> More and more people now realize that race is not biological, that there's no DNA of race, and so it's socially constructed. But what does that mean? What

does it mean to say it's socially constructed? There's a lot of confusion around that. And when [Dolezal] says things like, you know, "It's complicated," people are not sure how to make sense of that. But what it means to say it's socially constructed is that *it's socially constructed, it's not individually constructed.* It's based in social customs and practices and histories. And so, you know, we have decided together that a piece of paper counts as a dollar; everybody has to agree to that, or it's not going to work. That's what social construction means. (emphasis added)

After correctly observing that race is *socially* constructed, Martín Alcoff emphasizes that race is therefore not *individually* constructed. But there is a problem with this line of reasoning: the *social* is simply an aggregation of the *individual*. The idea of race—and it is an idea—exists in the heads of real individuals, not in the abstraction known as society. Or, rather, we can say that it exists in society if it exists in the heads of enough individuals. Every idea is individually constructed. Every social construction is also an individual construction. True, individuals are shaped by the society into which they are born, but this means that individuals are shaped by the other individuals around them. It's fine to refer to that aggregation of individuals as a *society*, as long as we don't forget that by society we actually mean a group of interrelated individuals.

In addition to this misunderstanding of the relationship between the individual and society—we could call it the Borg Fallacy—Martín Alcoff errs by putting race into the same category as the dollar. While both are social constructions, race is a *cultural* construction while the dollar is both a *cultural* and a *legal* construction. The state does not racially categorize its citizens, nor even provide criteria for how they might self-identify should they choose to do so. (There are, however, categories of nationality for Native Americans which may provide some benefits.) The power of race lies in the meaning given it by individuals. The state no longer imposes a common racial label on people with identical physical traits (like skin color) who adopt different racial identities.

The dollar, on the other hand, is not only widely accepted culturally (far more so than race) but has a legal foundation that would be almost impossible to fight. The state requires that we accept the dollar as the means to settle payments and debts. Every dollar has an identical value to every other dollar. I cannot pretend that my student loan payment or mortgage doesn't exist. Or, rather, I can default on my debts and the face sanctions that will be enforced by the state. Thus the comparison of race to the dollar is a false analogy.

There is yet another problem with the attack on Dolezal, an inconsistency that reaches the level of hypocrisy. Around the time that Dolezal was being criticized by Martín Alcoff and others, Bruce Jenner had just openly identified as female (and subsequently changed her name to Caitlyn). In contrast to Dolezal, Jenner was praised by many in the IDMP. Why the support for the deconstruction of the social construction of gender but hostility for the deconstruction of race? According to Martín Alcoff, race cannot be individually deconstructed because it's "based in social customs and practices and histories." OK, but gender has a social grounding that goes even deeper than race. Even the idea that gender can be separated from biological sex is relatively recent and many people still don't accept the idea that a biological male could have a female gender identity. I am certain that Martín Alcoff would agree that biology does not determine one's gender just as she notes that "race is not biological, that there's no DNA of race." If so, then why is it not acceptable to change one's racial identity? Both race and gender are based on social customs that can be rejected at the individual level. And neither is determined by biology.

Part of the problem might be what sociologists refer to as a "trained incapacity" on the part of the specialist to properly evaluate a situation. With a bit of cleverness it's easy enough to navigate through or around logical barriers in order to reach the preferred destination. But why is it necessary to defend the traditional social construction of race yet not gender? The reason, I believe, is that much of the academic study of gender ultimately rests on delinking gender identity from biological sex. Many of the questions in the field examine the nature of that decoupling and explore what is meant by masculinity and femininity. Indeed, the tension between the biological and the social creates a fertile area for investigation.

No analogous opportunity exists for race. The study of race must begin with the recognition that there is no valid biological basis for categories like black and white. With regard to biology, that's it. End of story. There is no potential for interesting back-and-forth between something biological, the analog of sex, and something cultural, the analog of gender because there isn't anything biological about race. Studies of race always carry the risk of reifying that fundamental error made by our ancestors. Of course, the study of the ways in which race is socially constructed, of the history of race, of the sociological differences between the socially constructed races, and so on, are perfectly valid. But there is still a big difference between the interplay between the biological and the social sides that exists with sex/gender and the analysis of the purely social construction of race. In any case, Dolezal was seen as posing a threat to the race side of the Program and thus was labeled a liar and a fraud; Jenner provided another case study for the gender side and thus was courageous and inspiring.

While the attacks on Dolezal are unjustifiably hypocritical, and we should defend her right to subjectively identify with any race, we must not forget that this is a controversy about a categorization that doesn't actually exist. Dolezal plays the role of a Protestant against (Catholic) Christendom instead of an Enlightenment thinker rejecting the folly of all religion. Rather than identifying as black or as white, Dolezal might better have identified as human. This would have been consistent with her leftist values. Even though she didn't go this far, the positive legacy of her experience will be its signaling of a shift in American culture. The hegemonic status of the concept of race no longer exists. Leftists can hope that the deconstruction of race in society will accelerate as more people like Dolezal (Diallo) come forward. It seems likely that a greater openness toward and acceptance of a flexible racial identity will follow a similar trajectory to that of transgender identity, albeit perhaps a few years behind.

The deconstruction of race should be good news for leftists and for anybody else concerned about racism. Today we are freer than ever before in this country to identify as any race or no race at all. We can affirm that race is nothing more than what we believe it to be. From the perspective of existentialism, the social forces that perpetuate the idea of race deserve condemnation. In this regard the Identity, Diversity, and Multiculturalism Program is a conservative force—one built on traditional beliefs—resisting the deconstruction of race. It shares a common cause with white supremacists. The Identity, Diversity, and Multiculturalism Program is in the business—quite literally for some people—of reifying race. Instead of acknowledging that race has no objective basis and affirming that race is nothing more than what we pretend it to be, many people insist on perpetuating the social construction we have inherited from the racists of previous centuries. The promotion of race is a deplorable act of bad faith. The Left should assert that race is fiction, nothing more than a pernicious cultural construction. It was made by humans, that is, our ancestors, and can be changed by us. It is bad faith to pretend otherwise.

The liberal defender of race should not misconstrue or obfuscate the ontological critique. Ontological colorblindness cannot be attacked by claiming that it denies the existence of racism. To be clear: Race is not real but many people believe in it and many people act according to those beliefs. That is, race has no objective reality but there are racist beliefs, actions, and outcomes. It's not a complicated statement so it should not be misconstrued. The allegation that the denial of race is tantamount to the denial of racism is yet another act of bad faith.

Nor does the distinction between objective phenomena and intersubjective beliefs correspond to a distinction between important and unimportant things. Indeed, the cultural structure, or superstructure, that we have created out of and on top of physical reality is probably more remarkable than nature itself. Some of these things, like the notions of justice and equality, are extraordinarily wonderful. Others, like religion and race, can be remarkably terrible. The social world we create out of our beliefs has real consequences for good or ill.

What remains of the tenet of *Race as Culture* after the ontological critique? Only by further weakening the meaning of the term is it possible to pretend that race exists. Race is nothing more than a word one may use to identify oneself. It has no biological basis and thus is not real in an objective sense. Even as a subjective social construction it grows increasingly weak, having lost it hegemonic status. There is no legal basis for race. Although many continue to believe that race exists, leftism as existentialism must reject this. "To deal with a human being," argues Peter Berger (1963, 157) "exclusively qua 'Negro' is an act of 'bad faith,' no matter whether these dealings are those of a racist or a racial liberal. In fact, it is worth stressing that liberals are often just as much caught in the fictions of socially taken-for-granted repertoires as are their political opponents; only they attach opposite valuations to those fictions." We should not accept as legitimate either the biological essentialism or the misconstrued social constructionism behind it. While we cannot prevent others from living in bad faith, we can expose it and we can refuse to play along. Walter Benn Michaels (2006, 39) puts it well: "Treating race as a social fact amounts to nothing more than acknowledging that we were mistaken to think of it as a biological fact and then insisting that we ought to keep making the mistake. Maybe instead we ought to stop making the mistake."

THE EMPIRICAL CRITIQUE OF RACE AS CULTURE

If the ontological critique is valid then there would seem to be little need for a second critique of *Race as Culture*. Recall the statement of the third tenet: Members of different races belong to different cultures. The ontological status of race would seem to make it impossible to actually put people into different races and thus creates an analytical impasse. There is a way forward but it requires that we weaken the tenet by making reference to race as a purely subjective, self-identified characteristic. For the sake of the empirical critique we need to revise the statement of the third tenet of the Identity, Diversity, and Multiculturalism Program as follows:

(3) Race as Culture: Members of different *self-identified* races belong to different cultures.

The original language implied that race is real, which we now reject as a false assumption, and thus rendered the claim untestable. It is a meaningless statement because it is impossible to determine any statistical patterns involving blacks and whites if we cannot objectively determine who is black and who is white. The revised claim avoids the ontological problems with race by giving it a fully subjective definition: an individual's race is simply whatever the individual says it is. Race is now amenable to measurement and thus empirical evaluation in the same way that religious affiliation can be matched against, for example, voting patterns without worrying about the ontological status of god. But the price that must be paid in order to make race a measurable variable is to give up on any objective basis for it. It can mean something different to each respondent. The person with the lightest-colored skin could claim to be black (and *mutatis mutandis*) and could not be challenged, as happened in the case of Dolezal. I trust that the liberal defender of race recognizes the extent to which this undermines the significance of the idea of *Race as Culture,* regardless of the empirical critique that follows.

The empirical critique is exactly that: it examines and finds wanting the evidence for the claim that blacks and whites have distinct cultures. Above I defined culture as a group with a set of distinctive beliefs and practices. The meaning of the tenet of *Race as Culture* now becomes clearer. *Race as Culture* supposes that those who identify as black have a distinctive *black* culture, that those who identify as white have a distinctive *white* culture, and so on. Blacks would thus have beliefs and practices that are different from those of whites. But the claim still can be interpreted in many ways. How distinctive must blacks and whites be? Is black culture completely distinct from white culture or can it share most traits and have only a few differences?

For the notion of culture to carry much weight two conditions are necessary: (1) individuals within the same culture must think and act in many of the same ways as each other and (2) they must think and act in a number of different ways from individuals in a different culture. The second part is typically emphasized by *multi*culturalists. They assume, for example, that collaboration between a black person and white person on some project is likely to get two different perspectives. But the first element cannot be overlooked. If one black person is likely to differ from another black person, or one white person from another, then what sense would it make to talk about a black perspective or a white perspective on a situation? As heterogeneity within any group increases, individual perspectives, not cultural ones, carry greater weight. We would get two different perspectives on any situation simply by having two different people regardless of the racial combinations. Thus the tenet of *Race as Culture* suggests a relatively high degree of homogeneity within each race as well as heterogeneity between races.

Homogeneity within and heterogeneity between are not completely independent. Under many circumstances as the variation within any group increases the differences between groups will necessarily decrease. For example, consider a society that has moved from a state of religious exclusivism to one of religious pluralism. Perhaps everybody at some earlier time was Christian and now individuals are more evenly distributed across many different beliefs. Consider another society that was entirely Islamic and then also moved to a state of pluralism. In the early period we could speak of homogeneity within each group and heterogeneity between the groups; that is, we could properly speak of distinct cultures (particularly if they also spoke different languages). Now, however, as the heterogeneity within each group has increased—we find a sprinkling of Christians, Muslims, Jews, Hindus, Buddhists, atheists, etc. in both—the two societies have come to resemble each other. The heterogeneity between has diminished. If we wanted to explain at the earlier time why somebody was a Christian in the first group and a Muslim in the second, we could plausibly invoke culture as the factor. At the later time, however, culture will no longer be of much use when we want to explain the religious affiliation of any person in either group. We might argue that culture is still relevant because it permits pluralism, but it would not help us explain any particular individual's affiliation because it is now a constant: religious pluralism is the norm in both groups and thus cannot explain variation between them. We would need to find other individual-level factors to explain the distribution in religious views. Furthermore, we could no longer assume that by selecting someone from the first group we would get a Christian perspective and somebody from the second group a Muslim. If our objective was to get two different perspectives, we could simply pick two from the first or two from the second. This would give the same odds of getting two different views as selecting one person out of each group.

Figure 4.1 helps us visualize the possible relationships involving homogeneity within and heterogeneity between races and thus the degree of importance of culture as a factor in explaining individual-level characteristics. Distributions of opinions on some culturally relevant issue could be represented in this way. They are drawn as more or less normal curves although the assumption of normality is not necessary and simply aids in visualization; more complicated distributions of categorical variables or non-Gaussian quantitative variables would lead to roughly the same conclusion.

At the top of figure 4.1 (labeled A), the distributions for blacks and whites on some cultural issue are totally distinct and thus reflect a high degree of homogeneity within and heterogeneity between the races. If the actual data looked like A for many traits, then it would be valid to speak of blacks and whites as coming from different cultures and to assume that individuals from the different races would have different perspectives. (Although this is not true of blacks and whites in the U.S., we could consider societies that speak different languages, practice different religions, perhaps due to geographical

Chapter Four

remoteness or distinct economic modes of production.) As we move down the figure the distributions within each race become more spread out (technically speaking, if the distributions are numerical and approximately normal, we would find an increasing standard deviation). Because I assumed that the set of possible opinions is bounded, as the heterogeneity within each group in-

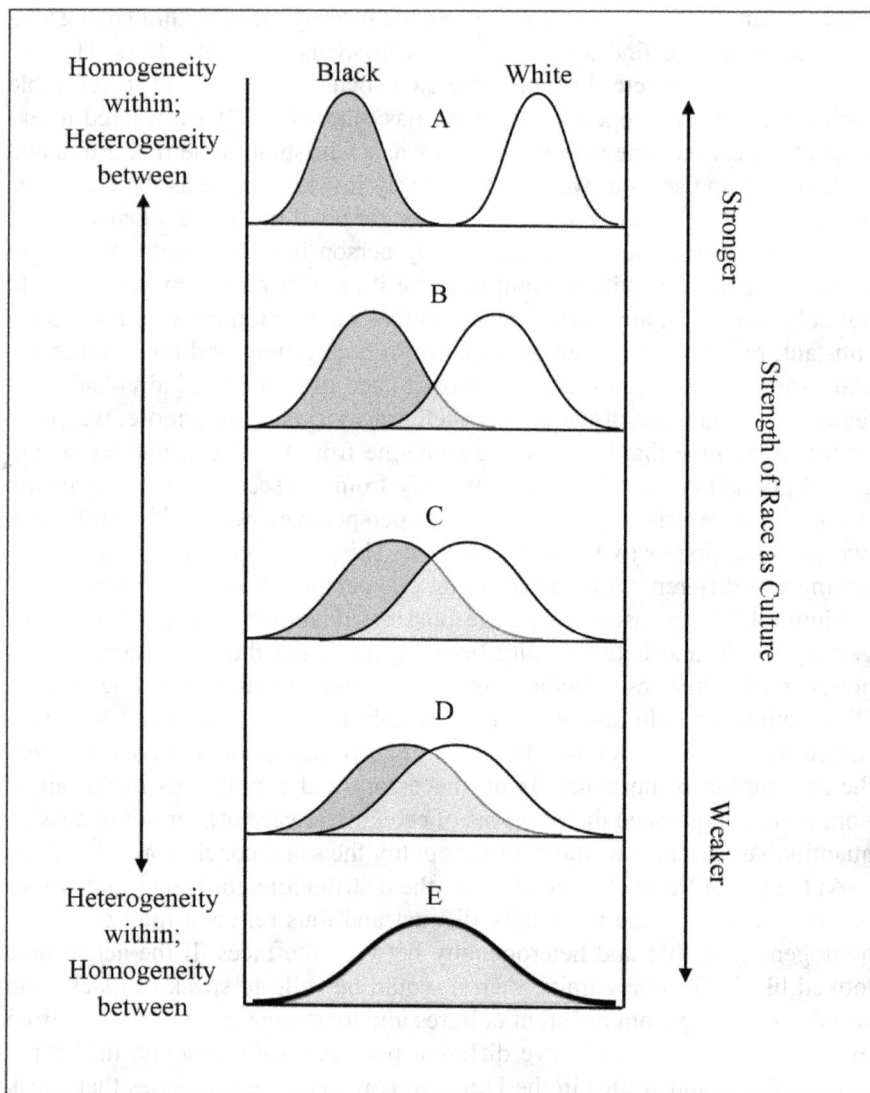

Figure 4.1.   Representation of Possible Distributions of Culturally Relevant Traits for Blacks and Whites

creases the homogeneity between them must decrease. The distributions must increasingly overlap. The racial distributions at E have come to completely overlap and the racial perspectives have become indistinguishable. Heterogeneity exists within each group and not between them. If the distributions were in fact normally distributed, then blacks and whites would have both equal means and equal standard deviations.

The distributions at C are the evenly split: half the area under each curve falls under the other. Assuming that even the most optimistic *multi*culturalist recognizes that completely separate distributions like A are impossible, supporters of *Race as Culture* might hope for a world like B or C. I will call this the *strong* tenet of *Race as Culture*. It claims that the distributions for blacks and whites are largely non-overlapping. But perhaps some IDMP supporters would be satisfied with something on the other side of the spectrum, something like that reflected in D. Thus I take the *weak* claim of *Race as Culture* to mean that the distributions are partially distinct, stopping some distance from the completely overlapping distribution shown in E. I shall not attempt to give quantitative precision to the notions of *strong* and *weak*. The representation of overlapping distributions provides a heuristic that will suffice to permit an empirical critique of *Race as Culture*. For each culturally relevant trait, a side-by-side histogram for blacks and for whites will reveal visually the degree to which the distributions overlap.

One final point must be resolved before proceeding to the data. Each distribution in figure 4.1 applies to only one culturally relevant trait at a time. Yet there are potentially a great many culturally relevant traits and each will have its own distribution. I argued above that language is the most important trait. In this case the races almost completely overlap because most (non-Hispanic) blacks and whites in the U.S. speak English. But there are many secondary traits and it may be that some largely overlap and some do not. It is thus necessary to modify the strong and weak claims to reflect the fact that many distinct traits exist in the totality of a culture. The new problem is this: how many traits must be in the neighborhood of B and C for the strong version of the claim of *Race as Culture* to be valid and how many in the neighborhood of D for the weak version to be valid? When dealing with culture there is no way to give a precise number so I will simply say that the strong version requires *many* traits to be largely non-overlapping (B or C) and the weak version claims that *at least a few* traits need to be not completely overlapping (D). There is obviously a large spectrum of possibilities that would fall somewhere in between the two. Cultural analysis is not an exact science and these qualitative statements might have to suffice.

THE GENERAL SOCIAL SURVEY

Having thus clarified as best we can the meaning of the tenet of *Race as Culture* we are now in a position to consider the evidence, which comes from the General Social Survey, the most important general purpose data set for sociologists in the United States. Conducted annually or bi-annually since 1972 it contains tens of thousands of randomly sampled respondents and thousands of questions. I use it to compare self-identified blacks and whites across a selection of beliefs and behaviors. There are, of course, other (self-identified) races on the GSS but the focus here is on blacks and whites. As mentioned previously, this racial division receives the most attention by those inside the Program (and in American society more broadly), and there are reasonable historical arguments why it should be so. Additionally, I do not wish to bring in other groups that might blur the line between race and ethnicity. The latter is a linguistic division and language is often the strongest basis for cultural boundaries. Many Americans who more recently immigrated from Latin America or Asia might still have linguistic and hence cultural differences compared to arrivers from an earlier time. Finally, the sample sizes for groups other than whites and blacks tend to be too small to draw strong conclusions.

The objective of the analysis is to determine whether the data fall closer to the strong version or the weak version of the tenet of *Race as Culture* for black and whites. Further comparisons can help with that determination. To give some reference, some sense of scale, we can compare the distributions for blacks and whites to other familiar groupings based on sex and age. It is useful to know whether the differences between blacks and whites are bigger, smaller, or about the same size as the differences between men and women, on the one hand, and the young and the old, on the other. In fact, it is via comparative data that we can best make sense of the significance of any absolute magnitudes.

Men and women differ on a number of variables but we do not, at least not in a strictly social scientific manner, take these differences to mean that men and women in the same country necessarily come from different cultures. Same for differences across the generations. The young and old will disagree on certain points on average but this doesn't mean they come from distinct cultures. Of course, we could say that any group difference, regardless of magnitude, is a cultural difference. This approach could save the notion of *Race as Culture* but only at the cost of diminishing the importance of culture. Social scientists argue that culture maintains some consistency within a society over time through the mechanism of socialization, which is simply the teaching and learning of appropriate beliefs and behaviors from one generation to the next. If generational differences are cultural differences, then we are forced to say that parents, who are key agents of socialization, are in a different culture from their children, who were the recipients of the socialization from their parents. And if sex differences represent culture, then brothers and sisters are also in different cultures from each other (and from their parents). This is not to deny the existence or importance of sex or generational differences, but rather to suggest that not all group differences rise to the level of cultural ones. The notion of *Race as Culture* would be strengthened if racial differences are larger than those based on sex and age.

Some final operational notes. The GSS currently uses a binary and biological measure of sex, not a multifaceted construct of gender. To measure generation, I have split the sample into those younger than 30 years of age, on the one hand, and older than 60 years, on the other.

Religion

We begin with three GSS questions on religion, plausibly regarded as the cultural trait second in importance only to language. Figure 4.2 shows the affiliations according to several religious categories for self-identified blacks and whites. The majority of blacks (67 percent) are Protestant, which is also the most common affiliation for whites at 46 percent, but many more whites than blacks identify as Catholic. A broader categorization of Christian that included Protestant, Catholic, and Christian as one category would find that blacks and whites are relatively close to each other (78 percent to 71 percent). Bringing sex and age into the analysis, we find that men and women have a high degree of correspondence while bigger differences emerge between the generations, on par with those observed between blacks and whites, although the generational change points to increasing secularization over time more than a sectarian divide.

Next we can consider the degree to which individuals feel engaged with their religion, regardless of affiliation with church or sect. For the question in figure 4.3, respondents were asked to report on their level of religiosity on a scale from *very religious* to *not religious*. Blacks clearly report being more religious than whites, with differences again much larger than those based on sex and comparable to those based on age. Finally, over and above religious affiliation and sense of religiosity is the matter of religious practice. It is relatively easy to state an affiliation and self-report as religious but it requires time and effort to engage in religious ceremonies, and thus may be a better indicator of true religiosity. Figure 4.4 shows the frequency of participation in an organized religious activity like church attendance. There are more whites than blacks who never attend (48 percent vs. 33 percent) and more blacks who attend weekly (12 percent vs. 6 percent). Men and women are nearly identical, while the old attend more often than the young.

The Important Things in Life

The GSS contains an interesting set of questions regarding the importance of different elements in the lives of the respondents. *Importance* is one of the primary cultural and personal judgments. The prefatory statement for the set of questions reads,

> I'm going to read you a list of some things that different people value. Some people say these things are very important to them. Other people say they are not so important. Please tell me how important each thing is to you personally, using the responses on this card.

The series of questions examined distinct aspects of the respondent's life: Importance of having a fulfilling job (figure 4.5), of being married (figure 4.6), of having children (figure 4.7), of being self-sufficient (figure 4.8), and of being cultured (figure 4.9).

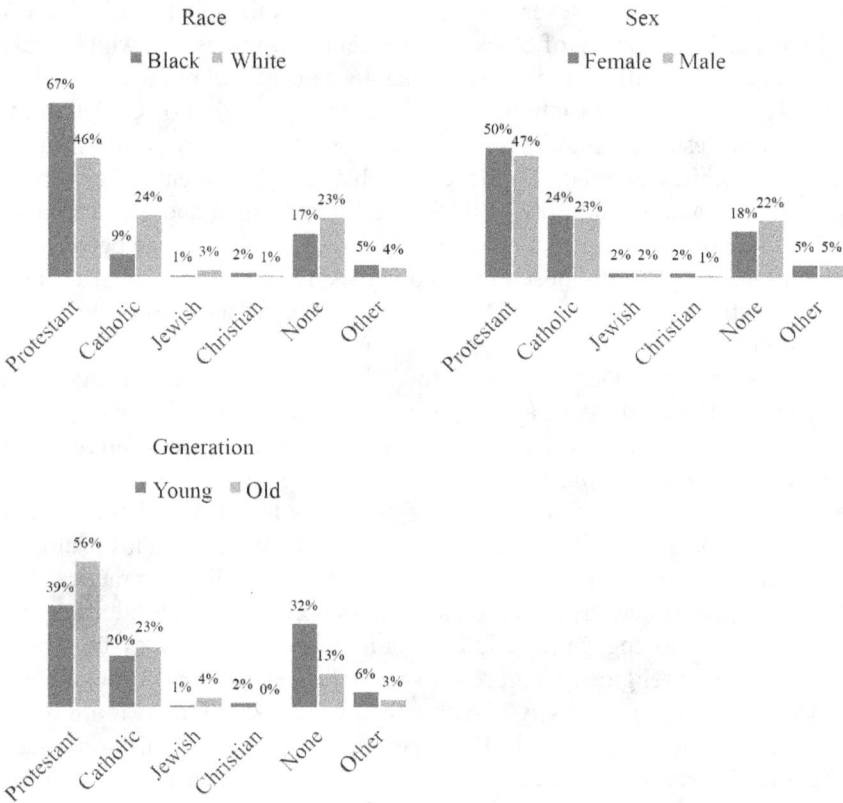

Figure 4.2.   Religious Affiliation by Race, Sex, and Generation

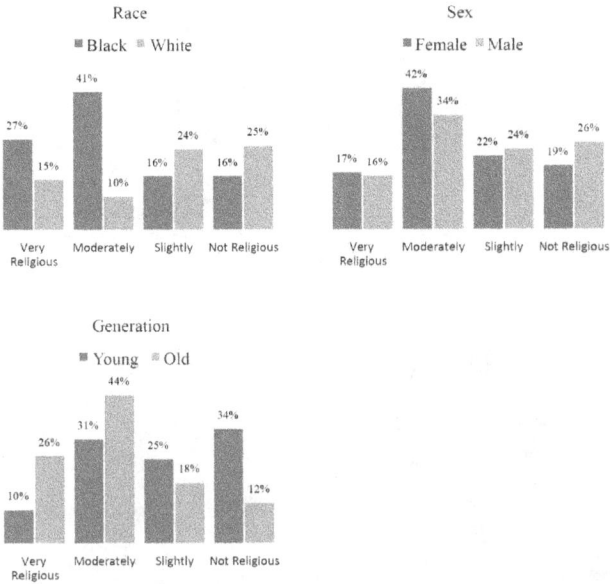

Figure 4.3. Consider Self a Religious Person by Race, Sex, and Generation

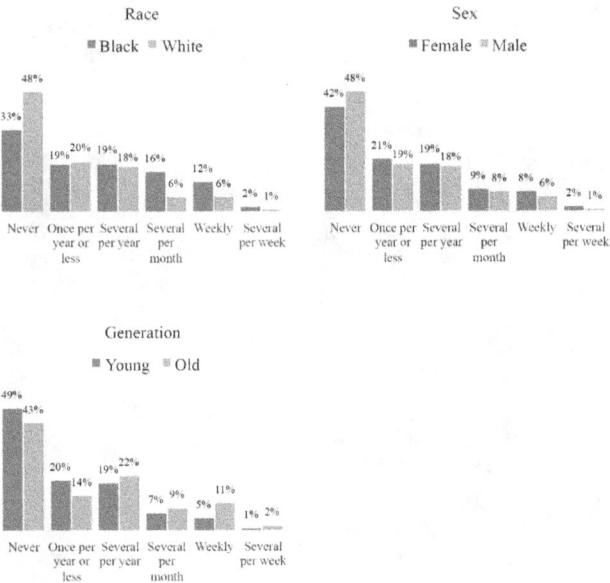

Figure 4.4. Frequency of Religious Attendance by Race, Sex, and Generation

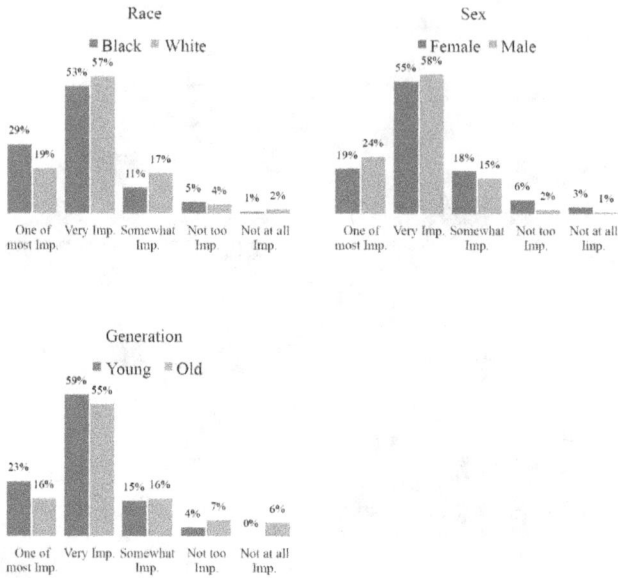

Figure 4.5.   Importance of Having a Fulfilling Job by Race, Sex, and Generation

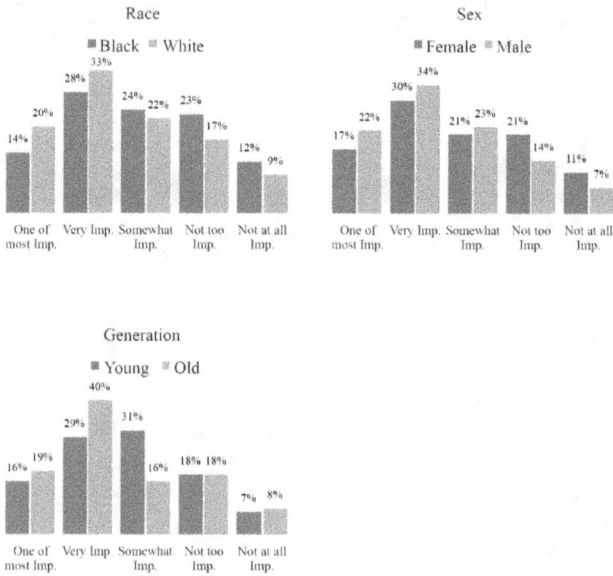

Figure 4.6.   Importance of Being Married by Race, Sex, and Generation

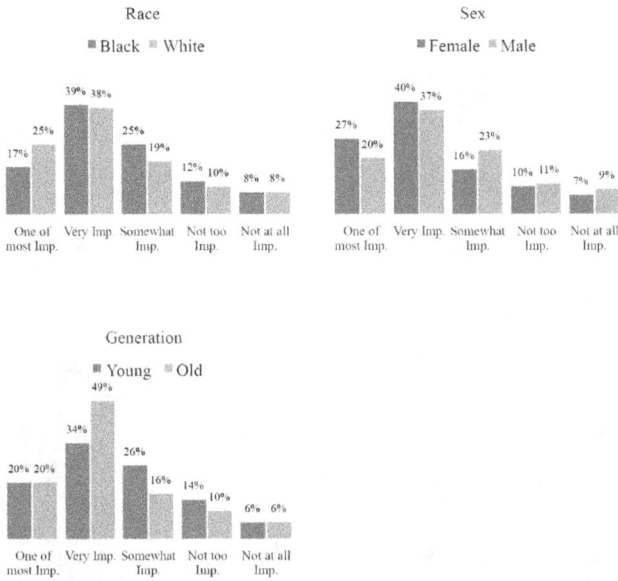

Figure 4.7. Importance of Having Children by Race, Sex, and Generation

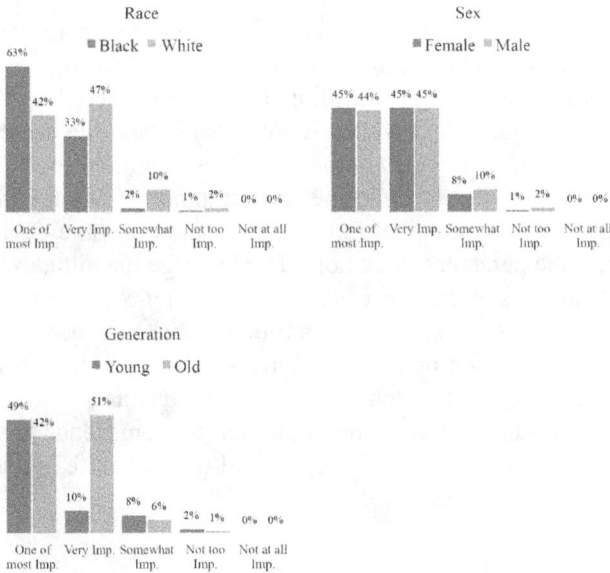

Figure 4.8. Importance of Being Self-Sufficient by Race, Sex, and Generation

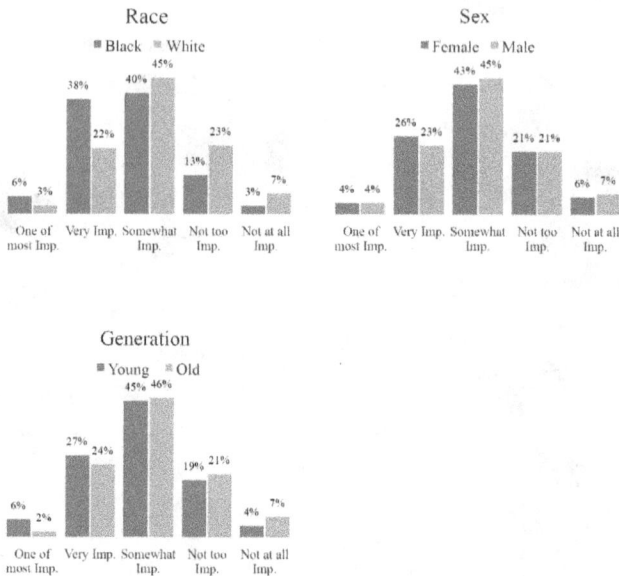

Figure 4.9.   Importance of Being Cultured by Race, Sex, and Generation

The distributions for all of these items largely overlap for blacks and whites. The exact numbers vary, of course, but the most common response for blacks is usually the most common for whites, the second most common for blacks is usually the second most common for whites, etc. Take figure 4.5, dealing with the importance of having a fulfilling job, for example. The most common response for both blacks and whites is *Very Important*, the second most for both is *One of the Most Important*, the third most common for both groups is *Somewhat Important*, and so on to the least common for both with *Not at all Important*. Considering the other three items, there are some deviations from this pattern but the percentages do not differ by large magnitudes, except per-haps for the responses to the *Importance of Being Self-Sufficient*, where blacks selected *One of the Most Important* at a much higher rate than whites.

The distributions based on sex and generation also overlap to a large de-gree. The numbers do not match exactly but the ups and downs of the bars tend to follow the same pattern. This set of survey items tends to suggest that the variation in the valuation of the important things in life is due to factors other than race, sex, or age.

Social Life

Another set of interesting questions from the GSS looked at the ways in which respondents spent their time socializing. The scenarios include spending a social evening with friends (figure 4.10), an evening with relatives (figure 4.11), an evening with neighbors (figure 4.12), and an evening at a bar or tavern (figure 4.13). The items used a seven-point response set ranging from *Almost Daily* to *Never*.

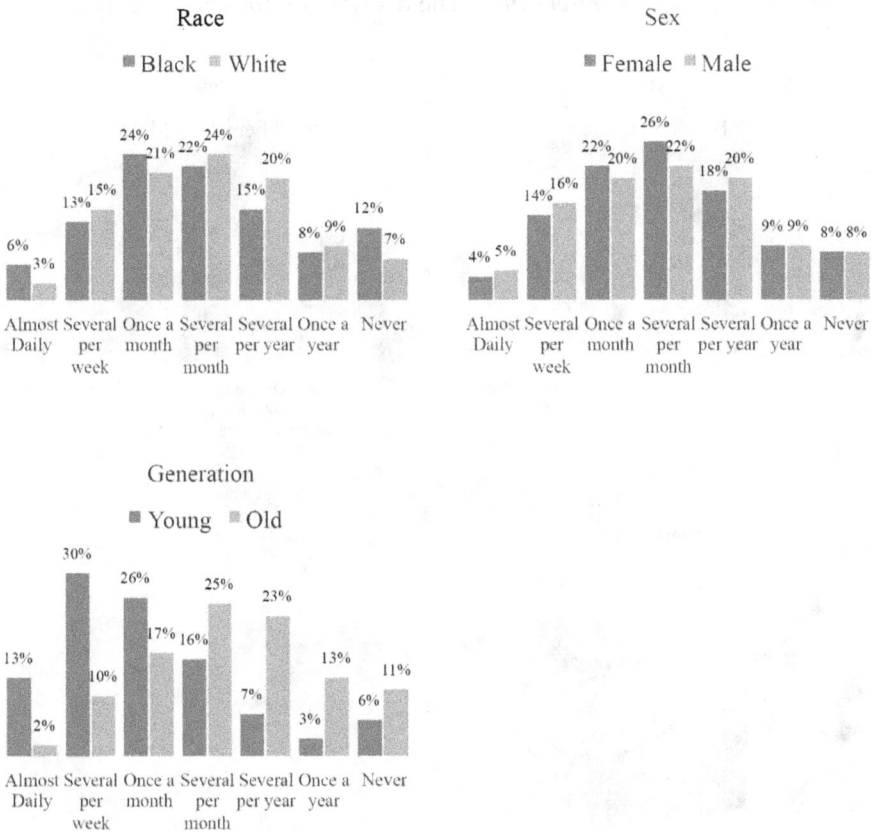

Figure 4.10. Spend Evening with Friends by Race, Sex, and Generation

There are many data points, but the overall impression from the charts is something like the largely overlapping distribution of blacks and whites at D in figure 4.1. One of the bigger differences between blacks and whites is the frequency of spending an evening with relatives, where 22 percent of blacks report *Almost Daily* compared to 14 percent of whites, although the rest of the distribution in figure 4.11 looks very similar. The distributions for men and women are also quite similar, while those for the young and the old show some substantial divergence.

Political Opinions

The GSS asks respondents about their political orientation. The first of these items is self-identification on the standard political spectrum from *Extremely Liberal* to *Extremely Conservative*. The distribution for blacks in figure 4.14

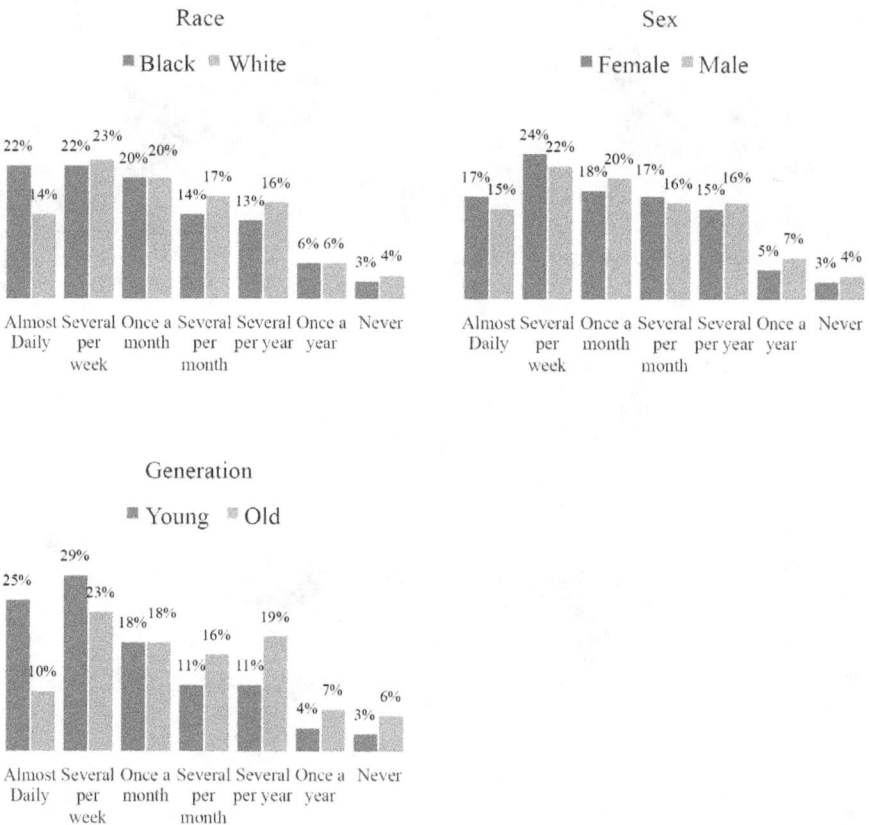

Figure 4.11.   Spend Evening with Relatives by Race, Sex, and Generation

is shifted just slightly in the liberal direction compared to the distribution for whites, although the resemblance far outweighs the differences. Much the same could be said of the distributions based on sex and age. Women and men are quite similar, and so are the young and the old, with the former of each group shifted slightly in the liberal direction. These data do not contradict the common political wisdom that women, blacks, and the young tend to support Democrats more than their demographic counterparts. In close elections, decided by just a few percentage points, the average position in each distribution will determine the outcome.

The GSS has several questions regarding positions on specific political issues, including five that are especially contentious today: economic inequality (figure 4.15), homosexuality (figure 4.16), capital punishment (figure 4.17), marijuana legalization (figure 4.18), and support for legal abortion

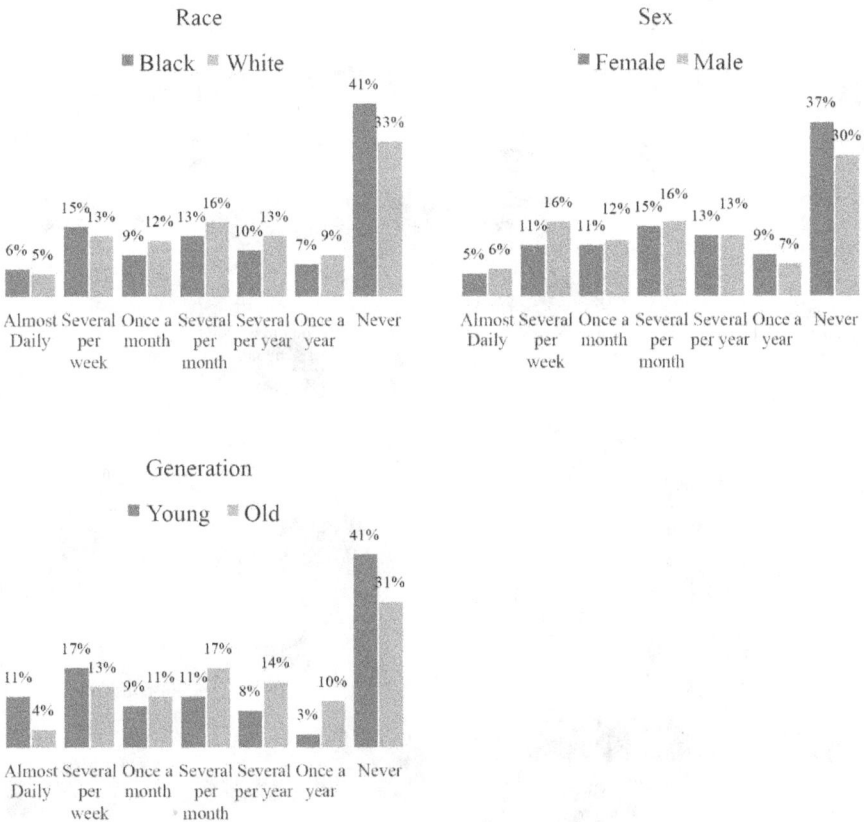

Figure 4.12.   Spend Evening with Neighbors by Race, Sex, and Generation

(figure 4.19). If cultural differences exist between the races they might plausibly show up as political disagreements on these.

We do see greater divergence at this level. A much higher percentage of blacks favor strong government action to reduce income differences than whites (36 percent vs. 19 percent in figure 4.15). The difference between the young and old, however, might be even stronger, considering the larger numbers of younger individuals who selected values 2 and 3 on the 7-point scale. Women are only slightly more progressive on this issue than men. In Figure 4.16 the ideological positioning reverses, where a majority of blacks (60 percent) see homosexuality as *Always Wrong* while a majority of whites (56 percent) see it as *Not Wrong at All.*[5] The magnitude of racial differences is matched by the generational split between those younger than 30 and older than 60. Support for capital punishment, in figure 4.17, similarly has a big racial divide, with a majority of whites (66 percent) supporting it and a majority of blacks (58 percent) opposing it. The sex- and age-based differences are

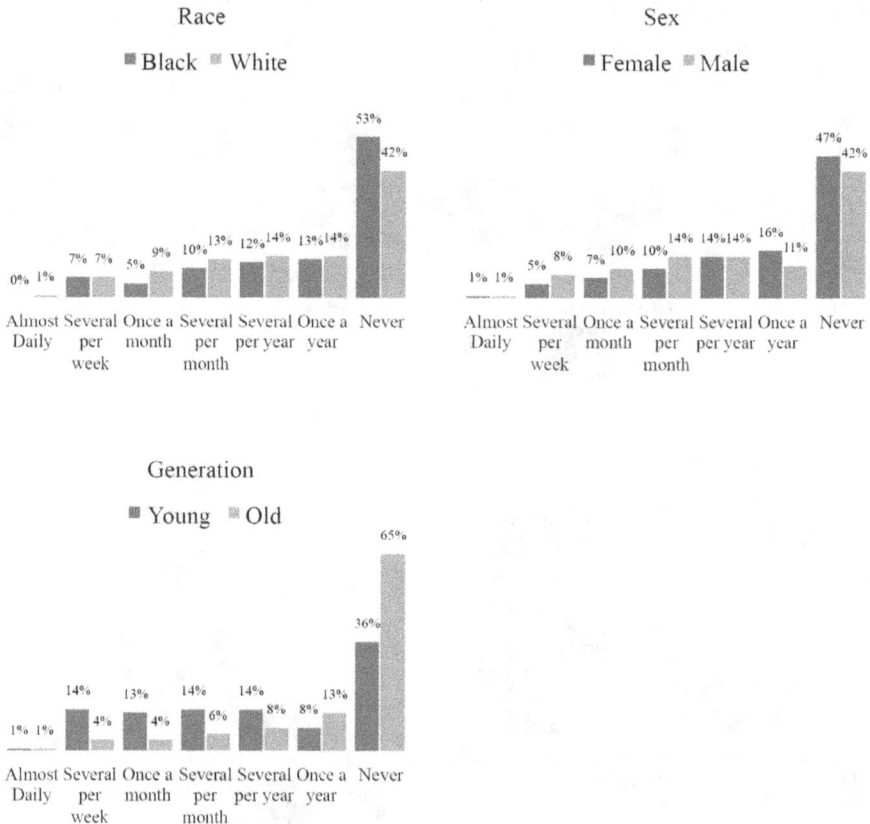

Figure 4.13.   Spend Evening at Bar by Race, Sex, and Generation

not quite as large. For the last two political issues—legalization of marijuana and support for legal abortion—we find nearly identical distributions based on race in figures 4.18 and 4.19. Men and women have modest differences on average while the gap is larger across the generations.

Taking Stock of the Survey Data

The reader is encouraged to glance back over figures 4.2 through 4.19. One will notice that, for the most part, the overall ups and downs are quite similar for blacks and whites across many of the items. Comparing these distributions, taken in their entirety, to figure 4.1 it is clear that the best matches would be near the bottom, meaning weaker versions of *Race as Culture*. Furthermore, we see considerable heterogeneity within each racial group. Blacks do not necessarily think or act like other blacks and whites do not think or act like other whites. It is not clear what either the black perspective or the

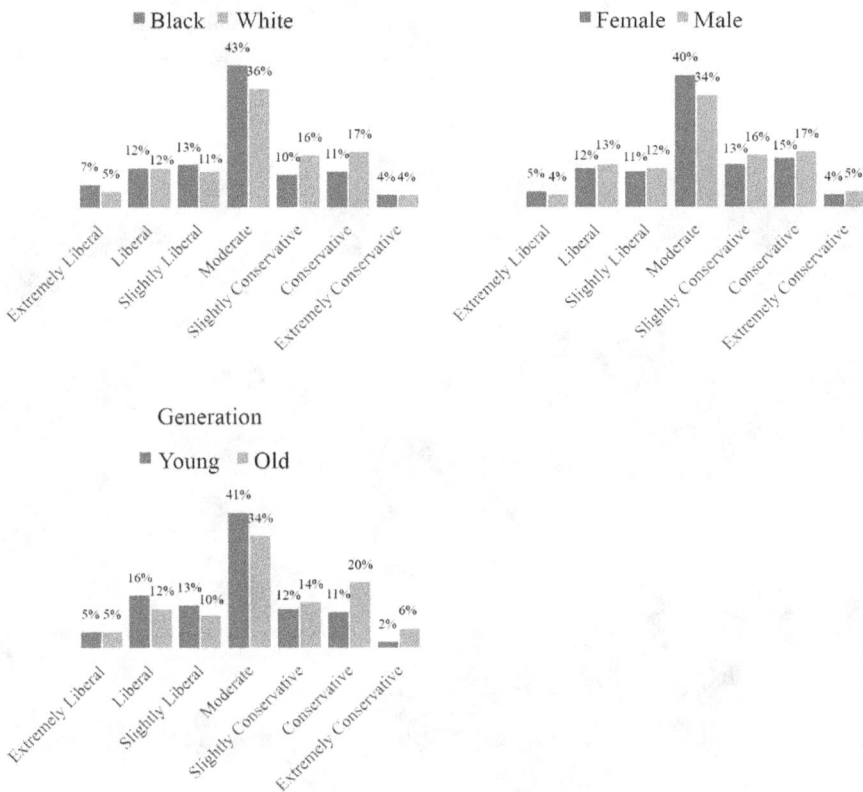

Figure 4.14. Think of Self as Liberal or Conservative by Race, Sex, and Generation

white perspective would be, that is, we find nothing that is distinctively black or distinctively white.

Religion might seem to be an exception. About two-thirds of blacks are Protestants while just under half of whites are. There are many more white Catholics than black. Blacks also self-identify as more religious and attend religious services more often. Do these add up to a cultural boundary between blacks and whites? This is both an empirical and a conceptual question. An alien anthropologist visiting earth would observe that all Christians believe in the same god, follow the same holy text, have the same creation myth, believe in heaven and hell, and so on. On the other hand, a theologian for each sect would presumably have much to say about the crucial disagreements between them and their important cultural consequences. In any case, data alone cannot adjudicate.

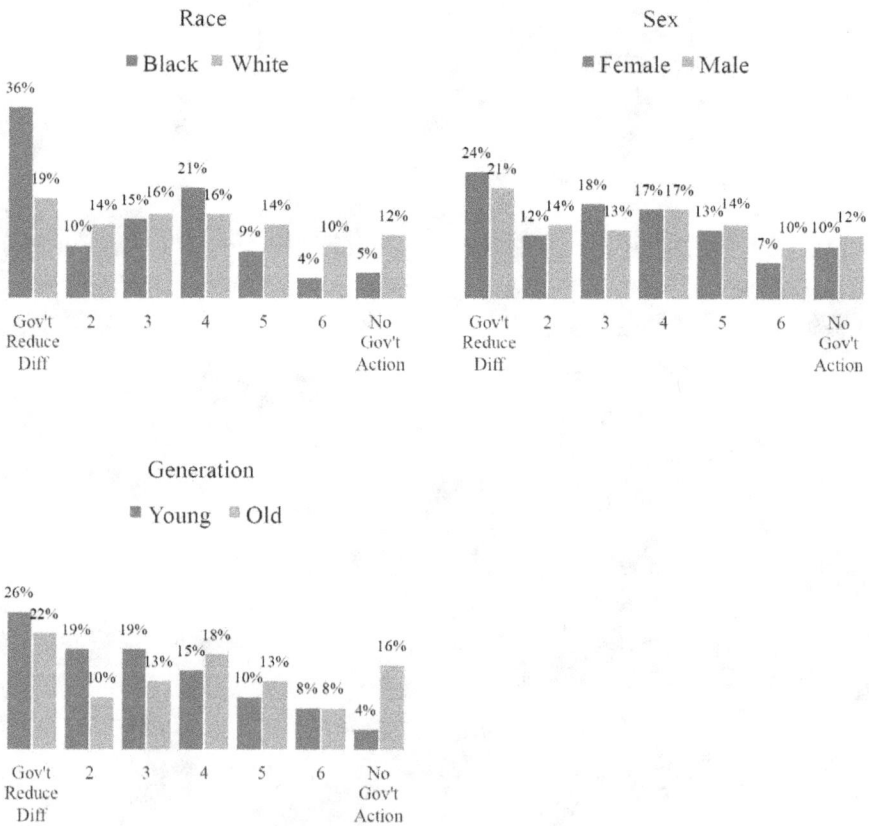

Figure 4.15.   Should Government Reduce Income Differences by Race, Sex, and Generation

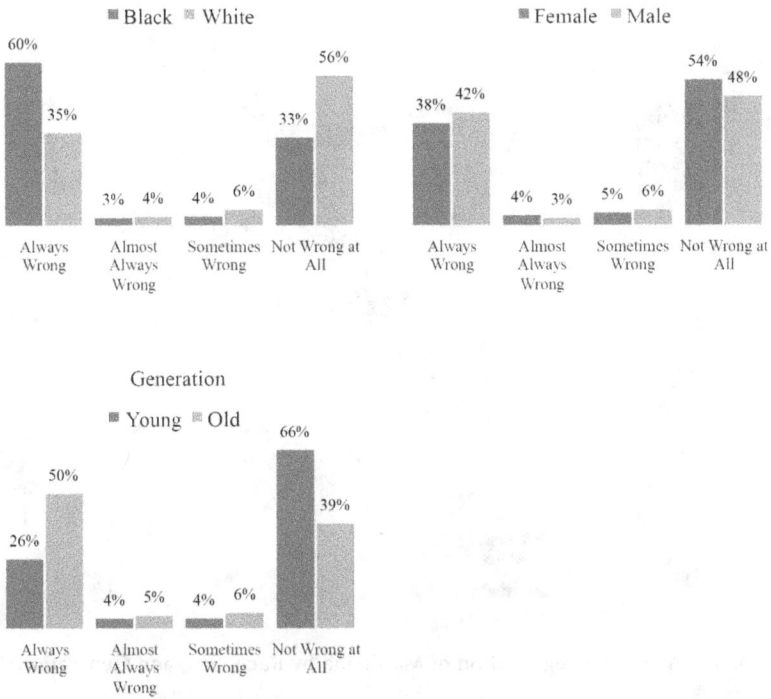

Figure 4.16. Views on Homosexuality by Race, Sex, and Generation

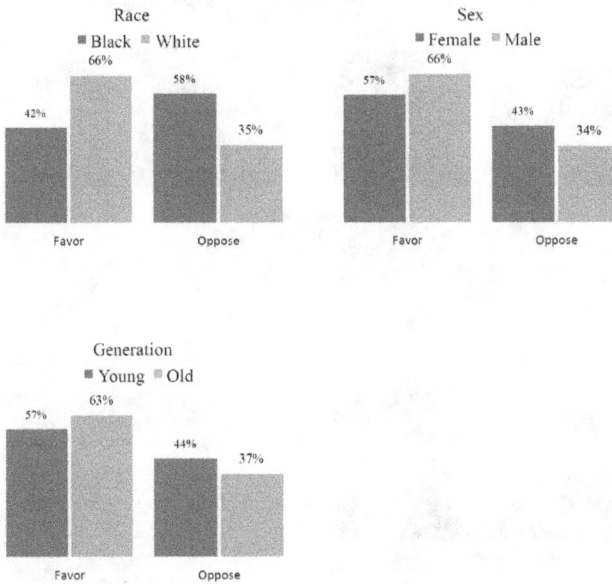

Figure 4.17. Views on Capital Punishment by Race, Sex, and Generation

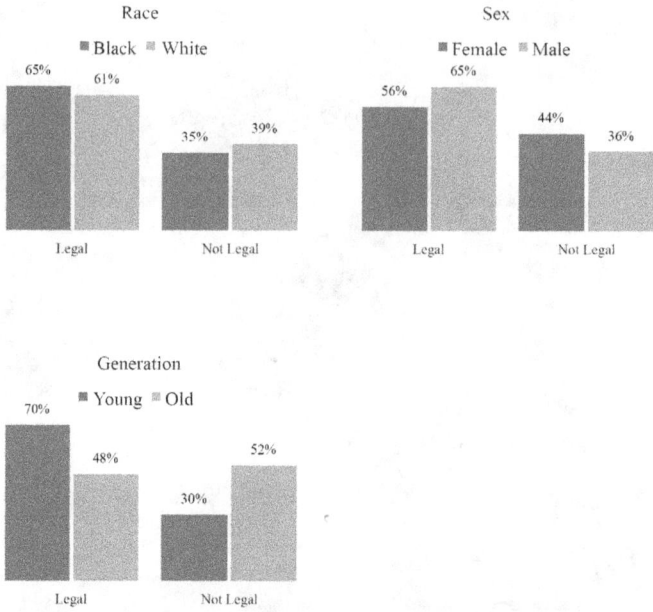

Figure 4.18. Views on Legalization of Marijuana by Race, Sex, and Generation

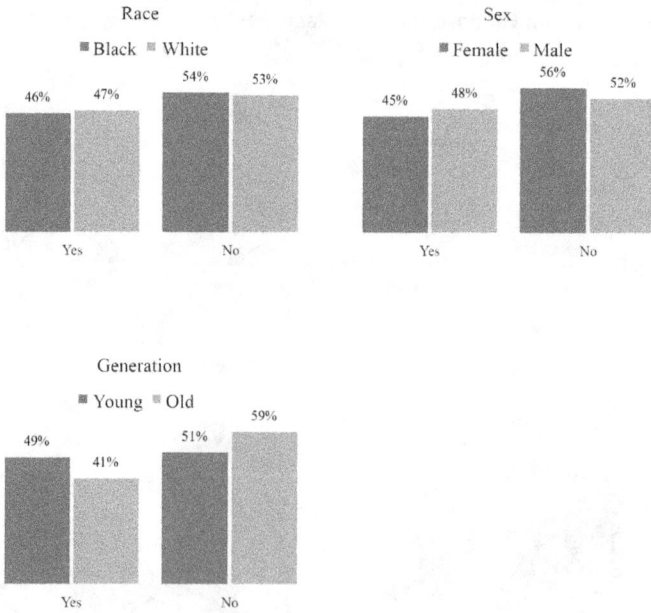

Figure 4.19. Views on Legal Abortion for Any Reason by Race, Sex, and Generation

So what can we do with of the data? A couple of things. First, we can draw upon our understanding of the differences between men and women, and young and old, and whether they reflect different cultures, on the one hand, or differences within a culture, on the other. Taken in their entirety, the distributions in figures 4.2–4.19 suggest that the differences between blacks and whites are on par with those based on sex and age. As a matter of logical consistency, if we believe that men and women come from different cultures and that the old and young come from different cultures, then we can believe that blacks and whites come from different cultures. *Mutatis mutandis* if we don't. We are free to choose our definition of the word *culture*, however, it would not be consistent with standard sociological or anthropological usage of the term to take men and women from the same society as coming from different cultures. Same is true for individuals from different generations. It undermines the notion of culture, which after all is passed along through socialization across the generations, to say that parents and children come from different cultures. When we find overlapping but not identical distributions for men and women, we do not therefore say that husbands and wives necessarily come from different cultures. If we did, into which culture would we put the sons and daughters whom they socialize? In a family with four people we could find ourselves in the awkward position of diagnosing four different cultures: the old dad, the old mom, the young son, and the young daughter. That seems to stretch the meaning of culture a bit too far.

There's a second analytical strategy. In addition to the qualitative heuristic comparison of race to sex and age, we can make a quantitative assessment of the strength of *Race as Culture*. Support for the notion of *Race as Culture* hinges on the presumption that blacks and whites bring different perspectives with them to any setting. Using the data above we can calculate the probability that a randomly selected black person and a randomly selected white person will have different opinions on any given issue.

For example, consider the question regarding attitudes about the responsibility of the government to reduce income inequality figure 4.15). Given the differences at the extremes we might suppose that randomly selecting one black person and one white person would likely give us two people with different positions. And indeed 83.7 percent of the time such a random drawing would produce two different responses, either supporting government action to reduce income inequality or opposing government action or some point in between. The black person and the white person would bring two opinions. Yet this would be true also by simply picking two black people or two white people. Two randomly selected black people are going to disagree with each other 78.2 percent of the time and two white people 84.9 percent. The disagreement within each race is about the same size as the disagreement be-

tween races, yet Identity, Diversity, and Multiculturalism supporters emphasizes the latter. We can't ignore the heterogeneity with each race, however, if
we want to assess the notion of *Race as Culture*. As heterogeneity within each
race increases, we should look for individual-level, not group-level, factors.

Some might suspect this outcome is simply an artifact of measurement
for this particular item. The GSS question on income equality uses a 7-point
response. Perhaps other items generate more difference between the races and
more similarity within each race. It turns out, however, that racial heterogeneity does not have much effect on the likelihood of getting different responses
to any of the survey items. Table 4.1 gives the probably of disagreement,
that is, two different opinions, for all 18 GSS items. In some cases, in fact,
the likelihood of different responses was higher with two people of the same
race. In all cases, the values were clustered rather tightly. The best case for
supporters of *Race as Culture* occurs with opinions on homosexuality, where
a black and a white will disagree 60.2 percent of the time, while two whites
will disagree 55.9 percent of the time, a gap of only 4.3 percent. (Of course,
from a leftist perspective, we shouldn't necessary celebrate disagreement on
this topic and would rather hope for universal acceptance. More on the significance of this point in the next chapter.)

I am tempted to say that the notion of *Race as Culture* is built around a
modest chance of getting an extra percentage or two in the likelihood of a
different opinion on some topic. In reality, race turns out to be a very poor
predictor of agreement or disagreement on many culturally relevant issues.
Let us not misinterpret this as an argument in favor of racially homogenous
groups. It's simply that one of the rationales offered by supporters of Identity, Diversity, and Multiculturalism doesn't hold up. On the other hand, if
we commit to the leftist notion of equal opportunity (as well as more equal
outcomes), then we should expect to find racially mixed organizations as the
norm. Support for racial heterogeneity receives a much stronger footing via
the fundamental moral principle of equal opportunity—one that is difficult
for even conservatives or neoliberals to denounce (in principle, that is)—instead of an empirical proposition that turns out, in fact, to be false.

In the end, I suppose supporters of the Identity, Diversity, and Multiculturalism Program can fall back on the claim that distributions for blacks and
whites are not *identical*. We are not in distribution E in figure 4.1. The distributions largely but not completely overlap, something like the distributions
in D. While I refer to this as the weak version of *Race as Culture,* one has to
take conceptual liberties to believe that blacks and whites are in reality two
distinct *cultures*. That is, belief even in the weak interpretation of *Race as
Culture* requires some abuse of the sociological and anthropological idea of
culture. Differences between individuals within a society are perfectly normal

Table 4.1.   Probability of Different Responses between and within Races.

	Chance of Different Responses between Randomly Selected . . .		
	Black and White	Black and Black	White and White
Religious Affiliation (figure 4.2)	62.9%	51.1%	*67.5%*
Religious Person (figure 4.3)	84.0%	70.8%	*84.7%*
Frequency of Religious Attendance (figure 4.4)	75.2%	*77.9%*	69.0%
Importance of Fulfilling Job (figure 4.5)	*62.2%*	62.0%	60.8%
Importance of Being Married (figure 4.6)	*77.7%*	*77.7%*	76.6%
Importance of Having Children (figure 4.7)	*74.3%*	73.6%	74.1%
Importance of Self-Sufficiency (figure 4.8)	57.8%	49.4%	*59.2%*
Importance of Being Cultured (figure 4.9)	*70.3%*	67.4%	69.0%
Evening with Friends (figure 4.10)	*83.0%*	*83.0%*	82.2%
Evening with Relatives (figure 4.11)	*82.9%*	82.2%	82.8%
Evening with Neighbors (figure 4.12)	79.1%	76.6%	*80.7%*
Evening at Bar (figure 4.13)	72.0%	67.0%	*75.4%*
Liberal or Conservative (figure 4.14)	77.7%	75.5%	*78.5%*
Reduce Income Differences (figure 4.15)	83.7%	78.2%	*84.9%*
Homosexuality (figure 4.16)	*60.2%*	52.9%	55.9%
Capital Punishment (figure 4.17)	*52.0%*	48.7%	44.2%
Marijuana Legalization (figure 4.18)	46.7%	45.5%	*47.6%*
Abortion (figure 4.19)	*49.8%*	49.7%	*49.8%*

Note: Highest value for each item in italics.

and should not be lightly recast as different cultures. The IDMP should claim no more than that the two self-identified racial groups are not identical.

A final point about the data. The supporter of *Race as Culture* could argue that blacks and whites come from different cultures, but the survey items on the GSS do not capture it. As with all scientific undertakings, a healthy skepticism is appropriate. But this can be pushed too far and become a non-falsifiable shield from facts that don't conform to one's ideology. It is not an especially scientific attitude to claim that blacks and whites have different cultures but it's simply not possible in principle to measure or quantify it. That is simultaneously making an empirical claim while declaring one's unwillingness to consider empirical data. Criticisms of the above analysis should point to specific problems with the items chosen and perhaps some suggestions for better cultural indicators. Absent this, it might be more reasonable to conclude that group differences that are too difficult to find are perhaps an insufficient basis for cultural boundaries.

SUMMARY AND CONCLUSION

The tenet for *Race as Culture* seems plausible on the surface only because of ambiguities in the meanings of both *race* and *culture*. By resolving these ambiguities, I suggest four possible interpretations for the claim of *Race as Culture*:

- Interpretation i: Members of *objectively* different races have *largely non-overlapping* distributions for *many* cultural traits (Objective-Strong).
- Interpretation ii: Members of *objectively* different races have *partially distinct* distributions for *at least a few* cultural traits (Objective-Weak).
- Interpretation iii: Members of different *self-identified* races have *largely non-overlapping* distributions for *many* cultural traits (Subjective-Strong).
- Interpretation iv: Members of different *self-identified* races have *partially distinct* distributions for *at least a few* cultural traits (Subjective-Weak).

Two arguments were made against the tenet that blacks and whites represent different cultures. First, the ontological critique called for abandoning the notion of objective race and adopting a subjective standard—race is nothing more than self-identification. The ontological critique is an assertion of biological colorblindness. Race is not, as we now understand genetics, objectively real. As a social construct it is only what we pretend it is. In a fundamental sense, therefore, it is meaningless to assert that races have different cultures because race does not exist. The empirical critique, on the other hand, provisionally accepts the notion of race as a self-identification and then goes on to consider the evidence for cultural differences between blacks and whites. The empirical data considered above reject any strong claim for distinctive black and white cultures; on every trait considered the distributions for blacks and whites largely overlapped.

A relationship between the various interpretations of *Race as Culture* and the two critiques is presented in a 2×2 format in table 4.2. The ontological critique applies whenever the someone speaks of race as an objective phenomenon. This covers the top row in table 4.2, interpretations i and ii. The IDMP supporter must either rebut the ontological critique by establishing some objective basis for race or must accept race as no more than self-identification and move to interpretations iii and iv in the bottom row. The empirical critique grants this subjective notion of race and considers the degree to which cultural traits overlap. The strong version, where there are many largely non-overlapping traits, is completely rejected by the data. Taken together the ontological critique forces the notion of *Race as Culture* to the bottom row and the empirical critique forces it into the right column, that is, into interpretation iv. What remains of the tenet for *Race as Culture* is the (extremely) weak statement that self-identified blacks and whites are not identical on all beliefs and practices. This does not provide much of a foundation to promote the notion of *Race as Culture*.

The claim for *Race as Culture* is the first of the two cultural tenets that I critique from a leftist, existential-sociological standpoint. It is not simply that the Identity, Diversity, and Multiculturalism Program wants us to view *Race as Culture* but it further asks us to celebrate those race-cultures as well. In the next chapter, I will argue that the leftist position demands a more nuanced stance, requiring praise or criticism depending on the cultural trait.

Table 4.2. Relationship between Interpretations of Race as Culture and Type of Critique.

		Distributions of Cultural Traits	
		Many Largely Non-Overlapping Traits (Strong Version)	Few Partially Distinct Traits (Weak Version)
Meaning of Race	Objective	Interpretation i False due to Ontological Critique	Interpretation ii False due to Ontological Critique
	Subjective	Interpretation iii False due to Empirical Critique	Interpretation iv Valid claim, but of limited significance

NOTES

1. The school of existential sociology does not have a universally accepted set of principles (nor does existentialism, for that matter) but I follow the approach laid out in Peter Berger and Thomas Luckmann (1967), *The Social Construction of Reality: A Treatise in the Sociology of Knowledge* and Peter Berger (1963), *Invitation to Sociology*.

2. Previous chapters discussed the ways in which racist inequality is perpetuated. None of the contemporary mechanisms requires the existence of legal racial categories. We could say that the neoliberal state is in the business of enforcing economic inequality, not racial identities. The legal-economic system produces racial consequences but this is not the same as enforcing racial categories.

3. Here is how the U.S. Census Bureau answers the question, *What is Race?*, on its website: "The racial categories included in the census questionnaire generally reflect a social definition of race recognized in this country and not an attempt to define race biologically, anthropologically, or genetically. In addition, it is recognized that the categories of the race item include racial and national origin or sociocultural groups. People may choose to report more than one race to indicate their racial mixture, such as 'American Indian' and 'White.' People who identify their origin as Hispanic, Latino, or Spanish may be of any race." Beginning with the 2000 Census respondents were allowed to identify as having more than one race and in the 2010 Census 15 racial categories were provided, with space to write-in a *Native American tribe*, *Other Asian*, *Other Pacific Islander*, or *Some other race*. The quantitative explosion is an indication of the conceptual implosion.

4. Those who want to deconstruct the concept might respond with the *human race* whenever faced with such a question, although some care must be taken. A student who did this in a philosophy class reported to me that he was sternly corrected by the professor, who otherwise spent much of her time teaching her students to critically analyze human-made constructs and to adopt a universal humanism.

5. Over time both groups have become more accepting of homosexuality and we might expect that numbers will continue to move in this direction and thereby converge to some degree. For example, in 1973 only 4.5 percent of blacks and 12.2 percent of whites said that homosexuality was "not wrong at all." At the other extreme 84.2 percent of blacks and 70.7 percent of whites said it was "always wrong." We have witnessed remarkable improvement among both blacks and whites over a mere four decades.

Chapter Five

A Leftist Critique of Culture as Virtue

In this chapter I critique the fourth and final tenet of the Identity, Diversity, and Multiculturalism Program (IDMP), *Culture as Virtue*, which is the belief that cultures should be respected and celebrated. This is related to the critique of *Culture as Virtue* just considered in chapter 4, as both involve the cultural side of the program. The critique of *Culture as Virtue* is, however, independent of the critique of *Race as Culture*. In chapter 4, I offered ontological and empirical critiques of the notion of *Race as Culture*. Here I will argue that culture itself is a problem, regardless of whatever relationship it might have with race or any other phenomena. In other words, even if the reader still believes that blacks and whites come from distinct cultures, I will argue that leftists ought not blithely respect or celebrate either of those race-based cultures.

Yet I do not assert that culture *in toto* is bad. Rejecting *Culture as Virtue* is not tantamount to claiming *Culture as Vice*, which are the extremes on a continuum. I maintain that Multiculturalists position themselves on one extreme while leftists should fall somewhere in the middle. Culture is the medium through which humans create a social existence. I have suggested that the most important element of culture is language and I make no criticism of language in general or of any specific language. As the set of beliefs (and practices) that distinguishes a group, I argue that culture will have some good and some bad elements, and some leftist and some right-wing ones. To a certain extent my critique entails a rejection of cultural relativism, a viewpoint largely accepted by Multiculturalists, but the repudiation is not as direct as may initially be supposed. Cultural relativism, a foundational idea in anthropology, asserts that a culture can be evaluated only by the values of that culture. Loosely we might say that criticism of one culture made from the standpoint of some other culture lacks objectivity. Yet even cultural relativism does not prohibit members of a culture from criticizing their own culture, and this is closer to my task. I intend to criticize—as a participant—some parts of American culture. I argued in chapter 4 that blacks and whites are part of the same culture. Together we can criticize our common set of beliefs from within. Each of us, as a matter of proper intellectual health and wellness, should perform a cultural self-examination. Only if everything turns out to be working properly would a celebration of our cultural health be in order. Otherwise some adjustments to our daily cultural routine would be advisable.

I make two related but distinct critiques of *Culture as Virtue*. First, many elements of culture directly conflict with the leftist principles of political liberty, economic equality, and existential freedom, all of which I have previously connected with the Enlightenment assumptions of moral equality and human reason. Many elements of culture are conservative or neoliberal. Other beliefs are simply unreasonable, that is, they cannot be supported by logic or evidence. Much of American culture is ill-founded and right-wing. An inventory of some of these elements I refer to as the *substantive critique* of *Culture as Virtue*. Second, the processes that generate much cultural "knowledge" are flawed because they rely on tradition or unqualified authority. Due to socialization and propaganda many of the beliefs in a culture will support the status quo and the interests of the powerful. I call this the *epistemological critique* of *Culture as Virtue*. After making these critiques, I conclude with an outline of a leftist approach to culture. In short, a commitment to leftist principles demands that we engage and often fight to change—not celebrate—our culture.

THE SUBSTANTIVE CRITIQUE OF CULTURE AS VIRTUE

By adopting a leftist standpoint, we can legitimately criticize several elements of our culture. Any belief that is clearly contradicted by empirical, scientific evidence can be criticized. After all, the modern Left comes out of the Age of Reason.[1] Science is not simply one among a number of equally plausible perspectives; empiricism does indeed hold a privileged epistemological position for certain types of questions. Note that this does not entail a naïve faith in the institution of science. Furthermore, leftist beliefs go beyond those that can be scientifically substantiated to include our values and principles, including a commitment to the notions of political liberty and economic equality. The existentialist perspective adds a commitment to human freedom and a condemnation of bad faith.

To organize the discussion, I put the cultural objects of leftist criticism into three categories: the *unreasonable*, the *conservative*, and the *neoliberal*.

Unreasonable beliefs are scientifically wrong. *Conservative* beliefs are those justified by reference to tradition and usually involve what are often referred to as social or cultural issues. *Neoliberal* beliefs are those that elevate the "free market" above equality. While I will refer to anti-scientific beliefs as wrong, I will simply label conservative and neoliberal values as non-leftist. For example, the belief in corporate personhood is not rejected as a false-hood—it is, after all, a non-empirical judgment—but it nonetheless violates leftist values because it threatens equality.

As with the critique of *Race as Culture* in the previous chapter, I turn again to the General Social Survey (GSS) for the substantive critique of *Culture as Virtue*. A complete catalog of all the unreasonable, conservative, and neoliberal beliefs in American culture would be impossible but I take a few instances from each category. The objective is to demonstrate that cultural beliefs in general do not deserve to be respected, much less celebrated, on the Left.

Unreasonable Beliefs

In order to call another belief "unreasonable" we must be quite confident that our own understanding of the matter is correct. This is a high, but not insurmountable, bar to cross. the safest approach is to identify those areas where the scientific approach has produced a strong consensus. As discussed in more detail below, science is a process, so no answer is ever definitive. Nonetheless, seeking out scientific consensus is the best we can ever do at any particular moment in time. When other types of knowledge are privileged over science, we can confidently find fault. I suggest, for example, that the high degree of religious faith relative to scientific understanding is one cultural source of ignorance.

The GSS measured the conflict between science and religion by asking respondents to agree or disagree with the following statement:

We trust too much in science and not enough in religious faith.

The responses were as follows:

- 6.8 percent—Strongly Agree
- 24.8 percent—Agree
- 25.0 percent—Not Agree/Disagree
- 31.3 percent—Disagree
- 12.2 percent—Strongly Disagree

While 31 percent of respondents disagreed with this statement, only 12 percent strongly disagreed. Nearly one-third either agreed or strongly agreed that we need more trust in religious faith and one-quarter could not form an opinion. A large proportion of Americans would prefer less reason in our affairs. An explicit rejection of Enlightenment values.

A specific instance of an unreasonable religious belief is creationism, that is, the rejection of evolution as the explanation for the origin of the species. In 2004 the GSS used the following question:

> After I read off three statements, please tell me which one comes closest to your views about the origin and development of man.

The responses:

- 42.5 percent—God created man pretty much in his present form at one time within the last 10,000 years.
- 12.2 percent—Man has developed over millions of years from less advanced forms of life. God had no part in this process.
- 41.6 percent—Man has developed over millions of years from less advanced forms of life, but God guided this process, including man's creation.
- 3.7 percent—Other

The most common response not only supports creationism but puts it within the last 10,000 years, thereby denying the fossil record for hominids stretching back millions of years. The softer creationist position, slightly less popular than the absurd version, asserts that creation occurred millions of years ago and that evolution was guided by God. Only 12 percent of Americans are able to do without the God Hypothesis. Survey data are subject to certain biases and I suspect that many who claim to deny evolution are insincere and do in fact secretly believe in some type of Darwinian explanation. Yet even if this suspicion is correct it would hardly help the notion of *Culture as Virtue* because it would mean that the socially appropriate response for many Americans is to lie in order to appear to be more ignorant than they actually are. On the grounds of reason, we can criticize culture regardless of whether the ignorance is genuine or feigned.

Climate change is potentially an existential threat to the species. The actions we take in response to it will be influenced by our understanding of the phenomenon. As a scientific issue, climate change is trickier than most because it is based on modeling and predictions about the future. We must rely upon theoretically derived probability distributions. Nonetheless, a large majority in the relevant scientific community has predicted dangerous con-sequences—coastal flooding, drought, more intense storms, flooding—from our current trajectory. In 2010 the GSS asked,

In general, do you think that a rise in the world's temperature caused by climate change is . . .

With the responses:

- 21.1 percent—Extremely dangerous for the environment
- 27.3 percent—Very dangerous
- 30.7 percent—Somewhat dangerous
- 13.9 percent—Not very dangerous
- 7.0 percent—Not dangerous at all for the environment

Perhaps the findings here are not completely gloomy; only 20 percent re-sponded that the temperature increase is not very dangerous or not dangerous at all. On the other hand, an additional 31 percent believed it to be merely somewhat dangerous. Thus less than a majority took the position that climate change is extremely or very dangerous, the position that seems to conform best to our current scientific predictions.

It would be possible to chart other examples, like the belief in astrology or geocentrism (as opposed to heliocentrism) or opposition to vaccination, but it should be obvious to any leftist observer that American culture contains many beliefs that are simply wrong. Would supporters of the IDMP deny it? Igno-rance deserves no celebration. There is no need to belabor the point because there are structural reasons for our ignorance and it smacks of speaking down and blaming the victim. Furthermore, it is equally true that American culture contains elements worthy of respect. Most people understand that the earth revolves around the sun and know that smoking causes cancer. Some people understand quantum mechanics and can translate ancient Greek. Of course, these are not uniquely American beliefs, so perhaps we should simply cele-brate and adopt the good ideas of the human species, wherever they originate. My point is not to beat up on the ignorant but rather to assert that we must be discriminating adopters of different beliefs and not celebrants of an entire culture. Naturally this entails a rejection of the notion of cultural appropria-tion, a logically and empirically dubious stance. The diffusion and adoption of beliefs and practices, with or without modification, has been feature of hu-man cultures throughout recorded history and, presumably, was a feature of life going back into prehistory for as long as different tribes were in contact.

Conservative Beliefs

I define conservatives as those who favor a traditional set of values and who are often willing to use coercive powers to promote them. Traditional values, however, are socially constructed in the here and now and need not have any connection to historical facts. Traditionalists face the further complication of choosing the correct distance in time that we must go back. Values were not static in the past and two competing values could both be justified on the grounds of tradition. For example, the conservative obsession with abortion is relatively recent.[2] For most of its long history even the Catholic Church was relatively unconcerned with it. That quintessentially traditional army of the Spartans institutionalized homosexuality. Polygamy has ancient roots. For blacks in the U.S., Christianity largely comes from the time of slavery, as many black Muslims point out. A deeper tradition—thus more authentic?—could be found in the religions, including Islam, practiced in western Africa prior to the slave trade. For that matter Christianity and Islam are predated by many large, organized religions and countless smaller, spiritual traditions over the prior millennia of human culture.

Despite the impossibility of finding one true tradition, I will review a few indicators of constructed conservatism today: abortion, homosexuality, and capital punishment. The question for abortion was worded as follows:

Please tell me whether or not you think it should be possible for a pregnant woman to obtain a legal abortion if the woman wants it for any reason?

The responses:

- 46.2 percent—Yes
- 53.8 percent—No

A slight majority opposes the right to abortion in this case. This particular context—a woman wants it for *any* reason—is the most permissive wording, and thus tends to get the lowest levels of support. Nonetheless, the leftist position is support for abortion in exactly this context.

Leftists also support a full set of rights for consenting adults to engage in sexual relations. The survey question on homosexuality was phrased,

What about sexual relations between two adults of the same sex—do you think it is always wrong, almost always wrong, wrong only sometimes, or not wrong at all?

The responses:

- 38.8 percent—Always wrong
- 3.6 percent—Almost always wrong
- 5.6 percent—Wrong only sometimes
- 52.0 percent—Not wrong at all

In 2016 American society was roughly evenly split between those who believed homosexuality is wrong, at least some of the time, and those who do not believe it to be wrong at all. Hostility to the rights of gays and to the rights of women to obtain an abortion are reasonable indicators of conservatism. In both cases, progressives must find fault with American culture.

A tough-on-crime stance is another good measure of conservatism, and there is nothing tougher than the death penalty. The GSS item was the following:

Do you favor or oppose the death penalty for persons convicted of murder?

The responses:

- 60.4 percent—Favor
- 39.6 percent—Oppose

A large majority still favors giving the state its most lethal expression of violence. The opinions on abortion, homosexuality, and the death penalty show substantial backing for conservative beliefs but we could tap into an even more foundational belief by directly examining the support for religious over secular authority. There is no ideal measure but as an approximation in 1991 the GSS asked respondents to agree or disagree with the following statement:

Right and wrong should be based on God's laws.

The responses:

- 28.8 percent—Strongly Agree
- 28.3 percent—Agree
- 21.3 percent—Not Agree/Disagree
- 12.5 percent—Disagree
- 8.6 percent—Strongly Disagree

Over half the population agreed or strongly agreed while only around one-fifth disagreed or strongly disagreed. A leftist might hope that many of those who agreed with the statement do not actually support some type of Christian theocracy in which the Bible becomes a legal document but even under an optimistic interpretation the data suggest widespread conservative, religious thinking.

We can get a good sense of how far people are willing to go to promote traditional beliefs by measuring the support for prayer in school. The GSS asks respondents the following:

The United States Supreme Court has ruled that no state or local government may require the reading of the Lord's Prayer or Bible verses in public schools. What are your views on this—do you approve or disapprove of the court ruling?

The responses:

- 41.6 percent—Approve
- 58.4 percent—Disapprove

The majority disapproved of the legal decision prohibiting prayer in school and therefore believed that local governments should have the power to re-quire students to recite the Lord's Prayer or a Bible verse. The wish to legally impose religious values is a conservative cultural trait, obviously unworthy of celebration.

I conclude this extremely brief audit of conservative beliefs by examin-ing attitudes toward race itself. Historically, a conservative view is to regard blacks as innately inferior to whites. The GSS measures this belief by asking the following:

On the average (negroes/blacks/African-Americans) have worse jobs, income, and housing than white people. Do you think these differences are because most (negroes/blacks/African-Americans) have less in-born ability to learn?

The responses:

- 8.3 percent—Yes
- 91.7 percent—No

Relatively few Americans hold the conservative opinion that blacks are inferior, although we might suspect that some who denied this belief did not respond honestly. Still, there has been progress, and perhaps the improvement deserves some measure of celebration. In 1977, the first year the GSS used this item, around one-quarter of Americans believed that blacks had less in-born ability.

Overall, the evidence indicates that American society has many conservative elements. It is strongly religious and many Americans object to abortion and homosexuality. While conservative positions do not always predominate they are certainly common. We could, of course, find many more conservative views but these few examples should suggest that a critical, not a celebratory, stance toward culture is warranted. As further evidence I next consider some neoliberal elements of American culture.

Neoliberal Beliefs

Both conservative and neoliberal beliefs are considered right-wing even though they have distinct logical foundations. Neoliberals are concerned not with the promotion of traditional values but rather of a relatively new societal model: "free-market" capitalism. Indeed, the latter can often undermine the former. Neoliberals typically downplay inequality and they certainly reject the Rawlsian principles of justice. At the libertarian extreme, whatever outcome the capitalist economy produces is taken as optimal, or at least as an outcome that could not be improved upon by state action. State regulations, except for the coercive elements required to maintain capitalist property rights, are typically disapproved. The GSS has several good indicators of neoliberal beliefs.

Whereas the Difference Principle uses the well-being of the least advantaged group as the standard by which economic policies should be designed, neoliberals are not terribly concerned with the situation of the poor. The GSS item that best captures this attitude is the following:

> Some people think that the government in Washington should do everything possible to improve the standard of living of all poor Americans; they are at point 1 on this card. Other people think it is not the government's responsibility, and that each person should take care of himself; they are at point 5. Where would you place yourself on this scale, or haven't you made up your mind on this?

The responses:

- 18.3 percent—1: Government responsibility
- 14.9 percent—2
- 42.5 percent—3
- 15.2 percent—4
- 9.1 percent—5: Not government responsibility

Although more take the leftist position (18 percent) than the neoliberal (9 percent), the largest segment agrees with both. On this issue it seems that confusion is the norm, a cultural situation that certainly benefits the interests of the powerful, and an epistemological point I explore later.

An item on the 1993 survey directly examined support for inequality. Respondents were asked to agree or disagree with the statement:

> People should be allowed to accumulate as much wealth as they can even if some make millions while others live in poverty.

The responses:

- 11.2 percent—Strongly Agree
- 46.4 percent—Agree
- 10.9 percent—Neither Agree nor Disagree
- 26.1 percent—Disagree
- 5.4 percent—Strongly Disagree

A solid majority (58 percent) either agreed or strongly agreed, taking the neoliberal position, while only 5 percent strongly disagreed with the notion of unlimited wealth amid poverty. Perhaps it was simply due to the heady days of the internet bubble economy, and we might hope for different responses now. Even if so, it would indicate the susceptibility of many Americans to an irrational capitalistic exuberance.

The GSS measures opinions regarding the government's role in healthcare. The format follows the same pattern as the question regarding government help for the poor:

> In general, some people think that it is the responsibility of the government in Washington to see to it that people have help in paying for doctors and hospital bills; they are at point 1. Others think that these matters are not the responsibility of the federal government and that people should take care of these things themselves; they are at point 5. Where would you place yourself on this scale, or haven't you made up your mind on this?

The responses:

- 31.0 percent—1: Government should help
- 19.2 percent—2
- 31.6 percent—3
- 10.0 percent—4
- 8.2 percent—5: Individuals take care of self

Unlike assistance for the poor, government help with medical expenses finds much more support. It is possible that the change in opinion reflects a large dose of self-interest; almost everybody has been affected by rapidly rising healthcare costs while a smaller percentage of respondents fall under the poverty line.

In addition to limited redistribution and direct help for the poor, the neoliberal position calls for limited state regulation of business organizations. The GSS item on this issue:

Here are some things the government might do for the economy. Circle one number for each action to show whether you are in favor of it or against it: Less government regulation of business.

The responses:

- 17.4 percent—Strongly in Favor
- 34.7 percent—In Favor
- 29.4 percent—Neither
- 14.1 percent—Against
- 4.4 percent—Strongly Against

Note that the numbers show the degree of support for *less* regulation. The neoliberal responses are those in favor or strongly in favor, and these represent a majority at 52 percent. Additionally, more than a quarter seemingly support the status quo, which is tantamount to a neoliberal position given the comparatively weak regulation of the U.S. economy.

In the private sector, given the absence of effective state regulation of the market, the only real threat to capitalist interests is an organized labor force. Thus neoliberals seem to be even more hostile toward unions than toward the poor, who are effectively powerless in the American political-economy. In 2014 the GSS asked respondents to agree or disagree with the following statement:

Workers need strong trade unions to protect their interests.

The responses:

- 10.0 percent—Strongly Agree
- 37.8 percent—Agree
- 41.6 percent—Disagree
- 10.5 percent—Strongly Disagree

The country is fairly evenly split but a majority (52 percent) took the neoliberal position by disagreeing or strongly disagreeing with the need for strong unions. Only 10 percent took the leftist stance of strongly agreeing with the need for unions.

To summarize, the substantive critique of *Culture as Virtue* claims—and empirically demonstrates—that many beliefs are wrong, conservative, or, as we have just seen, neoliberal. These beliefs deserve explicit criticism instead of respect, praise, or even accommodating silence. Any celebration of culture that is unqualified and unsophisticated is unacceptable. In the next section, we turn to the epistemological critique to argue that the flaws in culture are not random or accidental but instead are the result of systematic processes that generate cultural "knowledge." After that discussion I expand the argument by offering an explicitly leftist orientation to one's culture.

THE EPISTEMOLOGICAL CRITIQUE OF CULTURE AS VIRTUE

Epistemology is the branch of philosophy that studies the nature of knowledge. I refer to as *epistemological* a critique of the cultural mechanisms that produce objectionable beliefs like those discussed above. Epistemologists refer to three broad categories of knowledge, or more precisely, to three justifications of knowledge. They are the reasons we come to believe something to be true. First is traditional knowledge, something already identified with conservatism. Second, many beliefs are justified by claiming support from an authority. Finally, knowledge can be produced by scientific methods, broadly understood. Tradition, authority, and science are not mutually exclusive and I consider some of the combinations below. Neither are they exhaustive; other bases for knowledge can be found. Nonetheless a brief review of these three categories will clarify some of the systematic problems with much cultural knowledge. While the epistemological critique has a different focus, it complements the previous substantive critique and advances the same conclusion: cultural beliefs should not in general be respected or celebrated because many of the mechanisms that produce cultural knowledge can be challenged from a leftist standpoint.

Many beliefs are justified on the grounds of tradition. The very fact that a belief or practice existed for a long time persuades some people that it should continue to exist. The factual, historical basis for the belief need not be examined by the contemporary believer and would probably be irrelevant in any case. It might be taken for granted that these cultural customs have always been true or morally correct. In any case, even if traditions may have been reasonable for their time, we should not assume the practices should continue given changes in environmental, political, economic, and other cultural conditions. Established practices, however, seem to have an inertia of their own, which carries them along even after the cessation of any reasonable justification. Perhaps the Old Testament injunctions against certain types of food made sense prior to modern techniques of sterilization and preservation. On the other hand, traditional beliefs like misogyny or homophobia never had morally valid foundations but still continue to exist simply because they somehow became established.

I do not assert that traditional knowledge is necessarily wrong and should automatically be rejected. Much human knowledge was obtained by trial and error over countless generations, the cultural analog to natural selection in biology. It is likely that most hunting, gathering, and early farming techniques were discovered and refined by this process. The very fact that they were successful does give considerable backing to these traditions. Here there is no conflict between tradition and science: tradition simply came across a good result before science could offer a physical, perhaps microscopic, explanation.[3] Even today we accept that certain things may work according to some functional criteria or causal mechanisms that we don't exactly understand. A leftist approach toward tradition presumes neither validity nor invalidity but rather maintains that tradition, by itself, is an insufficient or incomplete argument. Some additional basis can reasonably be sought.

The second of the main justifications of knowledge, authority, refers to those whose opinions are held in esteem, that is, those individuals who have willing followers. As such, authority is not intrinsically bad. Some people deserve to be esteemed in certain contexts. Leonhard Euler was an authority in mathematics. Richard Feynman was an authority in physics. We may accept as valid a theorem by Euler even though we may not be able to follow all the steps of the proof. We may accept Feynman's model of the subatomic world even though a full understanding goes beyond our reach.

At the same time, however, we should challenge the validity of knowledge that comes from *unqualified* authority. The difficulty, of course, is sorting out the qualified from the unqualified. In many cases we might accept that there is no reasonable way to adjudicate. There are some questions that have competing answers from seemingly equally qualified authorities. If so, a wait-and-see position might be the most reasonable. But there are other questions where we can be so confident in our answer that we can consider others to be wrong. Take, for example, a specific empirical question: how old is the earth? The answer according to geologists is about 4.5 billion (4,500,000,000) years. The answer according to some who take the Old Testament literally is about 6,000 years. We accept the first number, allowing for slight refinements up or down as theory and technique change, and confidently pronounce the second number as absurdly wrong: it misses the mark by a factor of a million.

Assuming the reader is neither geologist nor theologian, both numbers come to us from some outside authority. One a scientific authority, the other religious. What makes the former more valid than the latter? Science, the third leading justification of knowledge, should be seen not as a body of facts but rather as a process, indeed as a social or cultural process (one worthy of qualified celebration). The main advantage of science over other ways of knowing is that it uses open, replicable methods. A scientific finding is, above all, the outcome of some technique or method. The technique used by one scientist to estimate the age of the planet is available to other scientists. Anybody else (with a mass spectrometer, say) could replicate the method and should come up with a similar finding. If the findings do not agree then we should be cautious in believing either result. If a great many replications all cluster in the same area, then we have reasonable confidence in the result.

Thus the finding of the earth to be 4.5 billion years old comes from re-peated radiometric dating techniques, which measures the proportion of uranium that has decayed into lead. It is possible that even older rocks will be found and the age may be adjusted upward. It is even possible that the technique somehow overestimates the age and will need to be revised down-ward. But such corrections should not be seen as a problem with science but rather as a strength: given open, replicable methods science has a built-in tendency to catch errors, at least in the long run. Thus, at its essence, science is a process that has the best chance of catching mistakes; any particular sci-entific *fact* is our best understanding at any moment in time. If we as outside observers have reasonable confidence that the question of the age of the earth has been studied by geologists who published their open methods, then we can consider our knowledge to come from a qualified authority.[4]

The belief that the earth is only 6,000 years old, on the other hand, lacks a reasonable foundation. The number originally comes from Archbishop James Ussher who, in the seventeenth century, attempted to work backwards from dates and events in the Bible. But why should we trust the biblical account of creation? It gives no method by which we could corroborate the story. It has no mechanism to catch errors. If one of our Iron Age ancestors made a mistake (how could he have done otherwise?) or simply made something up while writing a story that ended up in the Bible then we are stuck with it. It depends upon a perfectly circular argument: The Bible is true because the Bible says it is true.

The age of the earth is admittedly a relatively easy case of qualified versus unqualified authority. In general, I do not pretend that we can answer all of our questions. Furthermore, we cannot even be completely confident in any single answer. My main objective is simply to suggest a leftist stance toward knowledge: of ourselves and of others we should demand reasons for beliefs.

Reasons that are—in a deep sense of the word—reasonable. We would seek justifications built upon logic and, whenever available, empirical evidence. Furthermore, the search for knowledge is a social undertaking; we can reason together. Ultimately the epistemological critique is less about exposing or mocking creationists and more about challenging the cultural norms and social institutions that impede collective reasoning.

I would extend this intellectual approach to include even questions of morality. Though they lack an empirical basis they can still be subjected to a critique on the grounds of reason and our leftist principles. As leftists we should make explicit our assumptions, like moral equality among individuals and existential freedom, and we should reason together about what sort of society that would require. We challenge ourselves as we make the same demands of others. What, for example, are the assumptions of Christianity, Judaism, Islam, and so on? Does the Bible or the Koran assume that all individuals have equal moral worth? Do they attempt to work out the implications of that assumption in everyday life? Clearly they do not. Admittedly these texts are internally inconsistent but one can easily find support for hierarchy and inequality based upon tribe, race, and gender. Such texts have great value as historical documents but they are quite limited as contemporary moral philosophies.

The same critical stance applies to secular and right-wing philosophies like libertarianism. The defining characteristic is the assertion of private property as the most important right.[5] According to libertarians this right should have almost unlimited scope and should be all but immune to trade-offs with any other desiderata. Libertarianism may be more reasonable in a strictly logical sense than religious fundamentalism but we reject it nonetheless because, for starters, it has no concern for equality of opportunity, disregards the threat to freedom and democracy from concentrated wealth, and is oblivious to ecological dangers.

But I do not want to get sidetracked here into a leftist critique of the Right. My concern is with the Identity, Diversity, and Multiculturalism Program and the liberals, leftists, and radicals who embrace it. The problem with the Program is that its tenet of *Culture as Virtue* renders it almost incapable of discriminating among the different cultural mechanisms that produce knowledge. Instead we need more reasoned debate between the Left, the libertarian Right, and the religious Right. What's more, because the beliefs of the libertarian and the religious conservative have certain systematic cultural advantages because of their value to the elite, the Left must work harder to get its ideas a fair hearing. Supporters of Multiculturalism not only abdicate the fight but their celebration of culture actually discourages the challenging of beliefs and thereby strengthens the status quo, one with a great many conservative and neoliberal beliefs.

Cultural knowledge is produced in many ways but next I consider the two that give the greatest advantage to the Right over the Left: socialization and propaganda. Socialization is the main transmitter of traditional knowledge, much of which is conservative. Propaganda disseminates right-wing ideology, for the most part neoliberal.

Socialization into Traditional Beliefs

Primary socialization includes all the ways in which children learn what is appropriate in their culture.[6] Almost every time parents interact with their children some type of cultural training takes place. The instruction first imparts and then subsequently requires language. Primary socialization is the main conveyer of traditional knowledge including, as a leading case, religion. Hence we see a very high correspondence in religious affiliation between parent and offspring. Many other beliefs are also successfully but not perfectly reproduced from parent to offspring. As surveyed in the substantive critique above, many of these beliefs are politically or philosophically conservative, including opposition to gay marriage and abortion, and support for prayer in school. Or the tendencies toward militarism, tribalism, and nationalism. Some traditions are both conservative and quite wrong, such as creation myths taken as literal truth.

As a mechanism for generating cultural traits, primary socialization has several strengths. First, the child may not be exposed to any other ideas or ways of living. The strongest traditional beliefs are those which are so firmly implanted that they need no explicit justification because they are never consciously questioned. And if a challenge were to be brought the defense would probably sound something like, "How could it be otherwise?" or "That's just the way things are!" Here I speak of a hegemonic cultural position or of the world completely taken for granted. Second, primary socialization usually occurs in the context of a strong emotional bond between parent and child. The attachment gives the ideas of the parent greater valence. The ways of the stranger, if encountered, would typically carry less weight. Finally, the ideas of the parents have both primacy—they were the first implanted—and frequency—they were heard more often—over any alternatives.

The beliefs and practices learned in primary socialization can, of course, be challenged later during adulthood but they have the upper hand. They must be dislodged from their well-defended positions. Again consider language. It is possible to learn another language later in life but it is uncommon for the new language to attain the level of naturalness held by the first. Religious conversion is more common but even in this case only a relatively few will adopt an entirely new pantheon. In addition to these two leading examples are a host of other habits and mannerisms that would be nearly impossible to reject because they are largely subconscious. Primary socialization explains how similar cultural traits can persist across the generations.

Notwithstanding the functional advantages of primary socialization, the leftist position is that traditional beliefs should be challenged, certainly by the time the child reaches the age of reason. Leftists seek to encourage a cultural stance whereby beliefs need reasonable reasons. "Because my parents said so," at least after a certain age, is no longer a reasonable response. In this regard the Left and the IDMP are clearly at odds. On leftist grounds one cannot adopt a reflexive defense of tradition, the traits imparted via primary socialization. The believer in *Culture as Virtue* presumes that familial beliefs are somehow more *authentic*, that they correspond to one's true self. This reflects a biological essentialism or tribalism incompatible with a leftist standpoint. Traditional beliefs may be stronger as a social-psychological fact but this is no cause for celebration. The accident of one's birth should bring no immunity from scrutiny.

Right-Wing Propaganda

The second cultural mechanism I criticize from a leftist standpoint is propaganda, by which I mean an ideology that is intentionally disseminated. An ideology is a set of beliefs that would benefit the interests of a certain group were the beliefs to be widely adopted in society. Propaganda, therefore, is the deliberate propagation of ideas intended to steer behavior in a certain direction. Neither propaganda nor ideology is necessarily right-wing or even bad. We may sincerely believe our cause is just and we may have good reasons for doing so. It is appropriate that culture is the arena for these competing worldviews. One problem with propaganda in the U.S. is that the superior economic resources of conservatives and especially neoliberals give their beliefs a systematic advantage in the cultural fray. Their ideas attract many adherents not because they are more reasonable but instead because leftist ideas have been systematically marginalized.

Humans have a remarkable capacity to absorb new ideas yet in order to learn we must first be exposed to information. Propaganda is an important source of secondary socialization, the learning of culture that occurs after the primary socialization of childhood, but the divisions between family and society are not, of course, sharp. In all cases, individual knowledge is largely socially mediated. We talk to others, we observe others, we read what others have written. It follows that ideas with greater circulation are more likely to be widely held. To some extent this flow of cultural information is determined by countless micro-level interactions, defying any large-scale social manipulation.

At the same time, however, powerful actors are able to significantly impact the flow of information, providing a material basis for the creation and dissemination of ideas. Resources can be converted into beliefs in the culture in much the same way that resources can be converted into electoral success in the polity. Every word or image in television, radio, and print costs money and shapes our thinking. Advertising, as an obvious instance, is narrowly designed to create demand for a particular commodity but it will also strengthen a capitalistic, consumer culture more generally. Furthermore, advertising often reinforces social stereotypes and promotes a neoliberal ethos of individual responsible for macroeconomic problems. Upon repeated exposure to an ideology something is bound to stick, that is, to become ideas lodged in our heads.

Under typical social conditions the success of propaganda should vary according to the amount of resources put into the messaging. Individuals and organizations with more resources can disseminate more information than those with fewer resources. In a neoliberal capitalist society, a small number of extremely wealthy capitalists will have the most resources. These wealthy individuals have a tendency to be neoliberal and, to a lesser extent, conservative. In short, the epistemological critique of *Culture as Virtue* can be stated as follows: In the United States individuals on the Right, and the organizations they control, have more wealth and power than individuals and organizations on the Left; as a result, right-wing ideology has wider exposure throughout society. The problem with *Culture as Virtue* is that it encourages a celebration of a set of beliefs without sufficiently recognizing the systemic right-wing bias. Celebrating culture often means celebrating right-wing propaganda, even implicitly.

Organizations with a leftist ideology certainly exist and they do produce leftist propaganda, yet they have far fewer resources. Information competes with other information for the finite attention of our eyes and ears. Labor unions and environmental organizations simply cannot outspend their capitalist competitors or influence the state to the same degree.[7] Think tanks, agents paid to help create or spread an ideology agreeable to their funders, receive more money from wealthy individuals and corporations than from unions, environmentalists, or other leftists. With regard to the dissemination of that ideology, the most important entity is the corporate media, which today combine movies, television shows, and news reporting. While the corporate news media ostensibly cover "both sides of an issue" a critique of the fundamental problems of capitalism and inequality are almost completely avoided. There are few think tanks and no mainstream media companies that put out an ideology that would benefit the unemployed or the working poor. With limited resources they are excluded from much of the cultural arena. As a sad example, if we were to judge the relative importance based on the framing of the topic in the mainstream media, the rate of inheritance tax on millionaires and billionaires would be a bigger social problem than the number of children without healthcare. Those with money can distort a fair evaluation of a social issue and elevate their own interests.

The powerful not only widely disseminate their own worldview but they have a capacity to choke off information contrary to their interests. The publishing of leaked information detailing the misdeeds of the powerful is a case in point. The release by WikiLeaks of public documents—public in the sense that they were produced by public officials in public agencies presumably working for the public—was greeted with extreme hostility by many governments, including the Bush, Obama, and Trump administrations in the United States. But the attack on WikiLeaks and its founder, Julian Assange, was not limited to an official, governmental investigation. At the request of the U.S. government, financial intermediaries broke their contracts with WikiLeaks by removing the add-ons that allowed online donations. Eric Snowden faced similar hostility when he revealed documents detailing a massive domestic spying program by the National Security Agency. Chelsea Manning was imprisoned for seven years, much of it under cruel and degrading conditions, for revealing U.S. war crimes. In response to this threat to free speech, many journalists in the mainstream press sided with the government and editorialized against WikiLeaks, Snowden, and Manning.[8] Those in power do not simply seek to increase the flow of their own propaganda but also to impede the spread of contrary information.

Even when on the losing side, propaganda can play an obfuscatory role and thus buys precious time. Tobacco companies were able to inject enough uncertainty into the discourse on cancer research that even simple regulations were delayed. The fossil fuel industry performed a similar delaying campaign regarding greenhouse gas emissions and global climate change. In these cases, ideology ran directly into conflict with empirically verifiable data but nonetheless took advantage of science as a deliberative and deliberate social process. At some point the truth is bound to come out but billions of dollars in profit can be made in the interim—a very healthy return on the investment of a few PhDs, several politicians, and some advertising.

The epistemological critique asserts that resources can be converted into propaganda and propaganda into beliefs. Because the Right has more resources than the Left, right-wing beliefs have a systematic advantage in the culture. This is a fact that leftists should not celebrate. It is likely that the right-wing reader will dismiss this treatment of propaganda as some Marxist conspiracy theory. That's fine. My goal is not to persuade those on the Right. My approach is openly leftist. It is not the opinion of the conservative or the neoliberal that matters but rather that of the IDMP supporter who also identifies as a leftist. This reader must decide whether American culture is heavily influenced by right-wing propaganda. If so, a reconsideration of the tenet of *Culture as Virtue* seems to be in order.

A LEFTIST APPROACH TO CULTURE

I have made two separate but related critiques of *Culture as Virtue*. The substantive critique considered empirical examples of unreasonable, conservative, and neoliberal elements in our culture; the epistemological critique explored some of the cultural machinery that gives these right-wing beliefs a systematic advantage. Although elements of a leftist standpoint on culture were sprinkled throughout the critiques, a more complete picture can now be provided. I organize the discussion into two parts. First, I propose the means by which leftists might evaluate elements of their culture and, second, I discuss the ways in which leftists should engage their culture.

Evaluating Culture

I begin by clarifying a few concepts or, rather, dimensions of concepts. When evaluating specific elements of culture, it is important to keep in mind and to keep distinct three levels of treatment or stances: the *moral*, the *discursive*, and the *political*. First, the moral stance is an individual judgment or evaluation of a belief, behavior, or some other cultural element. Each of us can decide whether something is good or evil, right or wrong, and so on. We should approve or respect those elements we favorably evaluate and disapprove or disrespect those we negatively evaluate. The second stance is discursive, which refers to ways in which we talk about the objects of our moral evaluations. This ranges from positive to negative statements and includes as intermediate cases either silence or morally neutral language. It is at this level that we speak of praise, at one extreme, and criticism or condemnation, at the other. Discourse is meant in a broad sense to include what is considered political speech, for example, protests, vigils, and other nonviolent demonstrations. It can include instrumental attempts at persuasion as well as expressive displays of passion.

Finally, by political treatment I refer to physically coercive power in society. The notion of tolerance, a term used frequently by those in the Identity, Diversity, and Multiculturalism Program, belongs here at the political level. Tolerance as a doctrine originated in the late Middle Ages and early modern period as a political response to ostensibly religious disagreements, and implicated in wars, pogroms, torture, executions, and the like. The Thirty Years War (1618–1648) involved most of Europe, killing over one-quarter of the population in many regions. As a result of this catastrophe, the political elite in Europe widely embraced a limited version of a doctrine of religious tolerance, formally codified in the Treaty of Münster, part of the Peace of Westphalia (Straumann 2008). The treaty granted each head of state the right to decide the formal religion of its territory. Citizens outside the established church were permitted some freedom to worship and freedom from persecution. In its time this represented progress but nonetheless soon proved to be an inadequate solution. Sectarian divisions continued to generate civil unrest in many places in Europe and even civil war, as happened in England during the 1640s. It was with this backdrop that John Locke (1983) issued his call for a stronger version of religious toleration at the individual level, asserting that the state (the Magistrate) should have no coercive powers over matters of faith and religious affiliation.

> What Power can be given to the Magistrate for the suppression of an Idolatrous Church, which may not, in time and space, be made use of to the ruine of an Orthodox one? For it must be remembered that the Civil Power is the same every where and the Religion of every Prince is Orthodox to himself. If therefore such a Power be granted unto the Civil Magistrate in Spirituals . . . he may extirpate, by Violence and Blood, the Religion which is there reputed Idolatrous; by the same another Magistrate, in some neighbouring Country, may oppress the Reformed Religion; and, in India, the Christian. (42–43)

The historical record for religious tolerance is, of course, spotty but criticism should be leveled against the violations, not against the doctrine itself. Like Locke, I will employ the concept of tolerance to mean nothing more than civil permission or coexistence. Tolerance does not require moral approval of the behavior and certainly not laudatory speech. "Covetousness, Uncharitableness, Idleness, and many other things are sins, by the consent of all men, which yet no man ever said were to be punished by the Magistrate" (Locke 1983, 44).

Thus, intolerance goes well beyond both disapproval at the moral level and condemnation as discursive treatment. I assume that in many cases there will be a close correspondence between the moral stance and the discursive treatment such that moral approval would lead to discursive praise, moral neutrality to discursive indifference, and moral disapproval to discursive criticism. But political intolerance is an extreme measure and must be used only when we can justify potentially violent measures to repress a behavior. Disapproval and condemnation are necessary but not sufficient for intolerance; criticism is logically compatible with either tolerance or intolerance. At the level of the state, intolerance is the criminalization of a behavior; at the institutional or organizational level, where the tools of legitimate violence are fortunately weaker although not insignificant, intolerance is expressed by various sanctions including suspension and expulsion; at the individual level, the intolerant person supports state and organizational punishment. Still, tolerance in the abstract is neither good nor bad. We should be intolerant, for example, of murder and rape. Some behaviors do indeed rise to a level that warrants repression.

In figure 5.1, I apply this schema of categorization to a few cases, which were selected to highlight crucial differences between the Left and the IDMP. The horizontal axis shows the moral stance, moving from greatest approval on the left to greatest disapproval on the right. The vertical axis shows the discursive treatment, ranging from praise to criticism. Inside the larger box in the bottom left we put everything deserving of tolerance, even those deserving disapproval and criticism. The smaller box, at the top right, would contain those elements that not only receive the greatest amount of disapproval and criticism but also rise to the level of formal repression, that is, intolerance. If we assume some rough sense of proportionality among the three dimensions, various elements should fall approximately on a 45° line from the bottom left to the top right: increasing disapproval leads to increasing criticism and, at some threshold corresponding to the highest levels of disapproval and criticism, crossing over into intolerance.

As figure 5.1 reveals, the contrast between the Left and the IDMP is quite stark. In general, the IDMP falls on the extremes of positivity or negativity, that is, moral approval and discursive praise, on the one hand, and political intolerance, on the other. As part of its tendency to celebrate culture, the Program respects and praises several sources of identity: race, religion, gender, ethnicity, and sexual orientation. At the same time, however, it is more intolerant than the Left for certain behaviors. Compare the examples in the *Intolerance* boxes. Both sides are, of course, intolerant of violence but there are some important differences. Many IDMP supporters believe that speech that they deem hurtful to the identities they respect can be punished, certainly within institutions like schools and businesses, and some even favor criminal penalties. Furthermore, many followers believe that violence motivated by hatred toward those identities should face punishment over and above that warranted by the physical violence itself. And it is not merely those who use "hate-speech" but even those who don't fully buy into the Program who could face sanctions. Tim Wise (2010) argues

[M]ost every college and university mission statement now includes reference to the value placed by the school on diversity, multicultural learning and the facilitation of global citizenship . . . With such missions in mind, schools would be well within their rights—and even ethical responsibilities—to evaluate appli-

The Left

Intolerance

Political Treatment

Violence

Tolerance

Criticism

Hate
Hate Speech
Racial Identity
Religion

Discursive
Treatment

Indifference

Gender Identity
Ethnic Identity
Sexual Orientation

Praise

Approval/   Neutrality   Disapproval/
Respect   Disrespect

Moral Stance

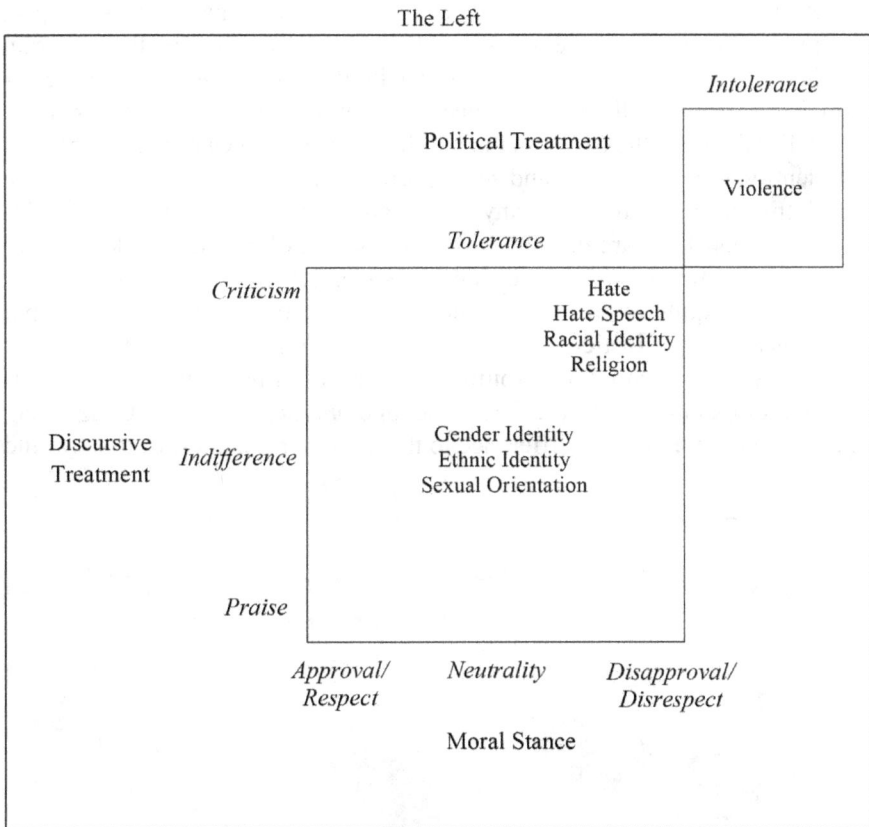

Figure 5.1.   Moral, Discursive, and Political Treatment of Selected Cultural Traits for the Left and the IDMP

cants (students and potential faculty) not only on traditional criteria of academic and professional excellence but on their commitment to the school's mission as well. If the reason a college exists is to promote a certain set of values within and throughout the institution, that school should feel under no obligation to admit or hire persons whose values run counter to that mission, *or even to those who are merely ambivalent about it.* (176–77; emphasis added)

The Left should be far more tolerant in this regard. The values of pluralism and free speech should protect ambivalence about various academic movements. While hate speech may often deserve a critical moral stance it generally does not justify coercive measures. One instance where the Left might be more intolerant involves cultural or religious excuses for truly harmful practices when children are involved, including genital mutilation or the denial of proper medical care by certain religious groups.

Yet the greater political tolerance of the Left is not tantamount to respect and praise. Indeed, the identities much beloved by those in the Program should be treated discursively with either indifference or else outright criticism, consistent with the moral stances of neutrality and disapproval, respectively. For the Left, the triplet in the middle of the tolerance box includes gender identity, ethnic identity, and sexual orientation as important cases. There is no leftist principle that gives any significance whatsoever to these identities or preferences. They are morally inert. One is free, of course, to adopt any or no gender identity on top on one's chromosomal sex. While a gender identity will likely be quite important for micro-level social interactions it does not matter as a point of justice. An IDMP adherent would almost certainly want to praise a person with XY chromosomes who does not identify as male as they do, for example, with Caitlyn Jenner and, *mutatis mutandis*, Chaz Bono. The Left should express indifference to this as a moral matter. Leftists would

The IDMP

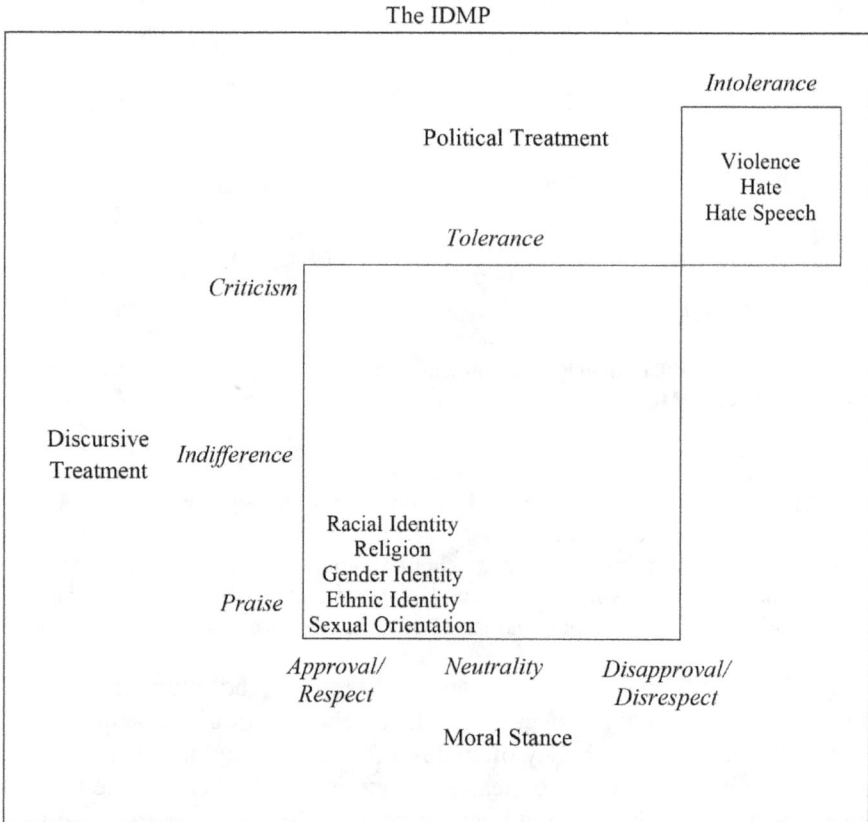

Figure 5.1.2.   Moral, Discursive, and Political Treatment of Selected Cultural Traits for the Left and the IDMP

express praise for individuals who defend their civil right to adopt any gender identity but this should not be confused with praise for the gender identity itself. Similarly for sexual orientation. The Left has no stake in sexual preferences or behaviors so long as consenting adults are involved. An individual has a right to be sexual, and political struggles for that right can be celebrated as virtuous, but the details of one's consensual sex life are morally irrelevant for parties not involved.

Although often conflated with race in everyday usage, ethnicity is best seen as a linguistic distinction. Hispanics are those who speak Spanish as their first language. Russians speak Russian first. Language as a human invention is important and praiseworthy but just about everybody has at least one language and none is better than any other and none carries any moral weight (although one could make a good leftist argument for Esperanto as an international second language in order to counteract the linguistic imperialism of English). It might be said that all languages are equally praiseworthy, but this rhetorical formulation adds nothing of substance to our position of discursive indifference: if they are equally good we can be indifferent among them.

The absence of praise does not mean that the Left needs to be humorless about ethnic identity. In the U.S. it is harmless fun to embrace an Irish identify on St. Paddy's Day. Wearing green, eating cabbage, and drinking a Guinness seem to capture the perfect degree of seriousness one should take with ethnic identity. A beer brewed according to the *Reinheitsgebot* along with a pretzel and a bratwurst is similarly appropriate during Oktoberfest. (The fact that currywurst is now considered German cuisine further suggests that some playfulness is in order when it comes to ethnic identity.) From a leftist perspective there is nothing particularly remarkable about mixing traits and going beyond the ethnic identity of one's childhood. Why should we care whether an Italian prefers kimchi and a Korean prefers gnocchi? The Left can merely insist that individuals be treated equally on the grounds of gender identity, ethnic identity, and sexual orientation. Their personal preference for cultural inventions have no more moral weight than whether they prefer the color red over blue. Cultural appropriation, whether light-hearted or earnest, is perfectly acceptable and often commendable.

Finally, consider the upper right part of the tolerance box for the Left. Here the Left should permit the things that it negatively evaluates. The important examples include racial identity, religion, and "hate" either as speech or as motivation. The positioning of these elements follows logically from leftist principles. First, religion should be tolerated but we should not celebrate the rejection of reason that is inherent in religious thinking. Faith is not an endearing defense for the irrational and unreasonable. Discursive challenges to religious positions are therefore appropriate; religious believers should feel somewhat pressed to defend their positions, or at least a bit embarrassed if they can't. For example, consider the issue of the banning of headscarves, currently a more prominent debate in Europe than in the United States. Leftists should not be afraid to denounce headscarves as sexist—a discursive response—but the banning of headscarves would violate civil liberties. They should be tolerated. (Furthermore it would likely be counterproductive and only strengthen religious conservatism.)

As a second case in the triplet of disapproval, criticism, and tolerance, leftists should place racial identities because, as argued in chapter 4, they are built upon the lie of race. It is either biological essentialism or metaphysical tribalism to pretend that race is real. Unlike gender identity, which is a reaction to the actual chromosomal trait of sex, or ethnicity, which is built upon actual language, race has no objective foundation. Not only is race a myth, and thus liable to critique on the grounds of reason, but it is also part of an ideology of hierarchy and oppression. It is both bad faith and bad politics to play along. Thus it is hard to justify even indifference or silence. The Left should openly criticize the notion of race and challenge those who believe in it to provide valid reasons.

The final example is "hate." The IDMP, as already discussed, is intolerant of hate and thus willing to punish the offenders. Leftists, on the other hand, should put hate into the category of disapproval, criticism, and tolerance. The leftist commitment to political liberty dictates that the proper response to our personal disapproval of hate is discursive. Simply put, speech is not violence. Bruised feelings are not the same as bruised bodies. Even on instrumental grounds it is better to engage racists, homophobes, and the like at the discursive level rather than to pursue political repression. Intolerance has a way of shifting the issue to the illegitimacy of the repression instead of the unreasonableness of the idea. As an example of such backfiring consider the case of Alex Jones, spewer of some of the most hateful right-wing propaganda through his platform, Infowars. In the summer of 2018 a number of social media sites, including Facebook and YouTube, banned him. Almost immediately his Infowars app jumped from number 47 to number 4 on the Apple store rankings (Breland 2018).

The leftist approach to culture is founded upon clearer moral principles and more consistent logic. It is, of course, correct for those in the Program to defend blacks against racism, gays against homophobia, and so on, but the defense leads to a more extreme position than needed or justifiable. Blacks and gays can be defended on the grounds of equality and civil liberties. It is not necessary for race or sexual orientation as individual traits to have their own positive moral quality. By taking a more reasoned approach to cultural traits, the Left avoids such contradictions. For example, the IDMP calls for respecting and celebrating religious and racial identities as well as sexual orientation. Yet many religions, including most Baptist churches, see homosexuality as contrary to God's will. Should the Multiculturalist approve and praise these religious teachings or seek to repress them as hate speech? Can one praise a religion that is homophobic yet condemn or punish its members for being homophobic? They can only adduce ad hoc responses to these contradictions. The leftist position, on the other hand, is internally consistent. One is politically tolerant of racial identity, religious identity, and even homophobic hate, but can challenge all of them discursively.

Leftist Engagement with Culture

The leftist position on most categories of identity is more critical (or at least less positive) both morally and discursively. Such criticism is not done for its own sake. Discourse in general, criticism as a specific manifestation, is a key element in social change. Indeed, criticism and change are logically connected. Criticism or praise of some behavior or outcome makes sense only given the possibility of some other behavior or outcome. Those things that absolutely must of necessity be, those that have occurred or will occur outside of human influence, have no moral content whatsoever. Human choice is a necessary element in morality. Thus, if a massive comet were to crash into the earth and kill billions of people, it would be a disaster but not an immoral act. On the other hand, the extralegal assassinations by U.S. drone aircraft, which kill comparatively fewer, are immoral because they reflect choices made by American presidents and CIA directors. It is the possibility of choice that determines whether an action will have moral significance.

Yet Multiculturalists assert that we should praise the culture and identities we were born into. We are either black or white or Korean or Mexican-American, Christian or Jew or Muslim. We are even, according to popular thinking, born either straight or gay; our sexual preferences, it seems, are fixed even before we are sexually active beings and we have no choice in the matter as adults. But if it were correct that our identities were fixed, then it would be senseless to celebrate them. We should feel neither pride nor shame in things beyond our control. The logical stance could be either resignation to or embracing of our fate.

Fortunately, they are wrong. Culture and identity are far more flexible than they suppose. The Left looks at culture not as an inheritance—or not simply as an inheritance—but rather as an ongoing process that human reason can, and should, direct. Thus at a fundamental level the leftist approach to culture is far more inspiring than the fatalistic alternative. We should see ourselves as the subjects, not the objects, of our culture. The best that the Multiculturalist offers is a false pride in things we did not do and for situations we happened to fall into. Perhaps if we lived in a world without options a delusional happiness with our fate might be the best we could achieve. In reality, choice and change are part of the human condition. The denial of this is, from an existentialist perspective, an act of bad faith.

Discourse itself is an important ingredient in cultural change, especially if we limit attention to nonviolent change. Just as language is the main way in which the world is socially constructed it is also the foundational tool we have for the deconstruction and reconstruction of unfavorable cultural traits. We are not talking about gravity or entropy, things that existed before humans and outside of us, objective things that we may come to subjectively and imperfectly understand. Cultural traits originate from mental concepts, which are intimately linked to language and which may, or may not, have an objective, real-world counterpart. The word for god, in a very real sense, is *god*. There is nothing more than whatever the word conjures inside the mind. Race is simply whatever that word, *race*, triggers us into thinking. But new word-concepts can be created. Old word-concepts can disappear or shift their meaning. This cultural process cannot, and should not, be stopped. To live in ignorance or denial of the process would put us at the mercy of blind cultural drift or of intentional currents of propaganda. A leftist stance calls on us to use our reason and our values to direct the future evolution of our culture.

Here we see the important role that criticism and debate play. The crucial distinction is this: the IDMP looks approvingly on cultural traditions and customs; for leftists, some ideas and cultural practices are better than others, and many are just plain bad. The communitarians might take some comfort in the fact that the discovery of new and better ideas is a collective process. Criticism and debate are part of the process of reasoning together. Furthermore the application of collective solutions must have democratic legitimacy. The social nature of human life requires that we achieve a certain level of agreement on the basic institutions that will govern us.

In practice, how do we move our culture closer to the values of the Left? We can start by changing the way we talk to each other. Let us take as an important example the notion of race on college campuses. When addressing the concept of race, we should clearly speak of it as a social construction that our ancestors created, one that served as an ideology of oppression and exploitation. It should be seen as something that we can and should change. So we might say, "Race is not real but many people believe it is." Or "Race is only what we believe it to be," or "If we can change our beliefs we can change the meaning of race," or "Racial identity is a subjective state in much the same way that religious affiliation is," and so on.

These statements are not too difficult for college or even high school students to grasp. This type of discourse has two significant advantages over the current approach that celebrates racial identity. First, it is true, or at least it conforms to our understanding of modern biology. It requires no flawed essentialist thinking. Fortunately, many of my students are already quite aware of the genetic research on race. Second, it moves the culture in a direction that facilitates leftist political change by asserting a universal humanity. Instead of attempting to rehabilitate the word-concept *race*—an idea that has been, and still is, used to divide and exploit—we simply move it into the same mental and historical category as demons or astrology: many people once believed in them, and some still do today, but they are wrong.

Analogous statements could be made about other categories of identity. Or in some cases no statements should be made at all. People should be neither praised nor criticized for their personal preferences and private behaviors regarding sexual orientation and gender identity. Again, we can properly praise those who fight for justice, including for equal treatment on the grounds of sexual orientation and gender identity, but we should distinguish between the personal identity and the political struggle. Many times the personal is not the political. It's just personal.

For those made of stouter stuff, it's possible to go beyond this somewhat academic and discursive approach, although I do not mean to diminish the importance of such a change. In Chicago in the late 1960s, an exemplary alliance—the original Rainbow Coalition—was formed between the Black Panthers, headed by Fred Hampton, and the Young Patriots Organization, comprised of poor whites whose symbol was the Confederate flag (Mc-Canne 2017). Later to join was the Young Lords, a group of radical Puerto Ricans, and relationships were made with the Native American community in Chicago. Where could such a "diverse" coalition find common cause? By fighting the enduring problems of police brutality and poverty. Contrast the political strategy of Hampton and the Black Panthers to contemporary anti-racist activists. Today, the "racist" is considered to be unworthy of any engagement. Indeed, the illiberal (and anti-leftist) impulse in the Program often calls for silencing and sanctioning those who practice hate-speech. I obviously do not condone racist beliefs. I am, however, suggesting that we might be able to work with racists on projects where we have common cause, just as the Illinois Black Panthers were willing to do with men who flew the Confederate flag. There's both a political and cultural angle to this recommendation. Politically, any victories against the oligarchy will take a mass movement. Culturally, I suggest that contact between anti-racists and racists might be good for both by getting them to question the ontological status of the social construct that unites them, that is, race. It might be for this very reason that Hampton was killed by the police shortly after forming this coalition. We might also note that Martin Luther King Jr. was murdered not long after forming the Poor People's Campaign, another movement based on class solidarity across racial lines. Again, this is the path for the stout-hearted.

I conclude this discussion with a lighter, pop-cultural example of the contrast between the leftist and IDMP approaches. At a performance on New Year's Eve 2011, Cee Lo Green changed the lyrics of John Lennon's song *Imagine* to "Nothing to kill or die for, and *all religion's true*" from the original "Nothing to kill or die for, and *no religion too*" (emphasis added). When challenged by fans of the original version Green responded, "It was all done out of love and out of peace and unity and tolerance and acceptance and all those many wonderful things that seem cliché and a little bit cheesy." Cee Lo may have had the best of intentions. The problem is the pervasiveness of Identity, Diversity, and Multiculturalism thinking. Instead of staying with the original lyrics and promoting a better culture, one free of religion, Cee Lo felt the need to celebrate the cultural traits we inherited. Furthermore, his statement is internally inconsistent. It is not possible for all religions to be true if the tenet of some (most?) religions is the belief that they alone are the followers of the one true faith. Polytheism, for example, is inconsistent with monotheism. Both can be wrong but both cannot be right. So not only did Cee Lo uphold a conservative cultural trait, he presented an incoherent defense. Cee Lo's revision and rather muddled logic is representative of the IDMP approach. Tradition should not save cultural elements that cannot be defended on the grounds of reason and justice. Leftists should seek to actively challenge their own culture.

SUMMARY AND CONCLUSION

In this chapter I made two related critiques of the tenet of *Culture as Virtue*—the substantive and the epistemological—and also offered an alternative, leftist approach to culture. First, the evidence in the substantive critique clearly demonstrates that large numbers of Americans hold many beliefs—the stuff of culture—that are unreasonable, conservative, or neoliberal. Why should leftists respect or celebrate ignorance, superstition, and inequality? Second, the epistemological critique brings attention to the cultural mechanisms that work against a culture of collective reasoning and encourage unreasonable and right-wing thinking. The economic advantage of conservatives and especially neoliberals gives right-wing propaganda a systematic advantage in the production of cultural beliefs. Furthermore, primary socialization tends to be a conservative force, at least if we assume a pre-existing set of mostly conservative beliefs. These mechanisms, instead of the defense or indifference given by the IDMP, deserve to be openly challenged on the grounds of reason and justice.

The difference between the approaches reflects fundamental disagreements over the meaning of tolerance, the very nature of culture, and the possibility for social change. First, the leftist commitment to political liberty requires tolerance in cases where the IDMP does not. But the Left, unlike Multiculturalism, does not equate tolerance with approval and praise. Many things that the program holds dear do indeed require toleration, but instead of celebration they deserve either disapproval and criticism, on the one hand, or neutrality and indifference, on the other. Furthermore, whereas the Multiculturalist takes culture as a preexisting, almost immutable, fact, leftists view it as a set of beliefs that we inherit as children but must take responsibility for as adults. Instead of tackling the entirety of a culture, something made up of a great many individual elements, we should engage it at the level of specific cultural traits. From a leftist perspective, which I believe is shared by most who identify as part of the Identity, Diversity, and Multiculturalism Program, many elements of our culture deserve rebuttal and not respect. We should jump into the cultural arena and argue for those things that correspond to our values and against those that do not.

NOTES

1. A commitment to science is leftist but not uniquely leftist. Those taking the right-wing path out of the enlightenment, particularly the liberal, can also stake a claim to science.

2. Abortion prior to the "quickening," that is, detectable movement by the fetus, was a legal and largely accepted practice in the United States until the second half of the nineteenth century (Brodie 1997). We could thus defend the re-legalization of abortion by Roe v. Wade as a return to a deeper tradition.

3. For example, even though humans have been making beer and wine for millennia, yeast was scientifically discovered by Louis Pasteur only in the middle of the nineteenth century.

4. I wish to avoid a more complicated review of the philosophy of science but my position in general accepts the Kuhnian (1970) and Quinian (1951) critiques of the naïve views of science held by logical empiricists or Popperians. But we must not forget that both Kuhn and Quine, although sometimes interpreted as critics of science, were in fact strong defenders of this type of human practice. Despite all the complications in applying it to the real world, the epistemology known as science is in general different from and superior to other means of producing knowledge.

5. I take Robert Nozick as the representative of an ideal philosophical libertarianism. See his classic *Anarchy, State, and Utopia* (2013) for a philosophical defense of virtually unlimited private property. Milton Friedman is a more famous libertarian

but his defense of deregulated capitalism in *Free to Choose* (1980) mixes liberty with utility, an argument that is less pure but perhaps more persuasive to the non-philosopher.

6. Here and elsewhere in this section I borrow heavily from Bucker and Luckmann's (1967) *The Social Construction of Reality*, a work to which I have already many times demonstrated my intellectual debt.

7. For the disturbing statistics visit the website for *The Center for Responsive Politics* at www.opensecrets.org.

8. For example, CNN legal correspondent Jeffrey Toobin has been one of the strongest critics of Julian Assange and Eric Snowden, and a defender of the NSA spying program. David Gregory, who worked at the time for the supposedly "liberal" MSNBC, asked journalist Glenn Greenwald why Greenwald should not be charged with a crime for aiding and abetting Snowden (Meet the Press, June 23, 2013).

Chapter Six

The Choice

Identity, Diversity, and Multiculturalism or the Left?

In this work I have argued that the Identity, Diversity, and Multiculturalism Program (IDMP) conflicts with the principles and objectives of the Left. In some areas it directly contradicts leftist ideals and in others it simply falls far too short of leftist demands, thereby abetting our movement in a neoliberal direction. Faced with this contradiction, many supporters of Identity, Diversity, and Multiculturalism, most of whom see themselves as falling on the left of the political spectrum, might feel some psychological unease. They regard the program as the vanguard of a brave and radical struggle against an unjust system. There are a few ways this psychological tension could be relieved.

First, the supporters could accept the incompatibility between the IDMP and the Left, and deal with the problem head on. If they hold their leftist values as the more fundamental then they would reduce their estimation of the former and hopefully work to advance the Left. This does not necessarily require abandoning the Program; instead they might work from within to push it to the left, which would entail a fairly radical restructuring. Such a reaction would, of course, be the principal objective of this work.

The second approach is a partial reversal of the first. Some might recognize the incompatibility between the two but decide that the problem lies with my statement of leftist principles. They would not reject the Left itself but rather my version of it. They might, for example, find it possible to reject my interpretation on the grounds that the Enlightenment is European and therefore the values are ethnocentric. Or they might say that Identity, Diversity, and Multiculturalism is meant to align with the Third-Way values of Bill and Hillary Clinton and Barack Obama. For them the Democratic Party might define the parameters of the Left. In this way they could continue to see themselves as leftist—the real Left, not the bad old European or radical Left. Although I would defend my statement of the Left, I acknowledge that this approach is perfectly logical. Opponents are free to offer alternative versions of leftist principles, although they should recognize that they have moved a long way from democratic socialism and social democracy, the leftist projects that have been dominant in western democracies for two centuries. They would essentially be moving neoliberalism from the right side of the political spectrum to the left. Definitions are merely conventions, and we can decide to change the meaning of words, but let us be honest about it. Perhaps these discussions might encourage some debate within the Program regarding what they mean by their leftist values. I would accept this as progress.

The final path toward psychological reconciliation draws upon the nearly infinite capacity of the human mind to work around contradictions and inconsistencies. Into this category would fall those who accept—more or less—my statement of the Left. They are not satisfied with the neoliberal agenda of the Democrats. They profess a belief in high levels of economic equality. They endorse the notion of individual freedom. Yet they wish to remain a part of the Identity, Diversity, and Multiculturalism Program. With a bit of cleverness almost any contradiction can be conquered, and I suspect that some will find a way to hold as perfectly consistent what I regard as inconsistent. Albert Camus (1955) observed that "From the abstract god of Husserl to the dazzling god of Kierkegaard the distance is not so great. Reason and the irrational lead to the same preaching. In truth the way matters but little; *the will to arrive suffices*" (47; emphasis added). Just as Camus calls on us to bravely and honestly face the reality of an absurd universe, so I hope to force an honest recognition of the choice between the Left and the IDMP. At a minimum I intend to make it as difficult as possible to slip away from the choice. In other words, I hope to provoke a crisis of cognitive dissonance among leftists who support the Program.

This work did not, of course, attempt to demonstrate the superiority of left-wing values. The values of the Left were the premises of the argument; they have simply been taken as valid, playing the role here that a Euclidian axiom might in a geometrical proof. I am speaking not primarily to those on the right but rather to supporters of the IDMP who identify as progressives, liberals, radicals, or any other type of leftist. I ask leftists to consider whether their current agenda is consistent with their ideals of social progress. Over time, as both neoliberalism and Identity, Diversity, and Multiculturalism continue their forward march, I expect many will come to recognize the compatibility of the two.

SUMMARY OF THE LEFTIST CRITIQUE

The critique was built around what I identified as the four tenets of the Identity, Diversity, and Multiculturalism Program.

1. *Diversity as Justice*: The most important struggle for justice today is increasing the representation throughout society of individuals from historically marginalized groups by ending discrimination on the grounds of race, gender, sexual orientation, and similar characteristics;
2. *Colorblindness as Racism*: Race-neutral solutions to the problems caused by racism are harmful to blacks;
3. *Race as Culture*: Members of different races belong to different cultures;
4. *Culture as Virtue*: Cultures should be respected and celebrated.

Before examining some of the specific rhetorical strategies I anticipate will be used by IDMP supporters to avoid the choice, which is the main objective of this concluding chapter, the arguments made previously against the four tenets can be summarized.

Diversity as Justice

The leftist struggle for justice goes far beyond an opposition to discrimination on the grounds of race, gender, and sexual orientation. In fact, a neoliberal orientation rejects these forms of discrimination too. Leftists must take seriously the notion of the moral equality of all individuals. Under conditions of modern industrial capitalism, we can derive from this premise support for state regulation of the economy that would produce equality of opportunity and a high degree of equality of outcome. This commitment is not shared by the Right (conservatives or neoliberals) and not by the center or even by the center-left. And, most importantly, the commitment to equal opportunity and equality of outcome is *not* a part of the Identity, Diversity, and Multiculturalism Program. Individuals who support the Program may indeed share this belief in equality but it must come from somewhere outside the program.

Diversity demands instead an end to white, male, heterosexual privilege. That is reasonable, because privilege is an unjustifiable advantage, but it should not be confused with true equality of opportunity. Furthermore, privilege-talk is silent about the overall amount of inequality of outcome, except for palaver about equity. *Diversity as Justice* is therefore closer to neoliberalism than to the Left. The market—once we remove discrimination on the grounds of race, sex, gender, sexual orientation, and the like—can sort people out. Wealthier parents can buy more advantages for their children just so long as no distinction is made among blacks and whites, boys and girls, gay and straight. In contrast, according to the Left, resources can be distributed unequally only within certain bounds and only according to our innate ability and effort.

Colorblindness as Racism

Leftist policies follow from leftist principles of justice, namely, complete equality of opportunity and a high degree of equality of outcome. To achieve these objectives, the state would have to play a substantial role in our capitalist economy. The policies fall into three big categories: (1) redistribution of household income by means of a strongly progressive tax system coupled with generous social spending; (2) funding and regulation of public institutions like education, housing, healthcare, and the criminal justice system; (3) maintenance of high wages and low unemployment through Keynesian fiscal and monetary policy, among other labor market regulations.

The tenet of *Colorblindness as Racism* maintains that race neutral policies are, ipso facto, racist because they harm blacks or, at a minimum, fail to help them as much as they should. I argued that, as a general claim, it is simply wrong. If, however, we substantially modify the tenet to mean that *conservative* or *neoliberal* colorblind policies are racist, then it is quite possibly true, at least for many policies. Or it could by modified to mean that many individuals who support conservative or neoliberal colorblind policies are at least partly motivated by racist beliefs. Of course the (possibly) true new statements are rather weak; they add little to our common-sense understanding of social reality.

Beyond the rhetorical overreach there is another problem with the tenet of *Colorblindness as Racism*: Leftist colorblind policies would bring more economic benefit to blacks than the race-based policies advocated by the IDMP. True, affirmative action would probably do more to help blacks than race-neutral *conservative* or *neoliberal* policies. But it is only by ignoring the class-based policies favored by the Left that Diversity advocates can frame this as a choice between the center and the Right, a contrived lesser-of-two-evils. If the Program were actually a leftist project it would endorse and promote leftist policies rather than label them as racist. For the majority of blacks, leftist colorblind policies would be far better than even a strong version of affirmative action. Leftist colorblind policies would move millions of blacks—along with millions of non-blacks—out of poverty. Millions of blacks—along with millions of non-blacks—would have healthcare. Millions of college graduates of all colors of skin would be freed from student debt. Affirmative action, even a plan with quotas for blacks, would not come close to this leftist and colorblind outcome.

It will be said that these policies are unlikely, even utopian, given the current state of American democracy. True, but then the Program should abandon the tenet of *Colorblindness as Racism* and adopt a new version, something like *Leftist Colorblindness as Politically Unlikely Today*. This would be quite a bit less rousing. In any case, Diversity supporters—who claim the legacy of previous "impossible" victories like the abolition of slavery and the end to Jim Crow segregation—should probably not be in the business of lowering our political and moral expectations. The right wing, which is well-funded and has an interest in lowering the demands of the demos, can spread this propaganda without any help.

Race as Culture

Beginning with the third tenet the emphasis shifts away from the political-economic and into the cultural realm. As a consequence, it becomes necessary to expand the set of leftist principles to deal with new cultural phenomena. The values of liberty and equality say little, at least directly, about claims like *Race as Culture* or *Culture as Virtue*. Instead, I suggest that existentialism is the most appropriate standpoint for a leftist analysis of personal behavior and related cultural issues. Although it lacks the moral strictures of most faith-based religions, existentialism does allow us to criticize behavior on the grounds of bad faith, that is, dishonesty in the face of the choice embedded in the universal human condition. In a sociological context, bad faith is the belief in social constructions as natural laws.

Thus the belief in *Race as Culture* is an instance of bad faith. Race is not objectively real. This is heart of the ontological critique of *Race as Culture*. We have had enough time since the discovery of DNA and the subsequent finding that all humans are part of the same species to accept the facts. The absence of biological evidence for the existence of race leaves us with nothing more than a malleable social construction. Furthermore, because races do not exist, it makes no sense to claim that different races have distinct cultures. We simply cannot objectively put individuals into the black race or the white race in order to tell whether they have different cultures.

Even if we play along with the lie, even if we suppose that there is such a thing as the black race and the white race, we can find no cultural differences of any substance between the races. This is the empirical critique of *Race as Culture*. It permits race to be self-selected and then compares the distributions of cultural traits for blacks to the distributions for whites. What we find, as demonstrated in chapter 4 with numerous examples of religious, social, and political variables, is that the distributions for blacks and whites largely overlap. That is, there is far more variation on average among members of each race than there is a variation between the races.

The ontological critique of *Race as Culture* is obviously the more fundamental. It requires an acceptance of modern genetics and the desire to avoid bad faith. But for those who still cling to the notion of race, even if it is nothing more than a check-box on a form, the empirical critique applies.

Culture as Virtue

For the multiculturalist, almost everything about culture is considered wonderful and worthy of celebration. The Left should not be so naïvely enamored of culture. Culture does indeed have some wondrous elements. Language, the foundation of human culture, allows us to develop complex ideas and relationships. Literature, science, mathematics are fruits of the tree of culture. At the same time, however, culture provides some strong ideological tools for the construction of a hierarchical and exploitative social system. In chapter 5, I pursued this line of reasoning to make two critiques of *Culture as Virtue*: the substantive and the epistemological.

First, by adopting a leftist standpoint we should be able to point out and to make reasonable criticisms of elements of culture that seem to be in conflict with our values. I group these elements into three categories: the unreasonable, the conservative, and the neoliberal. American culture has numerous instances of all three. Belief in evolution and denial of climate change are simply wrong. Many Americans prefer a religious position on matters that are clearly scientific. There is insufficient support for legal abortion and gay rights. Neoliberal beliefs are seen in the commonplace opposition to government action to strengthen equality. In short, the substantive critique maintains that many common elements of America culture deserve criticism, not celebration.

The epistemological critique expands upon the substantive by exposing the mechanisms that produce cultural knowledge. Leftists should be skeptical, and often critical, of cultural "knowledge" that comes from tradition via socialization or gets disseminated via propaganda. Tradition means the perpetuation of many conservative beliefs, religion as the leading instance. Leftists should feel no restraint in their criticism of religion. The IDMP, on the other hand, would rather take the internally inconsistent position that all religions are true, or at least beautiful. Because propaganda is dependent on resources, neoliberals have a systemic advantage over the Left. Many are happy to criticize Fox News for spreading propaganda, but they fail to realize that propaganda deeply permeates almost all elements of our culture.

Most generally the leftist critique of *Culture as Virtue* calls for critical engagement with culture on an element-by-element basis. It is not intolerant to suggest that the wearing of a burqa is sexist. It is not intolerant to suggest that the Mormon religion (along with others of older vintage) was created by a hustler. Tolerance demands that we let others live as they choose. It does not demand that we respect those lifeways. Nor does it demand that we remain silent when we oppose something. To a leftist, culture becomes an arena for potentially contentious discourse. If we wish to move society in a direction more consistent with our principles then we can do no less.

RHETORICAL AVOIDANCE OF THE CHOICE

My critique of the IDMP presumes a fundamental commitment to rational discourse by participants on all sides of the issue. Rational discourse is played according to certain rules. I have attempted to show that, according to my definitions of the terms, we reach a contradiction between the principles of Left and the tenets of the Identity, Diversity, and Multiculturalism Program. Ideally supporters of the Program would evaluate the critique on its merit. There would be discursive back and forth and some refinements of the positions on both sides. Reality, I fear, will be quite some distance from the ideal.

Judging from my own experience and from the treatment of other critics of Identity, Diversity, and Multiculturalism, it is likely that many supporters of the program will respond to the leftist critique by not really responding to it. Instead a strawman will be built and then knocked over. Rebuttals to the actual critique will be tangential at best. Even ad hominem attacks are to be expected. The variety of the non-responsive responses is limited only by the "will to arrive" and imagination of the supporters. Still, I find five broad types of nonresponses to be the most common and probably the most effective rhetorical avoidance strategies. In this section I attempt to preemptively address them, to show how they avoid and obfuscate instead of engaging the leftist critique. I do not claim that my arguments are immune from criticism but I would hope that the rebuttals play by the rules.

The R-word

The most powerful rhetorical weapon of the Identity, Diversity, and Multiculturalism Program would be the suggestion that this work is racist or was written by a racist.

The allegation of racism is as potent as it is insidious. The very existence of the tenet of *Colorblindness as Racism* makes any reasoned debate difficult.

The true believer who dogmatically accepts the tenet can use the allegation to shut down conversation. Anybody who openly defends colorblindness can be dismissed as a racist. Or, as a colleague once told me, I may not be a racist but my ideas are. This subtle distinction—one which does little to soften the accusation in any case—is of little comfort. The unpleasant situation is recognized by skeptics of Identity, Diversity, and Multiculturalism and thereby encourages self-censorship. The bind is even more sharply felt for leftist critics; whereas conservatives may take it as a sign they are on the right side of the culture wars, none of us on the Left wants to be put on the defense against such an allegation from potential allies.

Nonetheless, intellectual progress requires an openness to discourse. Branding an idea as racist—before engaging with it rationally—undermines the discourse and impedes the progress. I accept that there will be leftist supporters of the IDMP who disagree with my arguments. I take that as a normal and healthy state. I look forward to a friendly back-and-forth with people who should be political allies. I would find it more difficult to accept that my critique of the Program can be fairly labeled as racist.

Of course, it hinges on one's definition of racism. In this work I have employed a tripartite conceptualization: there are racist ideas, racist actions, and racist outcomes. As argued in chapter 3 (and summarized above) leftist colorblindness cannot be considered racist according to any of the three components. It cannot be a racist belief because it does not maintain that any race is superior to any other, nor does it reveal any racial animus. Leftist colorblind policies are neither racist actions nor racist outcomes because, in point of fact, they would radically redistribute resources and eliminate the income differences between the races. Leftist colorblindness would be better for blacks than color-conscious affirmative action.

My definition of racism is both reasonable and comprehensive. Almost anything that would strike us intuitively as racist—from racial slurs to racist discrimination—is included. Yet if one wishes to find a way to consider colorblindness racist, one needs another approach. Many believe that a suitable formulation is offered by Eduardo Bonilla-Silva. He argues that " . . . color-blind racism is the ideology of the 'new racism' era" (2010, 173). But note *color-blind* is not the subject of the quoted sentence but rather a modifier of *racism*. He tells us which type of racism is linked to a modern racist ideology, namely, color-blind racism. It is therefore an unjustified inference to equate color-blind racism—a type of racism—with colorblindness—a belief about policies (in this context).

Bonilla-Silva's "new racism" era coincides with neoliberalism, which is indeed the real problem. A leftist will accept the claim that many forms of racism have continued into the post-civil rights era. The issue here is whether we can blame *leftist* colorblindness. Given the absence of leftist policies in the U.S. and even of leftist ideas in the mainstream political discourse, it would be difficult to assign responsibility for racist inequality to colorblindness on the Left. Bonilla-Silva's justifiable complaint is with neoliberal colorblindness, not leftist colorblindness. The term "color-blind racism" does not capture the rather significant difference between the two. The IDMP oddly rejects an ideology that has *not* been tried—colorblind leftism—in favor of an ideology with a long and painful legacy of racist violence and inequality—color-consciousness.

I am skeptical of the attempt to rehabilitate color-consciousness and put it into service as part of the solution to racism. I fear that it encourages tribal loyalty and its concomitant social divisions. Yet this point illustrates another difference in our approaches: I do not regard the color-consciousness of Diversity supporters as a sign of their racism. I simply believe they are in error. I furthermore recognize the possibility that I could be wrong. Perhaps color-consciousness could somehow be part of society built along leftist notions of justice. Some of us support leftist colorblindness. Some support color-conscious Identity, Diversity, and Multiculturalism. Very few of us involved in this debate are racists. Care must be taken to level that accusation accurately, lest it lose the moral impact it ought to carry.

Denying Racism

The second rhetorical strategy, almost as effective as the allegation of racism, will be the suggestion that this work denies the existence of racism. After giving a talk on my campus I received a lengthy email from a student who was quite irritated that I argued "that racism is no longer a social problem." Of course in my talk I had said exactly the opposite and argued that multiple types of racism are found in society. Indeed, I anticipated this reaction and on one of the slides on the big screen behind me I had explicitly written that a leftist critique does not deny the existence of racism. Racist outcomes, I claimed at the talk, are the result of both (1) a neoliberal political-economy that perpetuates our inherited racial inequality and (2) ongoing racist actions. Yet it seems that this student's commitment to Identity, Diversity, and Multiculturalism was so strong that my leftist critique of it had to be distorted into a conservative display of white, male privilege (which was also alleged in the missive).

Although I worry that others in the Program will wear similar cognitive blinders, I briefly restate the ways in which racism has been addressed in my approach. The easiest way to summarize the role of racism is to review the model of inequality presented in figure 2.1 (chapter 2). The model explains the perpetuation of economic inequality at the analytical level of the family or household. As the first instance of racism, the model begins with the empirical fact that economic inequality in the distribution of family capital has a racial component, which I take as one type of racist outcome. Blacks have higher rates of poverty, lower average income, and lower average wealth. Next, as we leave family capital, the model displays the fact that the development of embodied capital depends on family capital—more money typically translates into better institutional experiences—but also that blacks and whites are often treated differently. This is the second instance of racism. Third, the model explicitly includes different levels of labor market demand for blacks and whites. Finally, the model suggests that both neoliberal and racist motivations lie behind many state policies.

Thus instead of a denial there are actually multiple categories of racism in the model. And each will have numerous manifestations. Racism will vary, of course, over time and space but my approach can accommodate whatever degree of racism may be found in empirical research. What should not be taken as a denial of racism is the claim that political-economic processes are at work alongside these racist mechanisms.

Eurocentric Bias

The third rhetorical strategy is a case of guilt by association. My critique might be dismissed as an instance of Eurocentrism or as a manifestation of a Western bias. The import of this can be hard to pin down but I take it as something like a statement of cultural relativism: we should not critique one culture by means of the values of another. My leftist critique of the IDMP, it will be said, is really a western or Eurocentric critique. It is not valid once we step outside that western domain. And presumably Identity, Diversity, and Multiculturalism falls on the outside.

There are three problems with the allegation of a Eurocentric bias. First, any strong logical or empirical link between beliefs in political liberty, economic equality, and personal freedom, on the one hand, and European culture, on the other, cannot be substantiated. It might be possible to demonstrate that these ideas originated in Europe and later diffused outside. In this case, the values of the modern Left would reflect the fact that capitalism first took off in Europe. In its train came dense urbanization and the nation-state. The modern Left and leftist principles make sense only in this historical epoch. They would make no sense in pastoral, horticultural, or even feudal societies.

But for the sake of argument and to avoid a prolonged and unnecessary historical discussion, let me grant the claim that the values of political liberty, economic equality, and personal freedom reflect a European cultural bias.

What would follow from this premise? It would do nothing to invalidate the leftist critique of Identity, Diversity, and Multiculturalism. Even if the values reflect a western bias, I have critiqued the Identity, Diversity, and Multiculturalism Program in the United States, which is, of course, a western society. And not simply among whites. The language spoken by most blacks in the U.S.—English—is Eurocentric. The Baptist Church, the most common religion among blacks, is Eurocentric. Do Multiculturalists suppose that they could tell blacks that their Christian faith is invalid because it comes to them via Europe and was imposed on them during slavery? Speaking of black writers and artists, Jim Sleeper observed (1997, 109) that "even as they turned their backs on a racist America, some of them reflected insightfully on the discovery that they were irreversibly American—indeed, 'Western.' Attending a Pan-African conference in Paris in 1956, [James] Baldwin noted . . . that the strongest opponents of European colonialism depended on Western values and languages to make their case to their fellow Africans." In order for Eurocentrism to be a plausible objection we must be talking about a non-European or non-Western culture, yet many blacks in the U.S., just like many whites, do consider political liberty, economic equality, and personal freedom to be morally relevant concepts. Blacks may be referred to as African-Americans but they are above all Americans. Most have never gone to Africa and know as much about Africa as Americans in general know about any other continent, which is to say, rather little. Very few speak any of the indigenous languages or practice a religion that predates Christianity. (Of course, the same could be said, *mutatis mutandis*, for white Americans with European ancestors.)

There is one final problem with the Eurocentrism objection. Ultimately the principles of the Left must stand or fall on their own merits. The content—not continent—of the values is relevant. The issue is not whether a commitment to political liberty, economic equality, and individual freedom is European but rather whether they form the moral and political foundation for the Left today in the U.S. If they do, then the charge of Eurocentrism is irrelevant. If they do not, it means I have misconceptualized the Left and my critique is invalid for that reason. But Eurocentrism would still be irrelevant. Some will reject the critique because they are not leftists. Some leftists will reject the critique by arguing that I improperly conceptualized what it means to be a leftist. But Eurocentrism does not matter one way or the other.

Unreasonably Reasonable

The fourth rhetorical strategy often overlaps with Eurocentrism, but not entirely, and it can be reached independently. Proponents of the IDMP might claim that the set the leftist values introduced here is too limited. They might accept that political liberty, economic equality, and personal freedom are valid leftist principles but they would insist that certain important values go beyond these overly narrow and possibly Eurocentric concerns. The primary omission, it will be said, is the role of emotions in human affairs.

Such a critique has a certain surface plausibility. I do indeed ignore (at least explicitly) emotions. Yet this is quite different from a rejection or denial of the emotional dimension to the human experience. Instead, I claim that the Left is not defined by any particular set of emotions or emotional experiences but rather by its commitment to certain values and principles. It is possible that emotions—feelings of empathy, for example—are conducive to the belief in the moral equality of all humans but the conclusion is more important than the route. If emotions are to be considered as ends in themselves and not simply a possible route to general principles, then some plausible reason must be given. In fact, it would need to be established that emotions are as important as the three moral criteria I have offered: political liberty, economic equality, and personal freedom. If the moral significance of emotions is not equal to or greater than these, then the inclusion of emotions would do little to change my argument or alter the conclusion.

I see no way in which the introduction of emotions as a moral standard could significantly change the structure or conclusion of my argument. Emotions matter for many things, but emotions cannot turn a project that is not leftist into one that is. To illustrate my point let us make a leftist evaluation of Jim Crow. On the grounds of economic equality, political liberty, and personal freedom we can safely declare that Jim Crow conflicts with the Left. Somebody could object by saying, "Wait just a minute! What about emotions? How did people *feel* about Jim Crow? What was the emotional content of the lived experience?" I suspect all of us would reject such concerns as superfluous to the leftist condemnation. Strong emotions about Jim Crow certainly existed and still exist, and they might be very important at a personal, experiential level, but they are not necessary to make a leftist critique of the system. Furthermore, there is no possible distribution of emotions or personal feelings about Jim Crow that could alter our conclusion. It would change nothing even if every white person had intensely positive feelings about the system (or even if some blacks had positive feelings). The Left is not a variety of utilitarianism in which we somehow count emotional units and declare as just the system with the highest score.

Strong feelings do exist about race and culture and discrimination and all the other subjects dealt with by the Program. As important as those feelings may be at the level of lived experience they do not undermine the leftist critique of the program. We could say that the emotional dimension is orthogonal to the leftist axes of political liberty, economic equality, and individual freedom. We are free to talk about that additional dimension but we should recognize that in doing so we have moved away from the leftist critique and are now talking about something else. No amount of positive (or negative) feelings could sidestep the leftist critique. At best the supporter might say, "Well, OK, maybe the Identity, Diversity, and Multiculturalism Program isn't leftist, but I'm not interested in that, and I just want to talk about feelings."

A final caution. When emotions replace rational analysis it is easy to hold logically incompatible positions. It allows one to feel good about being a leftist, and to feel good about supporting Identity, Diversity, and Multiculturalism. While it would be nice to feel good about all our personal projects, it is more important to live in good faith. Emotions can quite easily lend themselves to a form of conservatism. The Romantic era, with an epistemological bias in favor of understanding based on intuition and knowledge based on personal experience, was a conservative reaction to the Enlightenment. The fault of the Enlightenment according to these critics, just like their modern counterparts, was its excessive emphasis of the role of human reason. The critics are doubly wrong. First, "reason is not the enemy of experience. Nothing is more foolish than to confuse a reactionary pseudo-universalism with the genuinely democratic universalism that underpins the liberal rule of law, the constraint of arbitrary power, and the free exercise of subjectivity" (Bronner 2004, 15). Second, Enlightenment thinkers actually celebrated the fullness of the human condition, and "sought not merely to educate their minds, but also to educate their sentiments and sensibilities."

Intersectionality, Identity, and the Real Me

The final strategy of avoidance can be stated in several ways but all, I believe, tap into a roughly similar sentiment. The problem with my critique, it will be said, is that it ignores intersectionality.[1] That is, it fails to recognize the multiple, complex identities that define who we are. Expressing this sentiment, a young person once told me, in response to a statement I made in support of ontological colorblindness, that if I don't see her color then I don't see who she really is. Intersectionality, so it is said, is important. Identity matters.

It is true that if somebody tells me that she values her racial category, that race is important to her identity, I will accept it. We all are free to decide what is important to us. But as argued in chapter 4, I consider personal identification with a race (other than human) to be an act of bad faith, and thereby find it to be in conflict with the leftist notion of existential freedom. I would reject as well the claim that she is the reincarnated spirit of Cleopatra. Some people believe in race and some believe in astrology, but the rest of us do not need to join them, or even to respect their beliefs. Thus I do not deny that a race-based identity matters to some people but instead I challenge the empirical and logical foundation of that identification. As argued in chapter 5, while we must be tolerant in the sense that we must recognize their right to believe whatever they want and to speak freely, we do not need to respect their ideas and we have a right to speak freely as we challenge them.

Despite its embrace by liberals, identity can be quite effectively employed by the right wing. Many people use their religious identity to oppose gay marriage, abortion, and even contraception. Identity is used strategically in the political realm to minimize legitimate criticism. Consider the growing number of conservative and neoliberal "people of color" and women appointed to government agencies and the courts. The Left should not permit identity to become a shield behind which harmful ideas can find protection.

Even putting aside the ontological and empirical critiques of *Race as Culture* (developed in chapter 4), the statement that "identity matters" has almost no meaningful content. The importance of something can be assessed only relative to the importance of something else, and often in some particular context. Things can matter more or less than other things in terms of some outcome. The presence of a racial identity or even *complex intersecting identities* may explain certain individual thoughts or behaviors. That is, it may matter in this context. Yet it need not matter in other contexts. For the consideration of leftist values, the only relevant identities that matter are those of *human* and *citizen*. Categories of race, gender, sex, sexual orientation, religion, and so on, do not matter in this context because we can derive no general principles of justice from them. Whether distinct or intersecting, these identities play a similar role to emotions discussed above. Whatever personal importance identities might have, there is no reason to elevate them above political liberty, economic equality, and existential freedom.

Finally, the categories of so-called *individual* identity are largely the categories provided by one's culture. Ironically there is often little individuality in those celebrated individual identities. Identity—especially racial and ethnic identity—is nothing more than what has been done to us by society. Individuals should instead take an active role in the creation of their identity, just as they should for their beliefs. One may have been born into a religious family or may have been placed by others into a racial category but adults are free to reject these ways of thinking. Passive, non-reflexive acceptance of such labels certainly deserves no praise. Recalling Sartre: god's will is realized only through individual interpretation.

It is therefore incorrect to claim that my critique is somehow flawed because I ignore intersecting identities. I ignore identity because it cannot save the Program from any of my critiques. Identity is quite often a self-indulgent distraction pervaded with bad faith. As free individuals we should not be enchanted with what we have been told to be. The Left is an emancipatory social project: we must work on what we can become.

A TYPOLOGY OF RACE AND EQUALITY

Having attempted to make avoidance a bit more difficult for the leftist supporter of the Program, I can now try to put the choice in the clearest terms possible. I wish to highlight two of the themes running throughout this work. First, I have made a high level of economic equality a central principle of the Left. Diversity, on the other hand, does not call for either equality of opportunity or equality of outcome but simply for an end to white, male, heterosexual privilege and for some fuzzy condition called equity. The second theme involves the status of race as political category. I have argued that policies consistent with leftist principles are colorblind, focusing on economic differences (along with political liberties, but those are not the focus of this section). Diversity, obviously, is color-conscious, offering either a stronger version of affirmative action or a strong defense of the extant weak version.

Using these as independent themes we can arrange various social, political, and economic movements into a 2×2 table. The horizontal variation represents the degree of equality that government policies are intended to effect. The vertical represents the racial component involved in the implementation of those policies.

The arrangement in table 6.1 starkly reveals the choice between the IDMP and the Left, at least with regard to these two themes. The Left would pursue strongly redistributive and colorblind policies to effect high levels of equality. The Program would pursue modestly redistributive and color-conscious policies that would scarcely change the overall level of inequality or rate of poverty. It does not call for an end to poverty but rather requires that the rates of black poverty equal the rates for whites. The stronger and colorblind policies of the Left—redistribution of income and wealth, funding and regulation

Table 6.1. **Typology of Movements according to Redistributive Objective and Racial Means.**

	High Equality	*Low Equality*
Colorblind	The Left	Post-Racial Liberalism Neoliberalism The Republican Party (part)
Color-Conscious	Black Separatism Black Marxism	The IDMP The Democratic Party The Republican Party (part)

of institutions, and the maintenance of strong labor market demand—would expand the middle class and eliminate poverty for all races.

I place a few other groups into table 6.1. When advocates of color-consciousness criticize colorblindness they fail to distinguish between the left and right columns in the top row of the table. They thereby lump together the Left with Post-Racial Liberals (as Tim Wise calls them), neoliberals, and even part of the GOP. The Program's hostility to the Right conceals a deep congruity: neither offers a fundamental challenge to the largely deregulated and savagely unequal model of capitalism currently dominant in the U.S.

Note further that the Identity, Diversity, and Multicultural Program falls into the same quadrant as the Democratic Party. The intellectual proximity of the two is worthy of some consideration. Neither is on the political left but both can be made to look good in comparison to those on the far right—the racists, homophobes, and other extreme conservatives. Indeed, just as the electoral success, such as it is, of the Democratic Party has come not by delivering a progressive program but rather by rhetorically posturing against the worst of the far right, so too does the Program appeal not to the core principles of the Left but instead positions itself as the social bulwark against racists, sexists, and homophobes. While we might allow for such bad faith among Democrats, who operate after all in the political realm, I suggest that the Left should not degenerate into the lesser-of-two-evils mindset of an American election. When elections come round one might behave in a narrowly strategic manner, deciding whether to support the lesser of two evils or "waste" one's vote on a progressive. But in the realms of philosophy and activism we are fortunate to have the opportunity to think critically, to pursue the truth, and to promote a genuinely just society.

The typology in table 6.1 clarifies part of the choice between the IDMP and the Left. It does not, of course, capture the full critique presented in this book but it does highlight the political context of inequality and colorblindness. If IDMP supporters wish to oppose neoliberalism they must move to the left, not embrace color-consciousness.

THE SOCIAL LANDSCAPE OF THE CHOICE

I have endeavored to present my case against the Identity, Diversity, and Multiculturalism Program as clearly as possible. My assumptions and definitions were made explicit. Theoretical models specified the causal mechanisms in operation. I provided empirical survey data where appropriate. The (anticipated) common objections were shown to be obfuscations. I do not, of course, expect to have persuaded every leftist who supports the Program. Yet

I do hope that leftist supporters recognize that they can no longer take for granted a correspondence between the Left and the IDMP. I further hope they no longer assume that critics are racists or conservatives. Leftist supporters of the Program should provide a comprehensive argument for their position. If they are willing to do so, our moral and political discourse will move forward.

I expect that the degree of honest, intellectual engagement with this critique will vary considerably. Individual reactions will not, however, be made in a social vacuum. The environment affects—both culturally and materially—our decision-making. Understanding this structure is important for leftist social movements because it points out the risks and rewards, our likely opponents and likely allies. The Identity, Diversity, and Multiculturalism Program typically has the full backing of people in positions of power in many businesses and schools—Chief Diversity Officers, Deans of Inclusion, and so on. It is not just a program, it's *The Program* one is supposed to get on board. This has cognitive and behavioral implications for both supporters, skeptics, and the undecided. There are, of course, the material rewards for going along. Bosses have the power to hire and fire, to promote, demote, or transfer, and to send resources to team players. Those who are not on board may be sanctioned or might be less likely to receive additional benefits. I believe that fear of retaliation (positive punishments) or the potential loss of benefits (negative punishments) accounts for much of the silence among skeptics.

Many skeptics do find subtle and safe ways to avoid playing along with the Identity, Diversity, and Multiculturalism Program. Doubts can be voiced with other skeptics, and I have heard many, but care must be taken when the boss or dean is around. I saw an amusing example of this at another institution as well. After my son was accepted into an engineering school (at a large state university) he, along with many other prospective entrants, attended the admitted-students day. They were shown around campus and the labs. The professors spoke about the program and their research. Current graduate students talked about their experiences. Folks went out for pizza and beer in the evening. All in all, a very nicely run program (and my son was more than happy to be wooed into attending). There was, however, one interesting modification to the agenda. Instead of talking about "Diversity" at the designated timeslot, the professors decided to take the guests on a walking tour of a neighborhood adjacent to campus. Presumably "Diversity" is an item that a dean or the president puts on the agenda of these events all across the university but the engineering faculty felt it was safe enough to ignore this directive around each other and around the engineering students. Instead of removing the item from the agenda altogether, which would require a confrontation with the administration, it was easier to sabotage it later. I imagine that many other skeptics behave similarly. Fighting the system is unpleasant and possibly risky to one's professional position. Secret sabotage is a reasonable maneuver under such conditions.

Yet there is an asymmetry here. While skeptics may play along when necessary because of fear of sanctions, I do not believe that most supporters of the Program are motivated primarily by the material rewards. They truly believe in the justness of the cause, a state that probably brings even greater psychological rewards than material. There is satisfaction in bravely fighting against an unjust system, of placing oneself in the tradition of the civil rights struggle. Objectively, the IDMP is part of the system; subjectively, the participants see themselves as fighting it. They get the best of both worlds: the psychological rewards of righteous rebellion alongside the material rewards of loyal service. This mutual reinforcement must account for the strong position of the Program in many institutions.

What does all this mean for the possibility of a vibrant leftist critique of the IDMP? The distribution of rewards and sanctions means that criticism will be muted until it becomes less risky. As with all social movements, there is safety in numbers. Of course, somebody must act first otherwise we'll never get to a safer spot. Here we take another important lesson from social movements: young people and college students will have to take the lead. Students do not operate under the same constraints as employees. They cannot be fired. And expulsion for criticizing the Program is an unlikely, although not impossible, event.

True, students depend on professors for their grades, and this creates an incentive to give the "right" answer, which in many cases means supporting Identity, Diversity, and Multiculturalism. Safer forms of disagreement could take place outside of class. Still, some young, progressive people must find the courage to challenge the dominant narrative of Identity, Diversity, and Multiculturalism. They will need to challenge professors in African American Studies, and risk being seen as racists. They will need to challenge professors in Gender Studies, and risk being seen as sexists. They will need to challenge professors in Queer Studies, and risk being seen as homophobes.

Thus, I conclude with an appeal to young people (of any age) who share a commitment to leftist principles of justice to take some risks. Unfortunately, social progress does not follow the path of least resistance. Yet we should acknowledge that the presumably safer path we are following poses some considerable risk as well. As we were focusing our efforts on the Identity, Diversity, and Multiculturalism Program, our level of economic inequality reached a level not seen since the Roaring Twenties, that is, right before the Great Depression. We should not comfort ourselves by believing that another New Deal is the inevitable response to a middle class in economic decline. Fascism, too, is a possible future and the failure of liberals to deliver greater equality through social democratic policies is largely responsible for the rise of the proto-fascist Trump. We might still have time to pursue a humane solution to the looming crisis but only, I believe, if the Left reaffirms its core values of political liberty and economic equality, recognizes that neoliberalism is the root of the problem for blacks, whites, and everybody else, and joins the political fray in large numbers.

NOTE

1. Kathy Davis, a gender-studies scholar, argues in *Intersectionality as Buzzword* (2008) that the secret to the success of intersectionality as an intellectual movement lies precisely in its vagueness and ambiguity. In other words, it can mean almost anything to the person who wields the concept.

References

Ainsworth, J. W. 2002. "Why Does It Take a Village? The Mediation of Neighborhood Effects on Educational Achievement." *Social Forces* 81 (1): 117–52.

Alexander, Michelle. 2012. *The New Jim Crow: Mass Incarceration in the Age of Colorblindness*. New York: The New Press.

Americans for Tax Fairness. 2014. a "Walmart on Tax Day: How Taxpayers Subsidize America's Biggest Employer and Richest Family." Washington, DC. https://americansfortaxfairness.org/files/Walmart-on-Tax-Day-Americans-for-Tax-Fairness-11.pdf.

Arrow, Kenneth J., and Gerard Debreu. 1954. "Existence of an Equilibrium for a Competitive Economy." *Econometrica* 22 (3): 265.

Bade, Rachael. 2018. "'It Would Look Ridiculous': Pelosi and Allies Warn against Ousting a Woman." POLITICO. November 12, 2018. https://politi.co/2qKpuoY.

Baker, Lee. 2001. "The Color-Blind Bind." In *Cultural Diversity in the United States: A Critical Reader*, edited by Ida Susser and Thomas C. Patterson. Malden, Mass: Blackwell Publishing.

Barndt, Joseph. 2007. *Understanding and Dismantling Racism: The Twenty-First Century Challenge to White America*. Minneapolis: Fortress Press.

Barnes, Julian E., and Shane Scott. 2018. "Cables Detail C.I.A. Waterboarding at Secret Prison Run by Gina Haspel." New York Times (Online); New York. August 10, 2018. https://search.proquest.com/docview/2091862051/abstract/4343CC6B008745A1PQ/1.

Berger, Peter L. 1963. *Invitation to Sociology: A Humanistic Perspective*. 1st ed. New York: Anchor.

Berger, Peter L., and Thomas Luckmann. 1967. *The Social Construction of Reality: A Treatise in the Sociology of Knowledge*. New York: Anchor.

Berlin, Isaiah. 1969. *Four Essays on Liberty*. Oxford: Oxford University Press.

Blanden, Jo, Paul Gregg, and Stephen Machin. 2005. "Intergenerational Mobility in Europe and North America." Centre for Economic Performance. https://www.suttontrust.com/wp-content/uploads/2005/04/IntergenerationalMobility-1.pdf.

Bonilla-Silva, Eduardo. 2002. "The Linguistics of Color Blind Racism: How to Talk Nasty about Blacks without Sounding 'Racist.'" *Critical Sociology* 28 (1–2): 41–64.

———. 2010. *Racism without Racists: Color-Blind Racism and the Persistence of Racial Inequality in America*. 3rd edition. Lanham: Rowman & Littlefield Publishers.

Bonilla-Silva, Eduardo, and David Dietrich. 2011. "The Sweet Enchantment of Color-Blind Racism in Obamerica." *The ANNALS of the American Academy of Political and Social Science* 634 (1): 190–206.

Bourdieu, Pierre. 1986. "The Forms of Capital." In *Handbook of Theory and Research for the Sociology of Education*, edited by John Richardson. Westport, Conn: Greenwood.

Brodie, Janet Farrell. 1997. *Contraception and Abortion in Nineteenth-Century America*. Ithaca: Cornell University Press.

Bronner, Stephen Eric. 2004. *Reclaiming the Enlightenment: Toward a Politics of Radical Engagement*. New York: Columbia University Press.

Brown, David. 2019. "How Women Took over the Military-Industrial Complex." POLITICO. January 2, 2019. https://politi.co/2BWjuP1.

Camus, Albert. 1955. *The Myth of Sisyphus, and Other Essays*. Translated by Justin O'Brien. New York: Vintage Books.

Carr, Leslie G. 1997. *"Color-Blind" Racism*. Thousand Oaks: SAGE Publications.

Carr, Paul R. 2016. "Whiteness and White Privilege: Problematizing Race and Racism in a 'Color-Blind' World and in Education." *The International Journal of Critical Pedagogy* 7 (1).

Central Intelligence Agency. n.d. "The World Factbook." Accessed July 30, 2018. https://www.cia.gov/library/publications/the-world-factbook/rankorder/2172rank.html.

Conley, Dalton. 2010. *Being Black, Living in the Red: Race, Wealth, and Social Policy in America*. Berkeley: University of California Press.

Cooper, Richard S., Jay S. Kaufman, and Ryk Ward. 2003. "Race and Genomics." *The New England Journal of Medicine* 348 (12): 1166–70.

Currie, Janet. 2009. "Healthy, Wealthy, and Wise: Socioeconomic Status, Poor Health in Childhood, and Human Capital Development." *Journal of Economic Literature* 47 (1): 87–122.

Danuta Walters, Suzanna. 2016. "Why This Socialist Feminist Is Voting for Hillary." *Nation*, January 25, 2016.

Davis, Kathy. 2008. "Intersectionality as Buzzword: A Sociology of Science Perspective on What Makes a Feminist Theory Successful." *Feminist Theory* 9 (1): 67–85.

Delgado, Richard, and Jean Stefancic. 2012. *Critical Race Theory: An Introduction*. New York: NYU Press.

Descartes, Rene. 1968. *Discourse on Method and the Meditations*. Translated by F.E. Sutcliffe. Harmondsworth: Penguin Books Limited.

Dijk, Teun A. van. 1989. *Communicating Racism: Ethnic Prejudice in Thought and Talk*. Newbury Park, Calif.: SAGE Publications, Inc.

Dilg, Mary. 2003. *Thriving in the Multicultural Classroom: Principles and Practices for Effective Teaching*. New York: Teachers College Press.

Domhoff, G. William. 1990. *The Power Elite and the State: How Policy Is Made in America*. New York: Aldine Transaction.

———. 2013. *Who Rules America? The Triumph of the Corporate Rich*. 7th ed. New York, NY: McGraw-Hill Education.

Ernst, Rose. 2010. *The Price of Progressive Politics: The Welfare Rights Movement in an Era of Colorblind Racism*. New York: NYU Press.

ExxonMobil. 2017. "Global Diversity: Creating Competitive Advantage through People." https://cdn.exxonmobil.com/~/media/global/files/other/2017/global-diversity-booklet.pdf.

Feagin, Joe R. 2014. *Racist America: Roots, Current Realities, and Future Reparations*. 3rd ed. New York: Routledge.

Feagin, Joe R., and Hernan Vera. 2008. "Confronting One's Own Racism." In *White Privilege: Essential Readings on the Other Side of Racism*, edited by Paula S. Rothenberg, 3rd ed. New York: Worth Publishers.

Featherstone, Liza. 2016. "Why This Socialist Feminist Is Not Voting for Hillary." *Nation*, January 25, 2016.

Ferber, Abby L. 2014. "We Aren't Just Color-Blind, We Are Oppression-Blind!" In *Privilege: A Reader*, edited by Michael S. Kimmel and Abby L. Ferber, 3rd ed. Boulder: Westview Press.

Forman, Tyrone A. 2006. "Color-Blind Racism and Racial Indifference: The Role of Racial Apathy in Facilitating Enduring Inequalities." In *The Changing Terrain of Race and Ethnicity*, edited by Maria Krysan and Amanda E. Lewis. New York: Russell Sage Foundation.

Foster, John Bellamy, and Fred Magdoff. 2009. *The Great Financial Crisis: Causes and Consequences*. New York: Monthly Review Press.

Friedman, Milton and Rose. 1980. *Free to Choose*. New York: Harcourt Brace Jovanovich.

Gerth, Hans. 1940. "The Nazi Party: Its Leadership and Composition." *American Journal of Sociology* 45 (4): 517–41.

Gilroy, Paul. 2001. *Against Race: Imagining Political Culture beyond the Color Line*. Cambridge, Massachusetts: Belknap Press.

Glazer, Nathan. 1998. *We Are All Multiculturalists Now*. Cambridge, Mass.: Harvard University Press.

Gould, Elise, Hilary Wething, and Natalie Sabadish. 2013. "What Families Need to Get By." Issue Brief 368. Economic Policy Institute.

Grassroots Policy Project. n.d. "Race, Power, and Policy: Dismantling Structural Racism." National People's Action. https://www.racialequitytools.org/resourcefiles/race_power_policy_workbook.pdf.

Hankins, Thomas L. 1985. *Science and the Enlightenment*. Cambridge: Cambridge University Press.

Hedges, Chris. 2011. *Death of the Liberal Class*. First Trade Paper ed. New York: Nation Books.

Hirschman, Albert O. 1970. *Exit, Voice, and Loyalty: Responses to Decline in Firms, Organizations, and States*. Cambridge, Mass: Harvard University Press.

Horkheimer, Max, and Theodor W. Adorno. 1969. *Dialectic of Enlightenment*. Translated by John Cumming. New York: Continuum.

Hout, Michael. 2012. "Social and Economic Returns to College Education in the United States." *Annual Review of Sociology* 38 (1): 379–400.

Jakobson, Roman. 1944. "Franz Boas' Approach to Language." *International Journal of American Linguistics* 10 (4): 188–95.

Jones, James M. 1997. *Prejudice and Racism*. 2nd ed. New York: McGraw-Hill.

Kant, Immanuel. 1784. "Beantwortung der Frage: Was Ist Aufklärung?" *Berlinische Monatsschrift*, December 1784.

Kenworthy, Lane. 2014. *Social Democratic America*. New York: Oxford University Press.

Keynes, John Maynard. 1964. *The General Theory of Employment, Interest, and Money*. 1st Harbinger ed. New York: Harcourt, Brace & World.

Kim, ChangHwan, Christopher R. Tamborini, and Arthur Sakamoto. 2015. "Field of Study in College and Lifetime Earnings in the United States." *Sociology of Education* 88 (4): 320–39.

Kousser, J. Morgan. 1999. *Colorblind Injustice: Minority Voting Rights and the Undoing of the Second Reconstruction*. University of North Carolina Press.

Kuhn, Thomas S. 1970. *The Structure of Scientific Revolutions*. 2nd ed. Chicago: University of Chicago Press.

Kymlicka, Will. 1989. *Liberalism, Community, and Culture*. Oxford: Clarendon Press.

Lareau, Annette, and Elliot B. Weininger. 2003. "Cultural Capital in Educational Research: A Critical Assessment." *Theory and Society* 32 (5/6).

Lilla, Mark. 2017. *The Once and Future Liberal: After Identity Politics*. New York: Harper.

Locke, John. 1983. *A Letter Concerning Toleration*. Edited by James H. Tully. Indianapolis: Hackett Publishing Company.

Marable, Manning. 1997. *Black Liberation in Conservative America*. Boston: South End Press.

Marshall, Gordon. 1998. *A Dictionary of Sociology*. 2nd ed. Oxford: Oxford University Press.

Martín Alcoff, Linda. 2015. Democracy Now Interview by Amy Goodman and Juan González. http://www.democracynow.org/2015/6/17/as_rachel_dolezal_breaks_silence_a.

Marx, Karl. 1977. *Capital: A Critique of Political Economy*. Translated by Ben Fowkes. Vol. 1. Vintage Books.

Mazumder, Bhashkar. 2005. "Fortunate Sons: New Estimates of Intergenerational Mobility in the United States Using Social Security Earnings Data." *The Review of Economics and Statistics* 87 (2): 235–55.

McCanne, Michael. 2017. "The Panthers and the Patriots." May 19, 2017. http://jacobinmag.com/2017/05/black-panthers-young-patriots-fred-hampton.

McCartney, Robert. 2018. "Leggett Not Ready to Endorse Jealous." *Washington Post, The*, July 28, 2018.

McIntosh, Peggy. 2008. "White Privilege: Upacking the Invisible Knapsack." In *White Privilege*, edited by Paula S. Rothenberg, 3rd ed. New York: Worth Publishers.

Michaels, Walter Benn. 2006. *The Trouble with Diversity: How We Learned to Love Identity and Ignore Inequality*. New York: Holt Paperbacks.

Miethe, Terance D., Richard C. McCorkle, and Shelley J. Listwan. 2005. *Crime Profiles: The Anatomy of Dangerous Persons, Places, and Situations*. 3rd ed. Los Angeles: Oxford University Press.

Moller, Stephanie, Evelyne Huber, John D. Stephens, David Bradley, and Francois Nielsen. 2003. "Determinants of Relative Poverty in Advanced Capitalist Democracies." *American Sociological Review* 68 (1): 22.

Monnat, Shannon M. 2010. "Toward a Critical Understanding of Gendered Color-Blind Racism Within the U.S. Welfare Institution." *Journal of Black Studies* 40 (4): 637–52.

Neville, Helen A., M. Nikki Coleman, Jameca Woody Falconer, and Deadre Holmes. 2005. "Color-Blind Racial Ideology and Psychological False Consciousness Among African Americans." *Journal of Black Psychology* 31 (1): 27–45.

Ney, Robert. 2013. *Sideswiped: Lessons Learned Courtesy of the Hit Men of Capitol Hill*. 1st ed. Cleveland, OH: Changing Lives Press.

Nove, Alec. 1991. *The Economics of Feasible Socialism Revisited*. 2nd edition. London: Harper Collins Academic.

Nozick, Robert. 2013. *Anarchy, State, and Utopia*. Reprint ed. New York: Basic Books.

Omi, Michael, and Howard Winant. 1994. *Racial Formation in the United States: From the 1960s to the 1990s*. 2nd edition. New York: Routledge.

Orelus, Pierre W. 2013. "Unpacking the Race Talk." *Journal of Black Studies* 44 (6): 572–89.

Pager, Devah, Bruce Western, and Bart Bonikowski. 2009. "Discrimination in a Low-Wage Labor Market: A Field Experiment." *American Sociological Review* 74 (5): 777–99.

Pager, Devah, and Bruce Western. 2005. "Race at Work: Realities of Race and Criminal Record in the NYC Job Market." Schomburg Center for Research in Black Culture.

Parijs, Philippe Van, and Yannick Vanderborght. 2017. *Basic Income: A Radical Proposal for a Free Society and a Sane Economy*. Cambridge, Massachusetts: Harvard University Press.

Peller, Gary. 2011. *Critical Race Consciousness: Reconsidering American Ideologies of Racial Justice*. Boulder: Paradigm Publishers.

Perkins, John. 2004. *Confessions of an Economic Hit Man*. San Francisco: Berrett-Koehler Publishers.

———. 2007. *The Secret History of the American Empire: The Truth about Economic Hit Men, Jackals, and How to Change the World*. New York: Plume.

Piketty, Thomas. 2014. *Capital in the Twenty-First Century*. Translated by Arthur Goldhammer. Cambridge, Mass.: Belknap Press.

Polanyi, Karl. 2001. *The Great Transformation: The Political and Economic Origins of Our Time*. 2nd ed. Boston, MA: Beacon Press.

Pollitt, Katha. 2016. "Why Didn't Bernie Get My Vote." *Nation*, May 23, 2016.

Press, Bill. 2016. *Buyer's Remorse: How Obama Let Progressives Down*. New York: Threshold Editions.

Quine, W. V. 1951. "Two Dogmas of Empiricism." *The Philosophical Review* 60 (1): 20–43.

Rawls, John. 2001. *Justice as Fairness: A Restatement*. Edited by Erin Kelly. 2nd ed. Cambridge, Mass: Belknap Press.

Regents of Univ. of California v. Bakke. 1978. U.S. Supreme Court.

Reich, Robert B. 2012. *Beyond Outrage: What Has Gone Wrong with Our Economy and Our Democracy, and How to Fix It*. New York: Vintage.

Reiman, Jeffrey, and Paul Leighton. 2016. *The Rich Get Richer and the Poor Get Prison: Ideology, Class, and Criminal Justice*. 11th ed. New York: Routledge.

Sainato, Michael. 2016. "Sen. Warren Turns Her Back on Native Americans After Exploiting Them." *Observer Online*, November 21, 2016. https://observer.com/2016/11/sen-warren-turns-her-back-on-native-americans-after-exploiting-them/.

Sartre, Jean-Paul. 1975. "Existentialism Is a Humanism." In *Existentialism from Dostoevsky to Sartre*, edited and translated by Walter Kaufmann. New York: Penguin Books.

———. 1993. *Being and Nothingness*. Translated by Hazel E. Barnes. New York: Washington Square Press.

Scheer, Robert. 2010. *The Great American Stickup: How Reagan Republicans and Clinton Democrats Enriched Wall Street While Mugging Main Street*. 1st ed. New York: Nation Books.

Schiff, Julia. 2018. "White Supremacist Posters on Campus: Administration Quick to Act and Slow to Follow Up." *The Trail*, November 16, 2018.

Semega, Jessica L., Kayla R. Fontenot, and Melissa A. Kollar. 2017. "Income and Poverty in the United States: 2016." Current Population Reports P60–259. Washington, DC: U.S. Census Bureau.

Sen, Amartya. 1995. *Inequality Reexamined*. New York: Harvard University Press.

Sleeper, Jim. 1997. *Liberal Racism*. 1st ed. New York: Penguin Books.

Smith, Robert C. 1995. *Racism in the Post Civil Rights Era: Now You See It, Now You Don't*. Albany: State University of New York Press.

Straumann, Benjamin. 2008. "The Peace of Westphalia as a Secular Constitution." *Constellations* 15 (2): 16.

Tamborini, Christopher R., ChangHwan Kim, and Arthur Sakamoto. 2015. "Education and Lifetime Earnings in the United States." *Demography* 52 (4): 1383–1407.

Tatum, Beverly Daniel. 2003. *Why Are All the Black Kids Sitting Together in the Cafeteria? And Other Conversations About Race*. New York: Basic Books.

Taylor, Paul, and Richard Fry. 2012. "The Rise of Residential Segregation by Income." Washington, DC: Pew Research Center. http://assets.pewresearch.org/wp-content/uploads/sites/3/2012/08/Rise-of-Residential-Income-Segregation-2012.2.pdf.

"The Agenda to Raise America's Pay." n.d. Economic Policy Institute. Accessed July 30, 2018. https://www.epi.org/pay-agenda/.

Walmart. 2018. "Road to Inclusion." Culture, Diversity & Inclusion. https://cdn.corpo
rate.walmart.com/11/0d/f9289df649049a38c14bdeaf2b99/2017-cdi-report-web.pdf.

Walsh, Joan. 2016. "Bernie Sanders Is Hurting Himself by Playing the Victim."
The Nation, May 19, 2016. https://www.thenation.com/article/bernie-sanders-is
-hurting-himself-by-playing-the-victim/.

Weber, Max. 1949. *The Methodology of the Social Sciences*. Translated by Edward
Shils and Edward Finch. New York: Free Press.

Williams, Dawn G., and Roderic R. Land. 2006. "The Legitimation of Black Subordination: The Impact of Color-Blind Ideology on African American Education." *The
Journal of Negro Education* 75 (4): 579–88.

Wilson, William Julius. 1980. *The Declining Significance of Race: Blacks and
Changing American Institutions*. 2nd ed. Chicago: University of Chicago.

———. 2010. *More than Just Race: Being Black and Poor in the Inner City*. New
York: W. W. Norton & Company.

Wise, Tim. 2010. *Colorblind: The Rise of Post-Racial Politics and the Retreat from
Racial Equity*. San Francisco: City Lights Publishers.

Zinn, Howard. 2003. *A People's History of the United States*. New York: Harper
Perennial.

Index

About the Author

Richard Anderson-Connolly is professor of sociology and anthropology at the University of Puget Sound. His academic background includes the areas of economic sociology, power and inequality, criminology, and urban sociology. As a political activist, he works on reforming the U.S. electoral system through the adoption of proportional representation. He lives in Tacoma, Washington.

www.ingramcontent.com/pod-product-compliance
Lightning Source LLC
Chambersburg PA
CBHW050423280326
41932CB00013BA/1970